PAUL DOUGLAS
PRAIRIE SKIES
The Minnesota Weather Book

Illustrations by Laurie Kruhoeffer
Photographs by Minnesota "Weatherspies"

VOYAGEUR PRESS

This book is dedicated to KARE 11 "Weatherspies," a talented group of photographers who just happened to be in the right place at the right time.

Printed in Hong Kong

Hardcover edition:
91 92 93 94 95 5 4 3 2
Softcover edition:
92 93 94 95 96 5 4 3 2 1

Library of Congress Cataloging-in-Publication Data

Douglas, Paul, 1958-
Prairie skies: the Minnesota weather book / Paul Douglas
p. cm.
ISBN 0-89658-118-7
ISBN 0-89658-208-6 (pbk.)
1. Minnesota—Climate. I. Title.

QC984.M6D68 1990
551.69776-dc20

89-48975
CIP

Published by
VOYAGEUR PRESS, INC.
P.O. Box 338, 123 North Second Street, Stillwater, MN 55082 U.S.A.
From Minnesota and Canada 612-430-2210; toll-free 800-888-9653

Voyageur Press books are also available at discounts for quantities for educational, fundraising, premium, or sales-promotion use. For details contact the marketing department. Please write or call for our free catalog of natural history publications and a free copy of our newsletter, *Wingbeat*.

Contents

Acknowledgments

I'm not sure where to begin. A huge hug and thank you to my family, who was patient while I spent endless weekends slumped over a Macintosh computer. My wife, Laurie, contributed all of the maps and illustrations, and that was no small task.

I have had the pleasure of working with some of the finest meteorologists in the nation at KARE-11. Thanks to Sunny Haus; Frank Watson, who helped me rummage through old, yellowing stacks of musty weather records; Ellen Ferrara; and Dennis Feltgen, who was kind enough to share his recent research into ozone depletion before leaving the Twin Cities for a new job opportunity in Tampa, Florida.

We are blessed with a top-notch National Weather Service office in the Twin Cities, and I want to tip my hat to the meteorologist in charge, Jim Campbell, and all of the men and women who work so hard to come up with a quality weather product twenty-four hours a day. Jim Zandlo and Greg Spoden of the Minnesota State Climatology Office graciously provided me with a plethora of useful weather facts and figures about Minnesota weather and climate.

Satellite photos are liberally sprinkled throughout the book, thanks to Kevin Marcus, director of Cropcast Services for Earthsat Corporation in Washington, D.C. He was a college roommate and a good buddy who got a "real job" in meteorology. Loren Johnson of Satellite Data Systems in Cleveland, Minnesota, is doing some amazing things with a simple satellite dish and an IBM-PC computer. We've included a few examples. For providing me with information and photos describing the cutting edge of meteorology and new and exciting advances in hardware and software, I thank William Smith of Tycho Tech-

nology, and Dr. Thomas Schlatter of NOAA (the National Oceanic and Atmospheric Administration), who is spending much time on the exciting PROFS program. Both gentlemen call Boulder, Colorado, home.

In 1985 I chased tornadoes (or more accurately, they chased me) in Oklahoma with Don Burgess of NSSL, the National Severe Storms Laboratory, and he was kind enough to update me on some promising advances in Doppler radar. Thanks to Dr. Walt Lyons, formerly of WCCO-TV, and founder of R*SCAN Corporation of Minneapolis.

Meteorologists often get sore necks from scanning the skies for fancy clouds and sinister-looking fronts, but we have a soft spot in our hearts for astronomy as well. A big salute to Lauren Nelson of the Minnesota Astronomical Society and Professor Terry Flower of the College of St. Catherine in St. Paul. Both provided me with some stunning displays of the aurora borealis.

I've been sensing a growing feeling of environmental concern and outright activism, a refreshing change from the "me-me-me" decade of the '80s. We are quickly realizing that we don't have much choice other than to keep our home clean. I mean, we have to live here (and so do our kids)! Many thanks to Cliff Twaroski of the Minnesota Pollution Control Agency for bringing me up to date on the acid rain threat facing Minnesota's lakes and forests. The MPCA's Peter Ciborowski helped out with helpful information on ozone depletion and how it may affect us right here at home.

Being away from an academic environment, it's easy to feel stale and somewhat out of touch. My sincere thanks to Paul Knight and Fred Gadomski of Penn State for helping to bring me up to speed

on what's new in the field of meteorology. Ken Reeves of Accu-Weather shed some light on the American and European computer models, and the considerable differences between the two.

I've had support from all of my colleagues at Channel 11. A big salute goes out to president and general manager Linda Rios Brook and to vice president of news Janet Mason. And I'll always be grateful to a former boss of mine, Nick Lawler, who now works for a TV news consultant in Iowa. He was the individual who first suggested including "Weatherspies" in my weathercast.

A medal of honor and a sincere thank you goes out to Helene Jones at Voyageur Press. As editor of *Prairie Skies* she offered wit and wisdom and seemingly endless patience as I made the awkward transition from broadcasting to publishing.

This project started out as an attempt to "show off" some of the amazing photographs we've received from viewers — a book of pretty pictures, a coffee-table book if you will. I hope it has turned into something more, thanks to help and input from all of the people listed above. My sincere gratitude goes out to every last one of them.

And finally, I'd like to thank my father, Volker, who was one of the first German exchange students to attend college in this country. In 1955 he landed a job as a proofreader at Science Press, in Lancaster County, Pennsylvania. Today he is vice president of sales and marketing of that same company. Over the years he has patiently listened to my gripes about a lack of books on weather. He encouraged me to write *Prairie Skies*, offering plenty of love and some good advice along the way. Thanks Dad.

Introduction

First, a true confession. I am by no means a weather expert. You see, there really is no such thing. Just about the time you think you have it all figured out, Mother Nature comes up with a new and exotic way of humbling you in front of hundreds of thousands of snickering souls. At times, it's a very painful way to make a living. My college meteorology professors wouldn't be thrilled to hear me say it, but the sad truth is that one can't learn the fine "art" of weather forecasting out of a book. The only way to learn how to predict the weather is to look at the maps until you're slightly cross-eyed, sneak a glance or two out the nearest window, roll up your sleeves, jot down a forecast—and then run to the window every fifteen minutes to see how you're doing! You learn from your mistakes, and if you make enough "busts" (slang for a blunder of mind-numbing proportions), you finally begin to see the light.

When I speak to schools and other organizations, I tell people that weather is a hobby that evolved into a career, and it's true. I was a Boy Scout, and the weather merit badge was my favorite. In fact, my Eagle Scout project was "tornado preparedness": talking to schools, nursing homes, and hospitals in my hometown of Lancaster, Pennsylvania, making sure people knew what to do if the unthinkable ever happened. When I was thirteen years old, our home was hit by the soggy remains of hurricane Agnes. Twelve inches of rain turned our basement into an indoor swimming pool. I can still remember wading through cold, muddy, waist-deep water in my undershorts, trying to plug up that hideous "leak." A man drowned in the stream behind our house, and as they carried him to the ambulance, I can remember wondering out loud why nobody had predicted a flood of this magnitude. From that day on I have been in awe of the weather, impressed by its subtle beauty, and amazed at its bouts of destructive fury.

Let's face it: Weather is just about the only thing we all have in common. You may not care about a tax hike in city A, or a sports score in town B, but it's hard to imagine somebody with no interest in the weather. Weather affects our travel plans, our weekends and vacations spent outdoors, the food on our dining room tables, the clothes we wear, the well-being of countless businesses, and our conversations. Weather is the ultimate ice-breaker, the source of more second-guessing and idle water cooler chats than probably any other topic. When in doubt, complain about the weather, right?

I'm writing this book out of frustration, too. There are weather-related books written for preschoolers, and college textbooks bursting with nightmarish math equations, but very little else. What follows is an attempt to come up with an introduction to weather that doesn't insult your intelligence. With a knowledge of clouds, a simple barometer on the wall, and some basic weather facts, you'll be able to make a pretty accurate twenty-four-hour forecast, and in some small way gain an edge on the elements.

But being Weatherwise is more than a convenience. If you live in Minnesota long enough, chances are very good you'll be confronted with a dangerous weather situation, what may literally become a matter of life and death. If you keep your cool, and know exactly what to do under these circumstances, there's absolutely no reason why you should become a "statistic."

In *Prairie Skies*, I'll attempt to capture the beauty and magic of Minnesota weather, and at the same time arm you with some facts and figures that could prove useful when the sky overhead turns threatening. You may want to browse through the pages that follow, picking and choosing those topics that interest you most. And for goodness' sake, keep this handy, just in case a goofy weathercaster in a three-piece suit ever tries to impress you with a mouthful of meteorological mush. The next time he or she tries anything funny, you'll be ready!

I hope you enjoy the book.

1 Welcome to the Super Bowl of Weather!

Some Memorable Weather Events

"In Minnesota, you have cold weather boasting rights for the nation!"

On a recent Christmas holiday, my wife and I rented a car in the New York City area. Much of our holiday was spent on the road, shuttling gifts between Laurie's home in New Jersey and my parent's home in Lancaster, Pennsylvania. Fiddling with the car radio one evening, we heard an all-news radio station announcer blurt out the following: "You'll really want to bundle up if you're heading outside. The forecast for the metropolitan area calls for windy conditions, with scattered snow flurries, turning bitterly cold with a low in the upper teens and low twenties. . . ." I turned to my wife, now shaking her head in disbelief, and then we both burst out laughing. We truly were traveling through the land of the weather wimps. You see, we live in Minnesota, where the cold fronts are "fresh," still reeking of the polar regions. Minnesota: land of squeaky snow and ice tingles up the nose—sure signs of a fine, invigorating, subzero day.

One of the simple pleasures of living in Minnesota is the God-given right to brag about the weather to friends and families stuck in other— okay, let's say it—dull parts of the nation. Some would call it complaining, but it's more of a boast than a sigh. Sometimes, when relating a particularly mind-boggling weather event over the telephone, I'm tempted to beat my chest and let out a

little primal yell. It's because Minnesotans are victors—predictable winners in the Super Bowl of weather, able not only to survive but also to flourish in one of the most extreme climates on the face of the earth. Greater temperature swings can be found in parts of Siberia and Mongolia, but there are few other places on the planet that experience summer temperatures near 110° and winter lows of -40°. A frontal passage that might take twelve hours on the East Coast can happen here in under an hour. And when it comes to weathering tornadoes and thunderstorms of every conceivable temperament—well, go ahead, pat yourself on the back and take another bow.

As you're about to see, anytime anyone, anywhere tries to impress you with a little local weather folklore from his or her hometown, you can safely chuckle under your breath and then proceed to skillfully one-up them. Welcome to the major leagues of meteorology!

THE COLD FACTS

"It was so cold, my backyard thermometer ran out of degrees. . . . "

There is a collective suffering in Minnesota that settles in during the month of November and lingers until March. Although it's easy to rationalize heavy snow (good for the skiers, farmers, more water in our lakes, etc.), it's more of a challenge to justify pleading with your car heater, chiseling frost off pets and small children, and writing out

A Few Thumb-numbing Statistics

Coldest Twin Cities temperature?
 -41° F. on January 21, 1888
 (Modern records: -34° F., January 1936)
Coldest Minnesota temperature?
 -59° F. on February 16, 1903 in Moorhead
Longest spell of subzero temperatures in the Twin Cities?
 186 hours, from 5:00 P.M. December 31, 1911 to 1:00 P.M. January 8, 1912
Statistically, the coldest day of the year? January 24
Average number of subzero nights in the Twin Cities? Twenty-eight
Average number of subzero days in the Twin Cities? Three

Cold Weather Facts

At . . .
 -20° F., motor oil becomes a thick gel and will not move through the engine of a vehicle
 -30° F., most piston-engine airplanes are grounded because they are prone to a kind of "mechanical hypothermia"
 -40° F., exposed flesh freezes within one minute
 -60° F., exposed flesh freezes within seconds
 -60° F., (or colder) breath turns to ice crystals that fall to the ground

(Source: *The World Almanac & Book of Facts*, 1989 edition, Copyright © Newspaper Enterprise Association, Inc. 1988, New York, NY 10166)

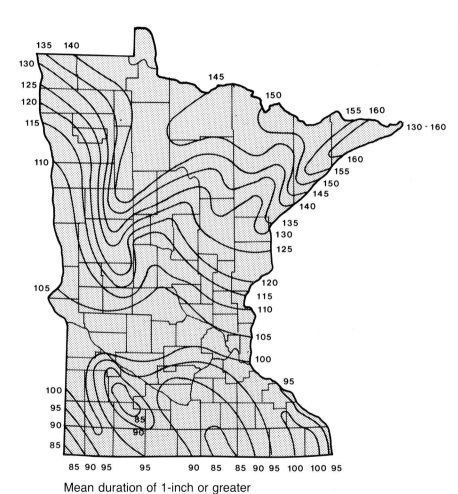

135 140
130
125
120
115
110

145
150
155 160
130 - 160
160
155
150
145
140
135
130
125
120
115
110
105
100
95

105

100
95
90
85

85
90

85 90 95   95   90 85 85 90 95 100 100 95

Mean duration of 1-inch or greater
snow cover in days. (1959-1979)

On average, the Twin Cities have an inch of snow on the ground nearly one-third of
the year, or one hundred days. The North Shore of Lake Superior is snow covered
almost half the year!

After the Armistice Day blizzard, Excelsior Boulevard, west of Minneapolis, resembled
a snowy never-never land. The blizzard changed highway design in Minnesota. Department of Transportation crews now elevate major roads, giving the plowed snow somewhere to go, reducing the effects of drifting. *Courtesy: Minnesota Historical Society.*

Phil Hadock and Sid Weber inspecting shoulder-deep drifts in front of Otto Schmalz-
bauer Jr.'s store on Fifth Avenue in New Brighton. The photo is from the *Minneapolis Star-
Journal. Courtesy: Minnesota Historical Society.*

heating checks that approach your parents' mortgage payments. But we try anyway. Minnesota: The Final Frontier, The Great White North, The Last Stop Before Anchorage.

How often have we heard, "It's good for you!" and "Look what it does to the crime rate!" or "Well, it keeps out the riffraff" (an oldie but goody). One thing is quite certain: This shared misery is good for the soul. In other, blander parts of the United States, folks may greet spring with a casual shrug. Elsewhere, the greenery and perspiration of a hot summer day may be almost an afterthought. But not in Minnesota. No, here we earn our summers!

THE ARMISTICE DAY BLIZZARD
NOVEMBER 11, 1940

It might have been the snowstorm of the century, and many people who lived through this great snow blitz still shake their heads when describing its fury. The death toll in Minnesota alone was forty-nine people. Thousands of farm animals were killed by the bitter winds and waves of drifting snow.

Most everyone was caught off guard that day. The forecast had called for a cooling trend with a chance of flurries. A storm approaching from Kansas intensified explosively as it passed between the Twin Cities and Eau Claire, Wisconsin, inhaling a fresh burst of icy air into the state, turning the rain to blinding sheets of snow that were whipped into two-story drifts by winds gusting to sixty miles an hour. Hunters, who had been enjoying sixty-degree temperatures early in the day, were found frozen to death days later, still in their shirt-sleeves. Many motorists became stranded, hopelessly stuck in towering snowdrifts.

By November 12, snowdrifts up to twenty feet were reported in Willmar. Officially, the Twin Cities received 16.2 inches of snow. Collegeville was swamped with 26.6 inches of snow, but the drifts were so thick that many roads remained closed until the end of November. In a narrow band from Albert Lea to Sandstone, glaze ice crushed trees and power lines. Everywhere,

streets were littered with abandoned cars, many with ruined radiators. The severe drop in temperature during the blizzard burst engines that hadn't been protected with antifreeze.

Since 1940 meteorologists have been blessed with supercomputers, satellites, more reporting stations, a network of radar sites, and a better understanding of the atmosphere. That means a similar blizzard in the future probably couldn't strike without some sort of warning. But the Armistice Day blizzard is a painful reminder that Minnesota weather can be truly unpredictable and deadly.

THE FRIDLEY TORNADO OUTBREAK
MAY 6, 1965

For nearly three hours on the evening of May 6, 1965, a family of tornadoes terrorized the northern and western suburbs of the Twin Cities. At least six twisters touched down, killing fourteen people and injuring 683 others, and leaving property damage in the tens of millions of dollars. The first tornado touched down shortly after 6:30 P.M. Minutes later, the Lake Minnetonka area was hit, with the greatest damage to Deephaven and Wayzata. At least three twisters swept through Fridley, Mounds View, and Spring Lake Park, leaving behind a pile of rubble and shattered homes nearly a quarter mile wide. One tornado sucked water out of a lake and created a new lake half a mile down the road! By the time the sixth and final tornado lifted into the clouds at 9:20 P.M., the Twin Cities had suffered its worst tornado outbreak in recorded history, a poignant reminder that twisters can indeed hit the metro area!

THE BROOKLYN PARK TORNADO
JULY 18, 1986

It might have been the most watched, most photographed tornado in history. Thousands of people stared, gawked, and pointed at this writhing, churning weather monster as it skipped across the northern suburbs of Minneapolis.

July 18 was a hot, stuffy, oppressive summer day. By midafternoon, the National Severe

How Snowy Was It?
Heaviest snow cover on the ground?
    Twin Cities, 38 inches in January 1982
    Minnesota, 70 inches on the Gunflint Lake Trail in February 1972

Twin Cities Facts
Heaviest snow in a season?
    Ninety-eight inches during the winter of 1983–1984
Heaviest snow from one storm?
    Twenty inches on January 22–23, 1982
Longest snowfall?
    Eighty-eight hours in 1969
Snowiest year?
    101.5 inches in 1983
Earliest snow?
    On September 16, 1916
Latest snow?
    On May 28, 1965

America's Worst Tornado Outbreak
On April 3–4, 1974, during a sixteen-hour period, a total of 148 tornadoes touched down in thirteen states. This "superoutbreak" of tornadoes left 307 people dead, more than sixteen hundred injured, and damage with a price tag estimated at $600 million. Many of the tornadoes were especially severe F4s and F5s, with wind speeds in excess of 250 mph, leaving behind a wake of total destruction. If you could have put the tornado damage end to end, it would have amounted to 2,598 miles of rubble. Had it not been for improved civil defense communications, teams of Skywarn weather spotters, and National Weather Service radar, the death toll would have been much higher.

Sky 11, are you out there? "My brother and I were loading a canoe onto the car for a trip to the Boundary Waters when we saw the funnel dropping from the sky. As my family headed for the basement, I ran to my jeep, and went after the twister for photos. At the time this photo was taken I was one-half to three-quarters of a mile away." (Look for the Sky II helicopter.) Michael Leschisin, Ocala, FL.

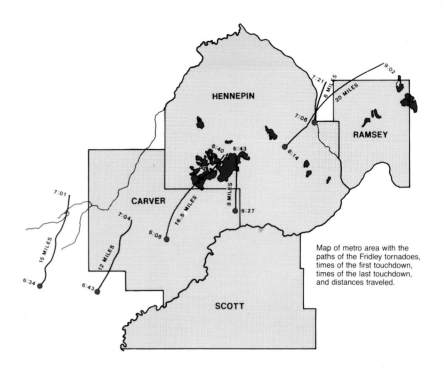

Map of metro area with the paths of the Fridley tornadoes, times of the first touchdown, times of the last touchdown, and distances traveled.

The Twin Cities metro area, showing paths, distances, and times of the Fridley twisters.

Fridley, after the tornado. Winds estimated in excess of 200 to 250 miles per hour left behind a quarter-mile-wide swath of total destruction. Photo from the *St. Paul Pioneer Press Dispatch. Courtesy: Minnesota Historical Society.*

Storms Forecast Center in Kansas City had issued a severe thunderstorm watch for portions of western Minnesota, but there was no indication that the skies would turn violent over the Twin Cities. At about 4:50 P.M., our police scanner in the KARE-TV newsroom picked up a report of a funnel forming over Brooklyn Park. Meanwhile, our Sky 11 helicopter pilot Max Messmer was airborne, on his way to a story, when he spotted the funnel beginning to drop out of the sky. Almost immediately, photographer Tom Empey began sending back extraordinary pictures of the tornado. Our 5:00 newscast was devoted exclusively to live coverage of the twister, the first time that a tornado had been tracked from beginning to end during an evening newscast. Frankly, we were just as amazed and spellbound as the viewers watching in disbelief at home.

The tornado's path had a length of about five miles, its 150- to 200-mph winds confined to a narrow swath of destruction some fifty to one hundred yards wide. Miraculously, there were no injuries or fatalities. The reason: The tornado spent most of its time in a park. Thousands of hundred-year-old oak and aspen trees at the Springbrook Nature Preserve were flattened. Had that tornado roared through a typical Minnesota neighborhood, the loss of life might have been considerable. Scientists worldwide have been analyzing the video, learning new things about what makes a twister tick. Experts were impressed with the violent upward motion near the funnel, and a lack of dirt and debris allowed tornado experts to peer into the inner core of the tornado.

Unfortunately, the pictures on TV might have been too spectacular. Instead of heading for their basements, many people were glued to their TV sets, or worse yet, lured outside to see the tornado for themselves. Folks watched from rooftops, backyards—anywhere they could get an unobstructed view of the chaos unfolding overhead. I want to stress that the Brooklyn Park tornado was not a typical Minnesota tornado. It moved very slowly, at times stalling over the same spot. Most twisters have a forward speed of twenty to forty miles an hour. The next tornado, there probably won't be time to stand outside and snap pictures with your Polaroid camera. You may have just seconds to take lifesaving measures.

THE TWIN CITIES SUPERSTORM JULY 23, 1987

"If you don't like the weather, don't worry, don't fret, and don't complain. Just stick around—'cause it'll change!"

It was the closest thing to a hurricane that residents of Minneapolis and St. Paul will ever experience. Over ten inches of rain swamped the metro area in six hours. Winds gusted to sixty miles an hour. The torrential rains were accompanied by nearly continuous lightning and a family of tornadoes and funnel clouds. Maple Grove, a northwestern suburb of Minneapolis, was hardest hit.

Unable to soak into the ground, the rainwater ran off into storm sewers and streets. Major freeways became impassable, and entire neighborhoods were cut off by the rising floodwaters. Countless thousands of basements were inundated with cold, muddy water, and many homeowners were horrified to learn that their insurance policies didn't cover flash flooding. Residents living on Lake Minnetonka who had forgotten to tie up their boats were surprised to find the boats missing the next morning. In a matter of hours, lake water levels had risen two to three feet!

The flood was a fluke, an extremely rare phenomenon known as a steady state storm. Two separate lines of thunderstorms merged over the Twin Cities, producing one sprawling megastorm. As old thunderstorms would drift out of the Twin Cities into Wisconsin and die out, new thunderheads would immediately take their place, bringing another wave of blinding rains to the metro area. According to the Army Corp of Engineers, it was a one-in-three-thousand-year storm. However, a storm of this magnitude is expected *somewhere* in Minnesota once every two or

The Five Deadliest Tornadoes in Minnesota's History

1. St. Cloud–Sauk Rapids tornado, April 14, 1886—Seventy-four dead
2. Fergus Falls tornado, June 22, 1919—Fifty-nine dead
3. Tyler tornado, August 21, 1918—Thirty-six dead
4. Rochester tornado, August 21, 1883—Thirty-one dead
5. Fridley outbreak, May 6, 1965—Fourteen dead

Superstorm Facts

Ten inches of rain falling on one square mile . . .

- translates into 170 million gallons of water!
- weighs about 720,000 tons!
- could fill 7,900 railroad cars with water!

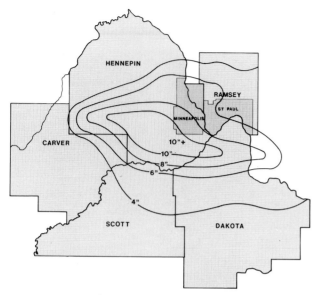

The Twin Cities superstorm, showing amount of rainfall in inches.

A rough guide: the taller the thunderhead, the greater the potential for flooding, tornadoes, and hail. The superstorm cells reached fifty-five thousand to sixty thousand feet, much higher than a "garden variety" thunderstorm. This is from a vantage point some ninety miles west of the Twin Cities. *Joe Ackerman, Atwater, MN.*

This chance shot of the Lake Gervais cyclone was taken about 5:00 P.M., July 13, 1890, from the west St. Paul Bluff, where the photographer, William F. Koester, happened to be with his camera taking pictures at the time of the disaster. The distance from the point of observation (Cherokee Avenue and Ohio Street) to where the funnel-shaped cloud touched the earth is a full six miles. *Courtesy: Minnesota Historical Society.*

A deadly one-two punch. The superstorm spawned more than watery headaches. At least half a dozen tornadoes and funnels skipped across the metro area. Hardest hit was Maple Grove in Hennepin County, where scores of homes experienced damage. Storms that result in both flooding and tornadoes are extremely rare. Usually, flooding results from slow-moving thunderstorms and light winds aloft, conditions unfavorable for tornadoes. *Kevin Swenson, Maple Grove, MN.*

three years. And engineers caution that urban sprawl, continued development of farmland, parking lots, and shopping malls, etc., has increased the risk of flash flooding in the metro area. The rainwater simply has nowhere to go but into storm sewers and streets, and that could mean more gulley-gushing thunderstorms and dangerous flash floods in the years ahead.

THE DROUGHT OF '88

"Only in Minnesota can you be hip-deep in mud with dust blowing in your face. . . . "

Nineteen eighty-eight was a devastating year for farmers, gardeners, and folks with lakeshore property. In the Twin Cities, the months of June, July, and August were the hottest since modern-day records began in 1892. For forty-four days the mercury sizzled above ninety degrees. The heat fried lawns and baked the moisture out of rich topsoil. For the year, rainfall was off by 30 to 50 percent, siphoning two to four feet off most lakes around the state. Thousands of wetland areas and smaller ponds dried up altogether. West of St. Cloud, underground water supplies went dry and bottled water had to be trucked in.

It was a frustrating summer for boaters and residents on lakeshore property, now confronted with too much lakeshore and not enough lake. Some boats were unable to reach the water altogether. One old-timer living next to Lake Minnetonka was still optimistic about the dry spell. "This is nothing. See those warning buoys out there?" he said, gesturing toward the lake. "Those used to be islands back in the '30s when lake water levels were down six to eight feet from where they are now. Lake water levels were unnaturally high back in the '70s and early '80s, but folks thought that was business as usual, so they built their homes and their docks assuming the lakes would always be brimming with water. Unfortunately for them, this is much closer to the long-term average for Minnesota lakes." Sobering news for many indeed.

It was a rude awakening for America's breadbasket, which had enjoyed twenty years of relatively wet weather. At the height of the drought in June of 1988, roughly 40 percent of America was suffering from severe or extreme drought. Climatologists tell us that nationwide, 1988 was the third hottest summer since accurate weather records were first kept in the mid-1800s.

"Weatherwise, it really was an incredible summer," said Jim Campbell, meteorologist in charge of the Twin Cities National Weather Service office. "If you look at what happened in the cities, we had the warmest June, July and August ever, since 1891."

Water was no longer taken for granted. The corn, soybean, and wheat harvest was off by 30 to 40 percent. The barge industry suffered a loss of $400 million. At the height of the drought, barge traffic was halted at nine places on the Mississippi River.

At least one scientific report concluded that it might have been the worst natural disaster in American history, costing the United States $30 billion, and resulting in close to ten thousand heat-related deaths. Most of the fatalities occurred in the inner neighborhoods of larger, older cities. Hardest hit: the elderly, the sick, and the disadvantaged. This makes the drought of 1988 deadlier than the hurricane of 1900, when six thousand residents of Galveston, Texas, were killed.

Frankly, meteorologists were at a ,loss to explain why a bubble of parched air remained anchored over the nation's heartland for month after month. Some thought it was the first signs of the greenhouse effect, but a majority of scientists believed that a strange cooling of the Pacific Ocean might have caused the jet stream to become locked in a peculiar pattern that favored hot, dry weather over North America. Minnesota was abruptly woken up; we had been spoiled during the 1970s, a decade of lower temperatures, heavy rains, and lakes brimming with water.

One pleasant side-effect of the drought: Thunderstorms were starved of gulf moisture, and for the most part, unable to strengthen to severe sta-

tus. There were only five twisters during all of 1988, and those were minor. A season with no tornado-related fatalities or injuries is a rarity indeed.

The dock to nowhere. *Charles l. Alden, White Bear Lake, MN.*

A sunburnt sky. *Casey Lotton, Mankato, MN.*

Dust and smoke. For the first time since the 1930s, dust storms swept across the prairie, hot winds filling the skies with precious topsoil. On at least one day, airborne dust combined with a rare rain shower to produce a "mud shower," which left cars stained with brown streaks! *Deb Lehrke, Aitkin, MN.*

Firestorm. The drought of 1988 left timberland tinder dry and vulnerable to catastrophic fires. Nationwide, over four million acres of forest went up in smoke. In this example, the hot ash from the fires seeded the clouds, sparking a few showers downwind. *Alphonse A. Thelen, Melrose, MN.*

Cumulus clouds are fair weather clouds — "popcorn" or "cotton" clouds. They are most common behind cold fronts and with the arrival of high pressure. A rising barometer, falling humidity, and cumulus clouds suggest at least twenty-four hours of dry weather. They appear weightless, but collectively the water droplets and ice crystals weigh millions of tons! *Jim Hawke, Eagan, MN.*

14

2 The Theater of the Seasons

"There is really no such thing as bad weather, only different kinds of good weather." —John Ruskin

Every day of the year, Minnesotans are treated to a beautiful and stirring performance, yet few take time out of their busy schedule to enjoy the outdoors. Weatherwise, days may be similar, but they are never exactly alike. This free show unfolding overhead is full of subtlety and nuance, boasting an impressive supporting cast of colorful rainbows, puffy popcorn clouds, bolting thunderheads, breathtaking sunsets, and a thousand and one more weather phenomena. They're all there, on permanent display, to be enjoyed and respected.

SPRING
"When the clouds appear like rocks and towers, the earth will be washed by frequent showers."

Spring comes reluctantly to Minnesota. In fact, if you sneeze you may just miss it altogether! Some years spring doesn't arrive at all, and we make the awkward transition from slush to perspiration and mosquitoes in a week or two, leaving some of us disoriented, feeling somehow cheated.

Without a doubt, spring is the most fickle of seasons. One day, the mercury nicks the fifty-degree mark, and we gleefully rip off our many layers of clothing and run around in shirt-sleeves and shorts, our pale bodies the color of white neon. And then, just hours later, heavy wet snow plasters the newly discovered lawns and token robins with a depressing layer of sandy slush and sludge, and we mope around indoors. Who among us has not experienced the utter despair of cabin fever?

Spring skies over Minnesota are irritable, and capable of explosive violence. The upper atmosphere is still extremely cold, suffering from a wintry hangover of sorts. But a strong sun is rising high into the sky now, heating the ground and the air immediately above the ground. The warm air wants to rise, the cold air tries to sink, resulting in instability. Here you have all the ingredients for severe thunderstorms and tornadoes.

What Is a Severe Thunderstorm?

A storm is classified as severe if winds greater than fifty-eight miles per hour are measured, or hail three-quarters of an inch or larger occurs. In Minnesota, fewer than 10 percent of all thunderstorms are severe. And how can you recognize thunderstorms? Look for cumulonimbus clouds. Cumulonimbus clouds are otherwise known as thunderheads, CBs, or if you prefer the pure scientific definition, electrostatic bipolar generators. These storms are characterized by intense updrafts and downdrafts, with wind speeds often exceeding one hundred miles per hour. Hail can be present, along with dangerous turbulence and frequent lightning. Generally, the taller the thunderhead, the greater the risk of severe weather. Some tornadic storms can reach heights of fifty-five thousand to sixty-five thousand feet, towering some twelve miles into the troposphere. Thunderstorms are often characterized by their anvil tips and the presence of lightning.

Anvil clouds are composed of microscopic ice crystals at temperatures of -40° to -60° F. An anvil is visual proof that a thunderhead is mature and capable of hail, lightning, strong winds, and heavy rain. The anvil is formed when a warm, moist updraft encounters the stratosphere, where temperatures rise with height. This causes the updraft to spread out, forming a funnel-shaped cap on top of the thunderhead. In the photo on page 16, the streaks are hailstones falling out of the anvil and evaporating in drier air surrounding the thunderstorm.

But not all thunderstorm anvils have flat tops. An overshooting top is evidence of a particularly violent updraft. This bulge on top of a anvil is a tip-off that the cell may "go severe." When you see this knob popping up above a thunderhead, there's a higher probability of hail, damaging winds, and possible tornadoes. An overshooting top is a warning sign that the thunderstorm may be maturing into something called a mesocyclone.

What is a mesocyclone? Ninety percent of all thunderstorms self-destruct—rain-cooled air eventually chokes off the warm updraft inside the thunderhead. But sometimes, when the upper-

A lonely shower. *Nancy Horn, Brainerd, MN.*

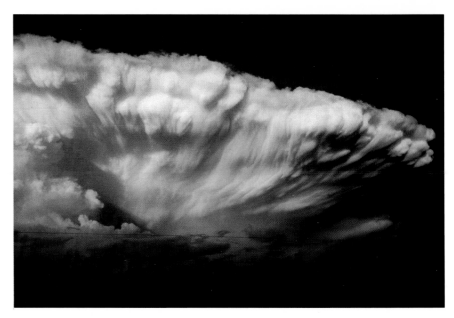

Anvil cloud and hail. *Nolan Jungelaus, Lake Lillian, MN.*

Overshooting top. *Paula Wiehoff, St. Cloud, MN.*

Mesocyclone.

Wall cloud over a lake. *Russell Dorn, Minnetonka, MN.*

This photo taken near Alexandria shows cumulonimbus mammatus clouds, the underside of a severe thunderstorm. *Barbara Lynn, St. Peter, MN.*

Cumulonimbus mammatus clouds are sure indicators that the atmosphere is explosively unstable. Often occurring at the tail end of a strong thunderstorm, "mamma" can signal the presence of hail and potentially damaging straight-line or tornadic winds. *Lou Morlino, Minneapolis, MN.*

Wall cloud. *Dan and Lisa Gombus, Foley, MN.*

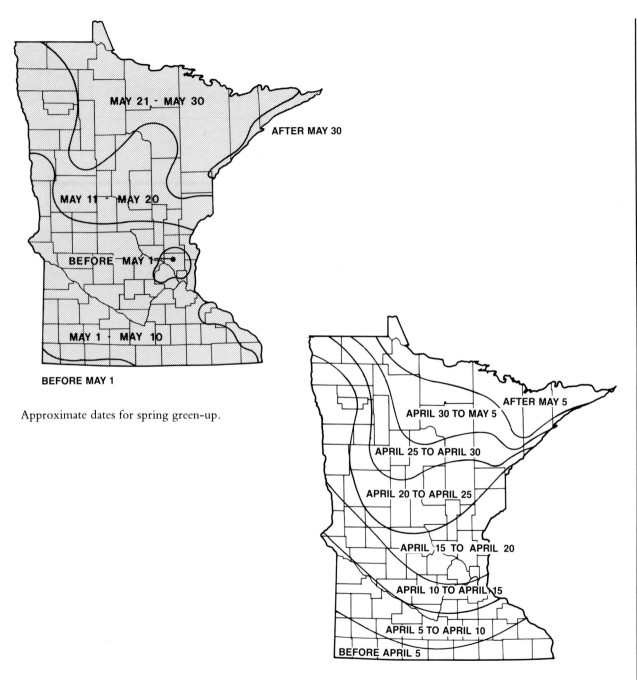

MAY 21 - MAY 30

AFTER MAY 30

MAY 11 - MAY 20

BEFORE MAY 1

MAY 1 - MAY 10

BEFORE MAY 1

Approximate dates for spring green-up.

AFTER MAY 5

APRIL 30 TO MAY 5

APRIL 25 TO APRIL 30

APRIL 20 TO APRIL 25

APRIL 15 TO APRIL 20

APRIL 10 TO APRIL 15

APRIL 5 TO APRIL 10

BEFORE APRIL 5

Average ice-out dates from 1960 to 1979. By the middle of April, ice is off most of Minnesota's lakes. But from the North Shore into the Boundary Waters, lake ice can linger into early May.

The tornado that swept through Fergus Falls on June 22, 1919 was probably an F4 or F5. The twister was the second deadliest in Minnesota history, killing fifty-nine people.

Roughly fifty days out of the year are potentially life threatening with a possibility of damaging winds, tornadoes, hail, blizzards, floods, or some other weather hazard that could conceivably kill you (or at least get your day off to a rotten start).

Funnel cloud: a tornado that has not yet reached the ground. Based on counterclockwise cloud rotation and the sighting of a developing funnel, tornado watches are immediately upgraded to tornado warnings for specific counties.

A "white tornado" is really the result of sunlight shining on the funnel. Some tornadoes have a whitish appearance due to rapid upward motion that condenses invisible water vapor into visible cloud droplets.

Waterspouts are most common over tropical waters. They tend to be less severe than tornadoes, with winds estimated at fifty to one hundred miles per hour, still powerful enough to capsize boats and threaten swimmers. Tornadoes passing over lakes can suck up enormous amounts of water into the air, producing showers of fish and frogs as the storm dissipates downwind!

level jet stream winds are strong, thunderstorms can tilt over slightly, allowing the heavy rain and hail to fall away from the warm updraft, keeping the storm alive for many hours. This increases the potential for destructive weather and creates the intense, rotating thunderstorms three to five miles wide known as mesocyclones. If the updraft is violent enough, the counterclockwise spin of a mesocyclone can spawn nature's deadliest wind, the tornado.

Many spinning mesocyclones go on to trigger wall clouds, found near the tail-end of severe thunderstorms. A wall cloud is any dark lowering of the clouds that rotates in a counterclockwise direction. Wall clouds should be watched very carefully. Here is where tornadoes are most likely to form. A wall cloud is evidence of an exceptionally strong updraft. The stronger this upward rush of warm, moist air, the greater the risk of an eventual tornado touchdown.

Tornadoes are nature's most violent wind. A narrow, violently rotating column of air in contact with the ground, this destructive updraft can have winds that exceed two hundred miles an hour, possibly reaching speeds as high as three hundred miles an hour. No wind instruments have ever survived a direct hit by a tornado, so wind speeds have to be estimated from the damage they leave behind.

Tornadoes form some two to four miles above the ground. Scientists believe that a sudden downward gust of rain-cooled air at the tail-end of the thunderstorm, called a rear-flank downdraft, may be the mechanism that actually pulls the funnel down to the ground.

What is a suction vortex? Many tornadoes, especially larger tornadoes, are composed of fierce miniature tornadoes some thirty to one hundred feet wide that swirl around the main funnel. It's here that tornado damage is most severe, and from the air, suction vortices appear as muddy scars scratched into the earth's surface.

Since 1950, more than 650 tornadoes have been spotted in the skies over Minnesota, leaving behind eighty deaths, sixteen hundred injuries, and hundreds of millions of dollars in damage.

Tornado Survival Tips

- At home: Studies show that the safest place to be during a tornado is in your basement, under the stairs. If you can crawl under a desk or table, the odds of injury drop even more. The real danger from a tornado is not being sucked up in a cloud and deposited in Kansas. Most injuries and fatalities are the result of people being hit by debris traveling at close to two hundred miles an hour, or being crushed by collapsing buildings. Statistically, the odds of being killed if you're under the basement stairwell are less than 1 percent. Avoid the southwest corner of your basement. Several years ago, the thinking was that this might be the safest area. New research suggests that in many cases, bricks, cinder blocks, and other debris accumulates in the southwest corner. If you don't have a basement, a small, windowless room on the ground floor offers the greatest protection. A storage closet, laundry room, or bathroom will work best. Many people have survived twisters by climbing into their bathtubs, and pulling a mattress over them. They hear a loud whoosh, kick off the mattress, and are shocked to see blue sky! The tornado has taken off the roof, and stripped away the outer walls, but the bathtub remains, reinforced by all the pipes leading into the bathroom. I've seen numerous pictures of damage where the only thing left and visible from the air is the family bathtub. And whatever you do, if you are already home and a tornado is sighted nearby, do not run to the neighbors' house or climb into your car and try to drive to safety. This is how many people become grim "statistics" every year.

- At the office: Avoid the elevators. If time permits, use the stairs to reach the basement or the lowest level in the building. Get away from outer walls and windows. There is little danger of a high-rise building tipping over. The real threat is from a eraser flying at two hundred miles per hour bonking you on the head. The safest area is a smaller room near the center of the office building, perhaps a windowless office or even a restroom.

- At school: Get the students as far away from the outer windows and walls as possible. If time permits, a basement offers the greatest safety. If there is no time, hiding under a desk offers some protection. Crouching up against lockers in an interior hallway is another option, but a wind-tunnel effect has been observed in some instances, with a very real danger of students being hit with flying debris. Avoiding large rooms, gymnasiums and auditoriums will lessen the risk of injury.

- Outside: Your first reaction is probably "Look for a ditch!" I don't know about you, but when I most need a good ditch, there's none to be found. Your first impulse should be to duck into a nearby house, office, or store. Any building will offer more protection than a ditch will. If you are truly out in the boonies with no sign of civilization in sight, a ditch will offer some help. A few lucky souls have survived tornadoes by climbing into giant storm sewer pipes underneath the highway. But be careful—tornadic thunderstorms are often preceded by copious rain, and the possibility of drowning in one of these storm sewers is very real!

- In your car: Use common sense. If the tornado is several miles away, drive away from the twister at right angles and don't look back! If the tornado is several blocks away, pull your vehicle over to the side of the road and run into the nearest building or house. It seems cars are among the first objects to become airborne when a tornado strikes. In 1979, a tornado swept through Wichita Falls, Texas. There was a good thirty-minute warning that the twister was on the way. But thousands of people got into their cars, and tried to beat the tornado home. The result was a massive traffic-jam just as the twister ripped across the city. Forty-five people were killed, most sitting in their cars. Had they stayed at the office, they all would have survived the tornado.

More Tips That May Save Your Life

Try to get as many walls between you and the tornado as possible. A small, windowless room near the center of your basement or ground floor will be safest. And, the smaller the room, the better!

And forget the windows! At some point in our lives, we've all been instructed, "If you have time, open up the windows on the side of the house away from the tornado to lessen the air pressure difference." It is true that a rapid drop in atmospheric pressure, as much as one hundred millibars in a few seconds, causes some homes to explode under the strain. But engineers have determined that opening a few windows is not going to save your house. In fact, so many people are injured and killed while tinkering with their windows when they should be high-tailing it for the basement that officials now recommend that you leave your windows alone.

Dumb, Dumb, Dumb. . . .

At all costs, avoid looking out the windows! Your first reaction to a tornado warning may be to run to the nearest window for a closer look, but you're asking for trouble. Shredded plate-glass windows hitting human flesh at upwards of two hundred miles per hour can have some very unpleasant effects. This is how most people are injured and killed.

Don't spend too much time searching for your pet. You'll lose precious seconds, and there's a good chance that Rover or Fluffy will seek shelter by themselves. Animals seem to have a sixth sense when it comes to bad weather. In many cases, they seem to be smarter than their owners!

Don't try to take a picture with your Instamatic or home video camera. Remember, the Brooklyn Park tornado was a fluke, traveling along at a slow five miles an hour. Most Minnesota tornadoes race along at twenty to forty miles an hour. The next time, you may not have time to load film — you may have literally a few seconds to do the right thing.

What Is Tornado Alley?

America has more tornadoes than any other country on earth. Desert-dry westerly winds blow over moisture-rich air flowing northward out of the Gulf of Mexico, resulting in explosive instability. The dry line, running through Texas and Oklahoma and Kansas, is a sharp boundary separating dry air from moist air. This is where the skies are most likely to turn black and deadly each spring.

Is it true there's a local tornado alley? Yes, although there is certainly no cause for panic. Statistically, there is a slightly higher probability of seeing a twister north and west of the Twin Cities, roughly from Lake Minnetonka to the Fridley — Coon Rapids area. Before you consider selling off real estate, I want to stress that this difference is extremely minor.

Tornadic thunderstorms thrive on high humidity. It's possible that the drier air over the immediate metro area may cause some severe thunderstorms to be deflected off to the north and west, staying close to the moisture-rich air necessary to sustain a tornado's violent updraft. But again, this is just a theory.

Is it true that tornadoes can't hit downtown St. Paul or Minneapolis? No, in fact, statistically it's just a matter of time before a large tornado dips into downtown Minneapolis or St. Paul. Tall buildings are not a deterrent. Twisters, especially the larger ones, pretty much go where they want to go.

Do mobile home parks attract tornadoes? Of course not, although at times it almost seems that way from watching the news. It's just that when a twister does hit a trailer park, the damage is always extensive, often with a tragic loss of life. Most mobile homes do not have suitable foundations and are not securely attached to the ground.

Weatherfact: Studies show that less than two-thirds of all severe storms are predicted ahead of time. Even so, when a tornado watch is issued, there's a 70 percent probability that a tornado will touch down somewhere within the watch box.

Tornadic Facts and Figures

- Every year, approximately one hundred thousand thunderstorms rumble across the United States.
- Of these, roughly ten thousand produce severe weather — hail or damaging winds.
- Of these, only one thousand or so spawn tornadoes. The bottom line: The odds of a given thunderstorm spinning up a twister are less than one in one hundred!
- Of these one thousand or so tornadoes, only twenty-five will be significant, leading to widespread damage and considerable loss of life.

Did You Know?

- If you live in Minnesota long enough, there's a good chance you'll see a tornado (hopefully from a distance). If you use your head and don't panic, there is no reason why you have to be a tornado "statistic."
- On average, some seventeen tornadoes skip across Minnesota every year. Most are minor tornadoes, with wind speeds under 125 miles an hour (but still capable of ruining your day).
- A typical Minnesota tornado (if there is such a thing) lasts ten minutes, has a path length of five to six miles, is nearly as wide as a football field, has a forward speed of about thirty-five miles an hour and affects less than one-tenth of 1 percent of the county warned!
- Tornadoes were called cyclones during the 50s and 60s. Today that term is rarely heard, but tornadoes are sometime called twisters.

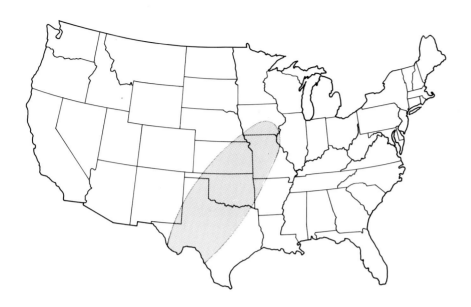

Tornado alley.

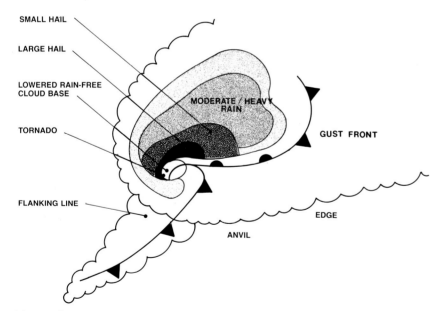

SMALL HAIL

LARGE HAIL

LOWERED RAIN-FREE CLOUD BASE

MODERATE / HEAVY RAIN

TORNADO

GUST FRONT

FLANKING LINE

EDGE

ANVIL

Too close for comfort.

Mesocyclones are intense, counterclockwise-rotating thunderstorms some three to five miles wide. They often tilt over slightly, the result of 100- to 200-mile-an-hour jet stream winds howling high overhead. This tilting prevents rain- and hail-cooled downdrafts within the thunderhead from snuffing out the fragile updraft. Rain and hail are swept away from the storm track, allowing the warm updraft to continue strengthening. Nearly all mesocyclones produce damaging hail and winds; about 50 percent spawn tornadoes.

It's not unusual for a mesocyclone to spawn up to half a dozen tornadoes over several hours. Here, the older twister (right) is being choked off by a rain shaft of cool, wet air that is sucked into the funnel's warm updraft. A secondary tornado has formed (left) where plenty of hot air still fuels the updraft.

More Tornado Trivia

- Tornadoes are most likely around the dinner hour, between 5:00 and 7:00 P.M. Less than 5 percent of all twisters strike late at night, but that is when many of the injuries and fatalities occur (because people are sleeping and not aware of impending danger).
- Prime time for tornadoes in Minnesota is June, May, and July—in that order.
- If this is a typical year, at least one or two Minnesotans will be killed by tornadoes.
- Nationwide, an average of ninety-nine people will perish from tornadoes every year.
- The ferocious winds in a tornado give off a tell-tale roar, which has been compared to "a hundred freight trains or a billion buzzing bees." If the rumble of thunder gives way to a steady rumble that gets louder with time, you may want to head for shelter.
- Scientists once believed that the load roar of a tornado was made by the winds that approached the speed of sound, nearly seven hundred miles an hour. After studying damage on the ground and videotapes of tornadoes frame by frame, researchers say that tornadoes are not capable of breaking the sound barrier. The top winds in a severe tornado may approach three hundred miles an hour or so.

Amazing, But True

- People have been picked up into the air by tornadoes and carried hundreds of yards, even a few miles, set down in trees dazed and covered with mud and garbage, but alive!
- A tornado once picked up a carton of eggs, carried it several miles into the next county, and set it down gently, without breaking one egg!
- A twister once picked up a locomotive train weighing hundreds of tons, lifted it up off the tracks, turned it around, and set it back down on the tracks—pointed in the opposite direction!

Tornado Tip-offs

Thankfully, tornadoes do not drop out of a sunny, powder-blue sky. Severe, rotating thunderstorms are necessary for tornado formation. There are some things you can watch for, subtle signs that the atmosphere is primed for a wild and windy display.

- Look for a dark, greenish cast to the sky. Severe thunderstorms tilt over into the wind slightly. Frequently, they are big hail producers. All this can leave the sky an eerie color.
- Lumpy, cumulonimbus mammatus clouds near the tail-end of a severe thunderstorm are an indication of extreme instability and possible hail.
- Nearly continuous lightning can be picked up as static on your AM radio dial. Tornadic mesocyclones produce enormous amounts of lightning.
- Watch for a wall cloud, any dark lowering of the cloud base that is rotating in a counterclockwise manner. Wall clouds are most often found at the tail-end of a severe thunderstorm, after a period of heavy rain and hail. Here, along the trailing, southwestern edge of a mesocyclone, is where a twister is most likely to touch down.

What is an F5 Tornado?

Tornadoes are classified by the destruction they leave behind. They are rated from F0 to F5, *F* standing for the *F* in the University of Chicago's Dr. Theodore Fujita, one of the nation's leading experts on tornado research. F0, F1, and F2 twisters spin up 73- to 160-mph winds, capable of considerable damage (but some walls will remain standing). An F5 tornado inflicts catastrophic destruction with wind speeds close to three hundred miles per hour or more, and the result is usually flattened rubble. Luckily, less than 2 or 3 percent of all tornadoes are F5s, and they tend to be in Kansas and Oklahoma rather than in Minnesota. Nearly 90 percent of all Minnesota twisters are "minor" F0s, F1s, and F2s, still capable of extensive damage and loss of life. Frankly, when you get right down to it, there are no minor tornadoes.

Tornado Category (F Scale)	Winds (mph)	Length (miles)	Width	Damage
0	Under 72	Under 1	Under 17 (yards)	Light
1	73–112	1–3	18–55 (yards)	Moderate
2	113–157	3–10	56–175 (yards)	Considerable
3	158–206	10–31	176–556 (yards)	Severe
4	207–260	32–99	0.34–0.9 (miles)	Devastating
5	261–318	100–315	1–3 (miles)	Incredible
6*	319–380	316–999	3–10 (miles)	Inconceivable

* An F6 is a theoretical calculation. No tornado has ever been classified as an F6.

When a tornado does touch down, the mobile homes are likely to be sent tumbling end over end. If you live in a trailer park, it's essential that there be an underground shelter or basement within a one-to-two-minute dash of your home. And when the siren sounds, don't assume the weather-casters are just crying wolf. Play it safe and head for safety.

Monitoring the Skies: Watches and Warnings

Tornado watches are issued by National Severe Storms Forecast Center (NSSFC) in Kansas City after examining satellites, radar, hourly airport observations, and upper air data. When conditions are ripe, a watch is issued for an area covering tens of thousands of square miles. Even with current technology, it is impossible to predict exactly when or where a tornado will touch down. A watch means go about your normal activities, but keep one eye on the sky and stay tuned for possible warnings.

Tornado warnings are broadcast on TV, radio, and NOAA weather radio when a tornado is actually sighted by Skywarn weather observers or law enforcement officials. Tornado warnings are also issued when Doppler radar detects violent rotation or a hook-echo, because both of these suggest a well-defined mesocyclone capable of dropping a funnel. This may tip off meteorologists, but in most cases the National Weather Service relies on a first-hand sighting from a trained, reliable observer before a warning is issued. Only the National Weather Service can initiate a tornado warning. A warning means that potential trouble is on the way, and it's time to go to the basement or the nearest shelter.

Remember, even when a warning is issued, a very small percentage of that particular county will be affected. Somewhere, someone is getting clobbered, but most of us will come upstairs only to find our homes and neighborhoods largely undisturbed. This leads some to believe that meteorologists are just over-hyping the weather.

It would be nice if we had the ability to call up individual homes in the path of a twister and issue personalized warnings to each family. Since this is neither possible nor practical, we are guilty of having to overwarn the public. But if anything, we want to err on the side of safety. As a profession, our worst fear is being caught with our "Dopplers down," not being able to give any warning to a town in the direct path of a tornado. Future refinements in Doppler radar, like the Nexrad program, should mean that fewer of us have to be warned unnecessarily.

Meteorologists working at the National Weather Service and the local media depend upon the eyes and ears of some twenty-five hundred trained weather spotters in Minnesota—a system called Skywarn. When a watch is issued, they go to assigned positions, waiting and watching for severe weather to strike. When a tornado or a damaging thunderstorm is actually spotted, these amateur radio operators call in their reports directly to the National Weather Service, and 95 percent of the time, based on their firsthand observation, a warning is issued for specific counties or parts of counties. There are approximately six hundred Skywarn spotters in a protective ring around the Twin Cities metro area alone, people from all walks of life who are on call at a moment's notice. Together with fire, police, rescue, and ambulance personnel, they provide the ultimate safety net.

And finally, you can keep an eye on the weather yourself with your TV set. You can pick up tornadoes on your TV set, you ask. True! Twisters seem to emit a very low-frequency electronic hum that sometimes shows up on your TV tube. Disconnect your TV set from the cable and tune to channel thirteen. Darken the screen until it just goes black. Now turn to channel two. Those occasional flashes are lightning strikes nearby. If the screen glows brightly on a nearly continuous basis, a tornado or funnel cloud may be within twenty miles or so of your house. This is a crude and often unreliable procedure, but it has saved lives!

SUMMER

Although I'm almost ashamed to admit it, I am not an impartial weather soothsayer. No, I prefer summer. I root and cheer for summer, grateful that these poor, tired, dusty warm fronts have found the strength to invade Minnesota. I am in awe of summer, amazed that a backyard punished by sub-zero cold can be transformed into something so green and lush. Even on the hot ninety-degree days a gusty wind offers some relief. On either coast, summer is a time of murky haze, of smelly pollution, and stale windless days dripping with humidity. But not in Minnesota. Here summers pretty much turn out the way God intended them to be.

The Sights and Sounds of Summer

Minnesotans are treated to a dazzling display during the summer months. These weather phenomena are treats for the senses, to be enjoyed by all weather-lovers (although sometimes from a distance).

Downburst: Mature thunderstorms contain intense updrafts and downdrafts, where wind speeds can top one hundred miles an hour at times. When these rain and hail-cooled shafts of downward-rushing air reach the air that is nearer the earth, they spread out into "gust fronts," with straight-line winds approaching 125 miles an hour, strong enough to take roofs off of houses. These downdrafts present the greatest risk to aircraft, especially during take-off and landing. Rapid changes in wind direction and speed can affect the lift on an airplane's wing, with potentially disastrous results. A number of airplane accidents are being blamed on nearby downbursts or smaller microbursts. Remote-sensing wind instruments near airport runways, and Doppler radar, which can "see the wind," hold the promise of giving pilots more advanced warning of this dangerous phenomenon.

Roll cloud: Sometimes called shelf clouds, these threatening, wedge-shaped clouds often precede severe thunderstorms. Triggered when a violent, rain-cooled downdraft within a thunderstorm advances into warmer air, these clouds are often accompanied by extreme wind shear and turbulence, capable of damage to aircraft. Along the leading edge of the storm, winds of sixty miles an hour or more are possible.

Pileus or cap cloud: As air rises, it cools and loses its ability to hold water vapor. As a result, water vapor condenses into visible water droplets and ice crystals. If the updraft in a thunderhead is especially strong, a brief cap or hood of ice crystals may form above the mushrooming cumulus cloud.

Altocumulus castellanus: Found in the midlevels of the atmosphere, at about ten thousand feet, these towerlike clouds are a sign of instability. Combined with a south or southeast breeze and rising dew points, they may be a tip-off that thunderstorms will develop later in the day.

Thunder: a shock-wave of superheated air, traveling away from a lightning bolt at the speed of sound. This expanding air literally piles into the air nearby, creating a rumbling sound.

How far away is that thunderstorm? That's easy to calculate. Since thunder travels at the speed of sound, roughly 650 to 700 mph (or about 950 to 1,030 feet per second), you know that thunder will cover a distance of one mile (5,280 feet) in about five seconds. Just count the number of seconds between when you see lightning and when you hear thunder, and divide by five. If you count thirteen seconds, the lightning strike was two and a half miles away. If you see the flash of lightning and hear the clap of thunder almost instantaneously, the lightning was dangerously close, probably less than a quarter of a mile away.

Lightning: a brilliant electric spark discharge in the atmosphere, occurring within a thunderhead, between clouds, or between a cloud and the ground—and an underrated killer. Lightning claims more lives every year than hurricanes and tornadoes combined, but since these fatalities tend to occur one at a time, they may not make the news as often as other natural disasters.

People struck by lightning receive a severe electrical shock. They may be burned, but they do not carry an electrical charge, and they can be handled safely. In many instances, lightning victims who appear to be dead are revived using CPR. Beginning immediate chest massage and mouth-to-mouth resuscitation before the ambulance arrives may save a life!

What is heat lightning? Here's a surprise—there is no such thing! What you are really seeing is the lightning of a distant thunderstorm over the horizon being reflected by haze or high cirrus clouds. Lightning from these distant thunderstorms can be seen as far away as 75 to 125 miles, especially on the prairie. Thunder is rarely heard from storms more than five miles away, thus the impression that these are silent, heat-generated thunderstorms. These distant flashes of lightning are most likely during the hot, hazy dog days of summer.

A mesoconvective complex, or MCC for short: a sprawling cluster of thunderstorms, sometimes over a hundred miles wide, capable of unleashing torrential five- to ten-inch-plus rains. They tend to form at night during the muggy summer months, and they can travel hundreds of miles before slowly dissipating the following morning. MCCs provide precious moisture for the plains and the Upper Midwest, but at times they can be too much of a good thing, leading to flash flooding and rain-swollen rivers.

Flash flood: If this is a typical summer, Minnesota will see seven to ten flash floods, defined as six inches of rain falling in six (or fewer) hours. Flash flooding is most likely to occur during late summer, when upper-level steering winds are light,

A downburst. *Cathy MacDonald, Eden Prairie, MN.*

A roll cloud. *Gene Grolla, McGregor, MN.*

24

Lightning. *Chris Grajczyk, Minneapolis, MN.*

"Cows lie down before a storm."

This is absolutely true! Cows tend to eat more before the arrival of a big storm, often to the point of indigestion. They too like to sneak in a nap after a particularly big meal.

"Cat's groom themselves before a storm."

Again, there is scientific evidence to back up this "old wives' tale." Thunderstorms generate static electricity, which separates the cat's coat hairs, making them feel dirty. Licking their coat smooths the hair, leaving them less self-conscious.

The safest places to ride out the storm?

When lightning approaches, avoid open fields, golf courses, and standing under trees or near metal poles or fences. Do not operate farm machinery. Swimming pools and boats provide easy targets. You don't want to be in or on the water when lightning strikes nearby. Remember, lightning is lazy — it usually takes the easiest path from cloud to ground. The bottom line: You don't want to be the tallest thing in the area!

- Stay indoors, away from large picture windows. Stay off the telephone during a severe electrical storm. (There have been cases of lightning striking a nearby telephone line and traveling into homes nearby.) Otherwise, go about your normal activities.
- If you are outdoors, any shelter will offer considerable protection. If there are no buildings nearby, crouch near a clump of small trees or shrubs. Crouch on all fours. Do not lie flat on the ground; this will increase the chances of receiving a dangerous electrical jolt if lightning strikes nearby. If you feel your hair stand on end, drop to your knees, and bend forward, putting your hands on your knees. If lightning strikes near you, the chances of your body acting as a conductor are minimized. Kneeling provides a low profile, while at the same time keeping only a small area of your body in contact with the ground. Don't lie in a ditch where surface water or saturated soil may act as a better conductor than the surrounding area.
- In your car? Relax, you are relatively safe. Rubber tires and the metal shell surrounding your body prevent you from being in direct contact with the ground. This measure of insulation means that even a direct hit probably won't be life-threatening (although chances are it will get your attention!).

"The hooting of an owl says the weather will be foul."
'When sheep gather in a huddle, tomorrow we'll have a puddle."

A cap cloud. *Wally Johnson, Eden Valley, MN.*

Altocumulus castellanus. *Deana Smith, Mora, MN.*

A pillar of precipitation.

Rainbows are most commonly seen at sunrise or sunset, when the sun is low and you are standing between a rain shower and the sun. White sunlight is refracted within each raindrop. A shower is made up of trillions of these tiny prisms, each separating sunlight into the colors of the spectrum. If the sunlight is bent once within each raindrop, a single rainbow will be visible. Sunlight bent twice within each drop results in a double rainbow. Triple rainbows are possible, but extremely rare.

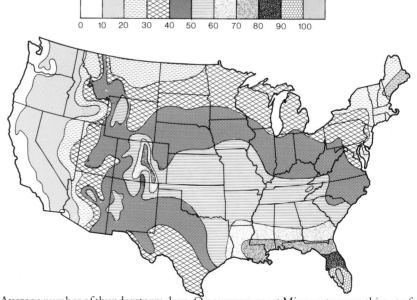

THUNDERSTORM DAYS

0 10 20 30 40 50 60 70 80 90 100

Average number of thunderstorm days. On average, most Minnesotans see thirty to forty days a year with thunder and lightning. (Alaska and Hawaii see less than ten days, and Puerto Rico and the Virgin Islands see about 50.)

WHERE MOST PEOPLE HAVE BEEN KILLED

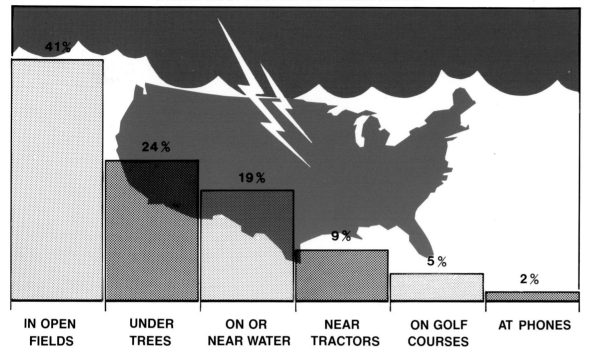

41%	24%	19%	9%	5%	2%
IN OPEN FIELDS	UNDER TREES	ON OR NEAR WATER	NEAR TRACTORS	ON GOLF COURSES	AT PHONES

Lightning dangers.

Lightning Facts
- It strikes the earth one hundred times a second, some eight million times a day!
- It is made up of charged particles that travel at roughly 81,000 miles a second.
- The United States is scarred by some fifty million strikes every year.
- Lightning kills two hundred to five hundred Americans every year, igniting twenty-two thousand house fires, and leaving behind over $100 million in property damage.
- Approximately ten thousand forest fires are sparked by lightning every year.
- Your typical, run-of-the-mill lightning bolt is five times hotter than the surface of the sun, roughly fifty thousand degrees Fahrenheit!
- Roughly 10 percent of all lightning strikes are

from the ground up! If the difference between negatively and positively charged particles is great enough, the lightning current can be initiated on the ground and work its way up into the thunderhead at roughly half the speed of light, or ninety-three thousand miles a second!
- At this moment, some two thousand lightning producing thunderstorms are rumbling around the earth. Nearly forty-four thousand electrical storms sprout up, worldwide, every single day.
- There is new evidence that airplanes can trigger lightning in clouds that are not producing the lightning naturally. Under certain atmospheric conditions, the passage of an airplane may disturb the cloud's electrical field, resulting in a lightning surge. Commercial air-

craft are struck by lightning on the order of once every three thousand hours.
- Lightning can strike in the winter, even as far north as Minnesota. Often winter lightning is a tip-off of an intense convective "snow burst" with snow piling up at the rate of up to two to four inches an hour!
- Recent research suggests that there are far more positively charged cloud-to-ground lightning strikes in tornadic thunderstorms. In 1995, NASA is expected to launch a satellite-based lightning mapper, capable of detecting cloud-to-ground and cloud-to-cloud lightning, and possibly able to highlight the electrical thumbprint of tornado-bearing thunderheads.

Old fashioned fertilizer!
Lightning combines with atmospheric gases to produce oxides of nitrogen and ozone, which act as natural fertilizers, helping to keep Minnesota a little greener during the summer months. This is what you smell before a thunderstorm, a pretty good indicator that you are about to get wet. It must be emphasized that 90 percent of all Minnesota thunderstorms are not severe. In fact they are extremely beneficial, squeezing out precious rains from March into September. Without these electrical storms, we might have a climate similar to that of western Kansas or Texas, and that of course would be very bad news for farmers.

Old fashioned (and cheap!) radar. Thunderstorms almost always trumpet their arrival, giving ample time to seek shelter. Thunder isn't the only tip-off. Your AM radio can detect lightning, both in-cloud, and cloud-to-ground. It shows up as static. Tune to a frequency where there is no radio station, preferably near 550 kilohertz (the left end of your AM dial). If you hear nearly continuous static getting louder with time, there's a high probability that a line of thunderstorms will be invading your town within a couple of hours.

and thunderstorms can stall, pouring out torrential rains in a short period of time. The greatest danger arises when people camp near small streams that can quickly overflow from a nearby cloudburst. There is evidence that flooding in the metro area may increase as development and the paving over of farmland continues. Rainwater simply has nowhere to go but into the streets and storm sewers. Nationwide, some twenty thousand communities are prone to urban flooding.

When a flash flood watch is issued, conditions are ripe for flooding. The air is exceptionally moist, and thunder storms may stall nearby. Stay tuned to local TV and radio, and avoid camping near streams and rivers.

A flash flood warning is issued if flooding is reported by the public, or a slow-moving storm looks especially threatening on radar. That means it's time to move to higher ground.

- Avoid areas prone to sudden flooding.
- Do not attempt to cross a flowing stream where the water is above your knees.
- Do not drive over a flooded road—you can be stranded or trapped by rapidly rising floodwaters. The depth of the water is not always obvious.
- If your vehicle stalls, abandon it immediately and seek higher ground. Rapidly rising water may engulf the vehicle and its occupants and sweep them away.
- Beware! The threat of hydroplaning is greatest during and immediately after a heavy rainstorm. At speeds greater than twenty-five or thirty miles an hour, a thin layer of water can build up between the highway and your tires, and your vehicle's tires may temporarily leave the roadway surface, leaving you with little control over steering or braking. To avoid an accident, slow down, pump your brakes gently, and try to avoid the well-worn ruts near the center of the roadway surface where excess rainwater is most apt to collect.

Wind: One thing that is not rare during a Minnesota summer is wind. On many days, wind can be more than a threat to your hairdo. It can make boating and fishing a downright risky undertaking. The local National Weather Service office issues a lake wind advisory when winds are expected to gust past thirty miles an hour for at least three consecutive hours.

The Minnesota Oven

Of course, summer is synonymous with heat. Thawing out and warming up can be a wonderful sensation, but hot weather can kill. It's hard to believe, but excessive heat claims more lives every year than hurricanes, tornadoes, floods, and earthquakes combined! Annually, some 175 to 300 people across the nation lose their lives due to heat-related ailments. An unusually hot summer may claim as many as fifteen hundred lives nationwide. The elderly and small babies are most vulnerable to the dangers of hot weather.

What's the difference between heat exhaustion and heatstroke? Symptoms of heat exhaustion include excessive perspiration, dizziness, nausea, and a low-grade fever. Bring the person affected into a cooler, shaded, or air-conditioned area and give them time to cool down. Heatstroke is much more serious, and if left untreated, can be fatal. Symptoms may include hot, dry skin, shallow breathing, a racing pulse, and total disorientation. Call 911 immediately!

When the weather pattern is humid, with dew points above sixty, the risk of heat stress is much greater. It's been estimated that at relative humidities greater than 60 percent sweat on the surface of your skin won't evaporate, and this poses a big problem. It is the evaporation of perspiration that triggers a cooling effect. When the relative humidity is very high to begin with there is little opportunity for this process to occur, leaving you even hotter under the collar than usual!

A Few Hot Weather Survival Tips
- Lightweight, light-colored, cotton clothing will keep you most comfortable. Try to avoid

"Crow on the fence, rain will come down. Rain will go hence when crow's on the ground."
"When swallows chirp and fly high in the sky, fair weather will follow."
"Houseflies bite before a storm."

There is some scientific evidence to back up these "old wives' tales." Birds and insects have extremely sensitive ears. They can detect even a slight drop in barometric pressure as a storm approaches. As a result, they tend to fly closer to the ground to compensate for this painful drop in pressure.

Weatherfact: A typical "cluster" of late afternoon thunderstorms may affect a one hundred-square-mile area. Just a one-inch layer of rainwater falling on this region would weigh 7,252,000 tons!

The costliest weather hazard? According to *The New York Times*, the federal government has spent some $20 billion on dams and levees this century in an attempt to control the ravages of flooding. In the past decade, annual flood damage ranged from $500 million to $6 billion.

Don't forget Fido and Fifi!

Pets—dogs, cats, and horses—feel the heat too. A few tips to keep your pet cool, calm, and collected:
- Offer them plenty of water and lots of shade.
- Limit their exercise. If listless and disoriented try applying cool water to their neck and head, and consider calling your veterinarian.

It's not the heat, it's the humidity! See the humature chart on page 122.

Multiple lightning strikes. *Jason Ryan, Verndale, MN.*

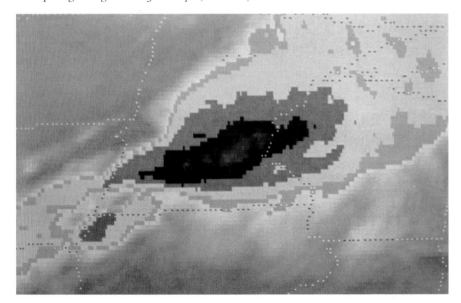

From twenty-two thousand miles above the equator, MCCs look like giant, black, late-night blotches marching across the map. This is an infrared satellite shot. The darkest colors indicate the coldest, thickest clouds, which are dropping the heaviest rains. (Look for the border of Minnesota, Iowa, and the Dakotas.) *Courtesy: Earthsat Corporation.*

"Dust devils" resemble mini-tornadoes, but wind speeds are usually forty to sixty miles per hour. They tend to form on sunny, dry days when the ground is warm and the air overhead cools rapidly with height. This extreme instability can lead to the formation of these tiny counterclockwise-rotating vortexes. This picture was snapped near the town of Silver Lake, Minnesota. The dust devil was nearly two hundred feet high and it "jumped around a dirt parking lot, picking up cans and bottles . . . and scaring a lot of bystanders!" *Dean Totushek, Hutchinson, MN.*

synthetic fibers.

- Drink more fluids than normal. Water still works best. Salt tablets probably aren't needed, but eating citrus fruits will help to replace lost potassium. Most people find that their comfort level in extreme heat increases if they cut down on the consumption of meats, eating more salads instead.
- Try to avoid the midday sun if at all possible.
- Use a highly protective sunscreen. A severe sunburn will just leave you feeling worse. Those rupturing microscopic capillaries reduce your body's ability to dissipate excess heat, actually increasing the risk of heat exhaustion and heat stroke.
- Don't be afraid to "sweat it out." Madison Avenue frowns upon perspiration, offering a multitude of products to help you stay dry. Unfortunately, these antiperspirants can get in the way of your body's automatic thermostat. The evaporation of sweat off of your skin cools your body (much like the chill you feel when you step out of the shower). That glistening glow on your skin may just keep you out of serious trouble!

I'm Going Buggy!

It seems everyone has their own tried and true remedies to cut down on bug bites. Here are a few that seem to work:

- Mosquitoes. There are numerous effective repellents on the market. Don't forget your wrists, ankles, and neck—favorite mosquito delicacies. Fogging your lawn may help temporarily, but you'll need to repeat it after a rainfall.
- Gnats. Would you mind wearing a snowmobile suit to the barbecue? That may be the only way to escape these pesky little critters. Staying in windy areas will help. Gnats prefer calm areas and shade. In addition, try to avoid dark colors and strong perfume, sure-fire gnat magnets!

The Great (and Hot) Outdoors

A period of abnormally dry weather of sufficient severity and duration to cause serious crop damage and water shortages is called a drought. Droughts can be devastating for the environment, wreaking devastation on water supplies, crops, and human and animal comfort.

Hear anything unusual? Recent research suggests that dry, thirsty crops emit a high-pitched noise as their cell structure breaks down. This high-frequency "plant scream" is found at one hundred kilohertz, much too high to be heard by people. However, these crop squeals may attract destructive insects that prey on the troubled leaves. Someday, special monitors may allow farmers to hear these cries of distress, and tell them exactly when and where to water during a drought.

FALL

Unlike spring, which can last all of a week or so, a Minnesota fall tends to be long and luxurious, sometimes hanging on into much of November. It's almost as if the atmosphere overhead is catching its breath, weary of the simmering summer heat, but not quite ready for a chilling visit from the tundra.

The bug olympics are winding down, and evenings are crisp and invigorating. Days are brisk and suitable for sweaters, and a tired sun is slipping ever lower into the southern sky. About this time, the North Woods begin erupting in vibrant colors, splashes of rust, lemon, lime, and cranberry decorating trees from the Boundary Waters to Lake Pepin. The sugar maples are first to turn, ripening just after Labor Day. The wave of color sweeps down the Mississippi, engulfing the Twin Cities by early October, and the landscape is transformed into a crazy paint-by-numbers quiltwork with colors that just can't be captured on canvas or film.

It is a treat for all of the senses, the pungent smell of family room fires and the muffled cheers of Vikings fans providing a faint reminder that

soon the first snowflakes of winter will be shaken out of a slate-gray sky.

Fall is prime-time for foggy mornings in Minnesota. The atmosphere is still mild and moist. The nights are getting longer, giving the air more of an opportunity to cool down to the "dew point." As air cools, it loses its ability to hold water vapor, and moisture condenses out into visible water droplets—dew or frost.

If there is enough moisture in the lowest mile or so of the atmosphere, a cloud may form on the ground, what we nickname fog. Most likely on a clear night when winds are light, fog tends to collect in river valleys. A nearby lake will help to moisten up the air, increasing the risk of fog. Look for fog to develop as the center of high pressure drifts overhead, especially if the previous day was damp and rainy.

Hurricanes in Minnesota?

Hurricanes, what, you have to be kidding, right? Yes, you'll be pleased to hear that although fall is prime-time for hurricanes, they are extremely rare in Minnesota. Every once in a great while, we experience the soggy dregs of an ex-hurricane, a shrinking blotch of gusty showers, weakening rapidly as it sloshes northward across the plains.

Unlike tornadoes, which wreak havoc and scare the heck out of people, hurricanes do seem to serve a purpose in nature. They are the atmosphere's automatic pressure relief valves, transporting excess heat and moisture away from the tropics. On occasion, they serve as drought busters for states south of Minnesota, squeezing out precious rains in time for fall harvest.

Hurricanes are huge, often two hundred to five hundred miles wide, but the most violent winds are concentrated in a narrow doughnut of thunderheads immediately surrounding the storm's eye. The hurricane eye marks the center of the storm, where skies temporarily clear and winds die down. The passage of the calm eye overhead can prompt many to think that the hurricane is over. A short sigh of relief can have tragic conse-

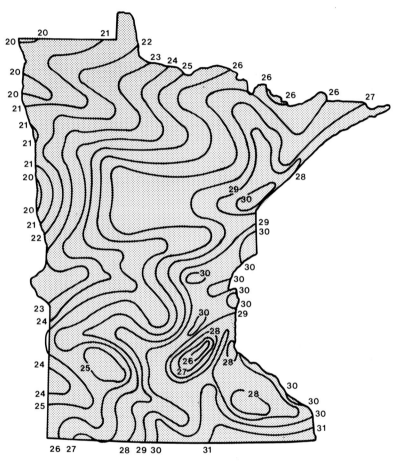

Data by National Weather Service
(All values in inches)

Average yearly precipitation for Minnesota.

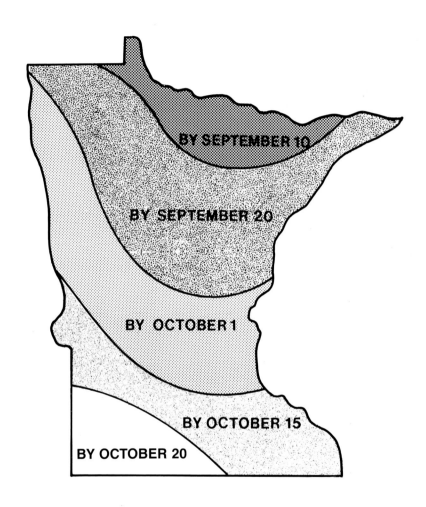

BY SEPTEMBER 10

BY SEPTEMBER 20

BY OCTOBER 1

BY OCTOBER 15

BY OCTOBER 20

Dates of peaking fall colors.

Fog is a common occurrence in fall. *Terry Cunningham, Minneapolis, MN.*

This was taken from an airplane window. Just some of the top floors of Minneapolis's skyscrapers are seen poking out from dense ground fog. *Beth Schmit, Woodbury, MN.*

Grace Anderson Schrunk, Blaine, MN.

Hurricane Allen was a category 5 storm that threatened the Gulf Coast in 1980. Mexico felt the brunt of the storm, which weakened dramatically before coming ashore. *Courtesy: Earthsat Corporation.*

Amazing, But True

Human reflexes tend to be slower when the barometer is falling. In the 1700s, the Bank of England sent its employees home when storms were approaching because they made more careless mistakes!

Many people are walking barometers, able to feel the approach of a storm. As the barometric pressure falls, fluids in their joints tend to swell, causing discomfort, even intense pain. Arthritis and bursitis sufferers are most apt to be affected as storm clouds begin to gather. The next time grandma or grandpa complains of pain in a trick knee, heed the warning and batten down the hatches!

How are Hurricanes Rated?

Hurricanes are rated on a scale from category 1 to category 5, 1 being a "minimal" hurricane, 5 being catastrophic. Less than 1 or 2 percent of all hurricanes ever become "cat 5s," capable of total destruction.

Category	Pressure	Winds	Storm surge	Damage
	(inches)	(mph)	(feet)	
1	28.94	74–95	4–5	minimal
2	28.50–28.91	96–110	6–8	moderate
3	27.91–28.47	111–130	9–12	extensive
4	27.17–27.88	131–155	13–18	extreme
5	under 27.16	156 +	18 +	catastrophic

Weatherfact: One pail of water can produce enough fog to cover 105 square miles to a depth of fifty feet!

quences, because the other side of the eye wall will literally sweep those who venture outside off their feet! Generally, the more severe the hurricane, the smaller the eye. A typical storm may have an eye some twenty to thirty miles in diameter, but a "category 5" storm can have an eye as small as six to eight miles across.

Hurricanes need warm ocean water to grow; heat from hundreds of thunderstorms causes the barometric pressure to drop, causing moist air to spiral into the storm's center. This infusion of wet air triggers more thunderstorms, the pressure drops even lower, and the storm intensifies. Once hurricanes move over land they lose this moisture source, and they weaken rapidly.

Most hurricane deaths are not from the strong winds, but rather from a storm surge, a five- to fifteen-foot-high wall of water that pushes ashore ahead of the storm's eye, drowning much in its path. Winds howling around the calm eye can top one hundred miles an hour, carving out huge, two-story waves. Tides can rise several feet in just seconds, cutting off roads, stranding many residents in their homes.

Hurricanes were given numbers in the 1940s and '50s, but this made tracking cumbersome and at times confusing. During the 1960s, these massive storms were given feminine names. Today, the hurricane center in Miami alternates between female and male names, using some Hispanic as well as Anglo-saxon names and following alphabetical order. Meteorologists meet yearly at a library in Geneva, Switzerland, to pick the names for the upcoming hurricane season.

A tropical depression matures into a tropical storm when sustained winds reach thirty-nine miles an hour. When winds surpass seventy-four miles an hour, the storm becomes a hurricane. Theoretically, winds in a "category 5" storm (the most severe possible) can reach two hundred to 225 miles an hour!

Hurricanes are energy monsters. They release an enormous amount of raw energy, equivalent to one moderate-sized nuclear explosion every

second!

On average, there are five hurricanes in the Atlantic and Caribbean each season. During a typical fall, three will hit the United States mainland. Hurricanes almost always move from east to west in this hemisphere. Thus, storms that form in the eastern Pacific tend to avoid land, affecting shipping and slow-moving whales. When hurricanes cross the International Date Line, they are called typhoons, and they may go on to threaten Japan, the Philippines, and other islands in the western Pacific.

A Potential for Disaster

Why do hurricane trackers and civil defense planners spend many sleepless nights from September through November?

In most cases, meteorologists can give only a six- to twelve-hour warning of where a hurricane will reach land. Unfortunately, in major metropolitan areas like New Orleans, Tampa-St. Petersburg, and Houston-Galveston, a complete evacuation could take at least twenty-four to thirty-six hours. It's estimated that only one in three people now living along the Gulf or Atlantic coasts have ever lived through a full-fledged hurricane.

The last "category 5" storm to score a direct hit on America's coastline was Camille, in August of 1969. Winds approaching two hundred miles an hour forced the waters from the Gulf of Mexico onshore with explosive force, wiping some coastal Mississippi towns off the map. Two hundred and fifty-six people died, with damage topping $1.4 billion. Since 1969, there has been rampant development along our nation's shores, with many high-rise buildings built on highly vulnerable barrier islands. This, combined with ignorance and a growing sense of apathy, has dramatically increased the risk of a hurricane disaster.

In late September of 1989, that potential for disaster became a reality as hurricane Hugo hit the South Carolina coast with 135-mph winds. Hugo was a "category 4" storm, and its monstrous

"Officer, I want to report a UFO!" A beautiful example of altocumulus lenticularis, this photo shows what a mountain ridge can do to a moist windflow. Many UFO sightings turn out to be weather related, but you can see why townsfolk might begin to panic. *Aaron Marple, Plymouth, MN.*

"Beam me up, Scotty!" No, this is not the stealth version of the Starship Enterprise, just a dramatic wave cloud found downwind of Mt. Rainier, Washington. This particular cloud lasted for several hours, much to the delight of hikers and campers nearby. *Curt Hewitt, Zimmerman, MN.*

Standing wave clouds forming "cloud streets" resemble jet contrails, but are formed by slight upward motion in a moist layer aloft. *L. H. Elder, St. Paul, MN.*

Fall streaks: Observed year-round, these unusual clouds tend to be most dramatic during autumn. Wisps of snow falling out of high clouds are swept downwind by powerful jet stream winds.

Crepuscular rays or "twilight rays" are fan-shaped patterns of light and shadows made visible by the presence of haze in the lower atmosphere.

fifteen- to twenty-foot storm surge took a heavy toll on coastal communities, washing many homes and businesses away. Although loss of life in South Carolina was small, scores were killed in Puerto Rico and the Virgin Islands. Hurricane Hugo will probably go into the record books as the most expensive storm in U.S. history, inflicting damage estimated at more than $10 billion. But for residents of Charleston, South Carolina, who escaped with little more than the clothes on their backs, the psychological damage and trauma will overshadow financial losses for many years to come.

The Lighter Side of Fall

In Minnesota, fall is perhaps the tamest of all seasons, with lingering summer warmth aloft creating a dry and stable atmosphere. The result can be delightful days filled with a golden haze and lots of lukewarm sunshine! We are often treated to an Indian summer, a spell of unusually mild weather after the first frost of autumn. The origin of the name is still somewhat in doubt, but it's believed that this dry, pleasant weather may have helped Native Americans complete their harvest before the first snows of winter arrived.

The northern lights, or aurora borealis, are often visible this time of year, especially when there's no moon to compete with. Magnetic storms on the sun spark enormous solar flares that give off a "solar wind." When this stream of charged particles reaches earth it accelerates toward both magnetic poles, hitting and "exciting" atoms of oxygen and nitrogen. As these particles vibrate back and forth, they emit light—pale, shimmering greens and blues that seem to ripple and dance high overhead, encircling the entire polar region. On many a night, the northern lights can easily be the best (and cheapest) show in town!

The northern lights, curtainlike bands and ribbons, are found some sixty-five to seven hundred miles above the poles. It's estimated that the electrical power associated with the auroral discharge is enormous, about one thousand billion watts, which is more electricity than the entire United States consumes in one year![1] Particularly intense displays of the aurora borealis have been known to disrupt radio transmissions and navigation and interfere with high latitude radar and satellite operations.

Getting Ready for Winter

A couple of gentle reminders that may prevent king-sized headaches when the arctic express begins to roll:

Your home:
- Check storm doors and windows for leaks.
- Have your furnace checked; clean your humidifier filters.
- Shut off outside water faucets to avoid pipe ruptures.

Your car:
- Double check your antifreeze.
- Make sure you have a few containers of dry gas to prevent fuel-line freeze-ups.
- Put heavier weight oil into your vehicle's engine (usually 5/30 or 5/40 but call your trusty mechanic first).
- Battery jumper cables can be a real life-saver.

Your fireplace:
- Every fall, there are hundreds of chimney fires in Minnesota, some that go on to consume the entire house. All of them were preventable!
- Burn dry wood. Wet, green wood releases creosote, which can build up on your chimney walls and catch fire.
- Check your chimney for blockage every month with a flashlight.
- If you see any kind of buildup, call a chimney sweep. It'll only set you back about $50, and you'll have some peace of mind as you lean back and enjoy the ball game. Better yet, do it your-

1. Akasofu, S. *Aurora Borealis*. Alaska Geographic Series, Vol. 6, No. 2. Bothell, Washington: Alaska Northwest, 1979.

self! Chimney cleaning brushes are available at many hardware stores.
- Be sure to store used fireplace ashes in a metal container outside. All it takes is one microscopic ember to spark a tragedy.

WINTER
"Tis very warm weather when one's in bed."
—Jonathan Swift

Winter certainly seems like the longest season of the year, and rarely do we ease into winter in Minnesota. Late in November winter arrives like a cold slap across the face. A snowstorm around Thanksgiving is customary, and unlike other towns around the nation, white Christmases are almost guaranteed in these parts.

The deep freeze settles in come January, but instead of hibernating in a cozy family room, many Minnesotans embrace the cold and the snow, charging headlong into the invigorating air outside. And there is no shortage of things to do outside—there's cross-country skiing, snowmobiling, ice-fishing, windshield chiseling, and battery-jumping to name a few. St. Paul even has a carnival to celebrate the lack of feeling in our extremities!

Family and friends living in other (warmer) regions of America gasp in astonishment when I rattle off the current temperature (and for God's sake, don't forget to hype the windchill!). I shrug and tell them that if you have a car that works, a garage, a warm coat or two, and a healthy dose of common sense, it's possible not only to survive, but to enjoy a Minnesota winter!

The White Stuff

Are the winters really getting snowier? Statistics suggest that we've all been doing a lot more shoveling in recent years. Potentially good news for skiers and snow-blower repairmen about the average yearly Twin Cities snowfall in inches is on the next page.

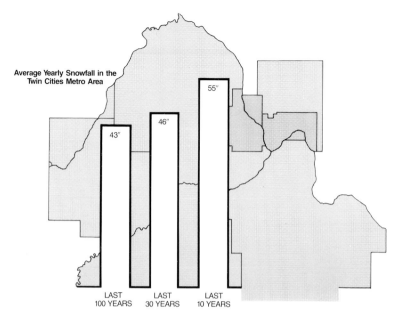

Average yearly Twin Cities snowfall (in inches).

Auroral bands. *Courtesy: Lee Snyder, Geophysical Institute, University of Alaska.*

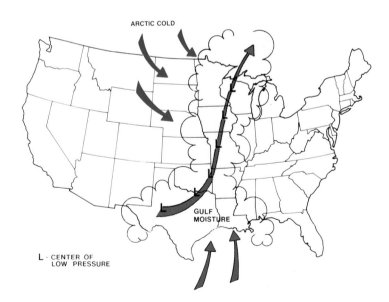

Beware of "Texas hookers," wet storms that brew in Texas or Oklahoma, appear to drift eastward, and then at the last moment hook northward and come right up the Mississippi. If the storm track is from Des Moines, Iowa, to near Eau Claire, Wisconsin, some part of Minnesota will receive a snowy clobbering! These storms can dump heavy wet snow, downing trees and power lines and closing secondary roads for days.

Parhelion: Sometimes called sun dogs, parhelia are bright spots on either side of the sun caused by sunlight being bent through microscopic ice crystals in the upper atmosphere. This spectacular example, shot at the South Pole, shows not only parhelia but also a parhelic circle intersecting the sun and running parallel to the horizon. The white spot at the top of the twenty-two-degree halo that surrounds the sun is an anthelion. Both the anthelion and the parhelic circle are relatively rare, the result of sunlight reflecting off of these same upper-atmosphere ice crystals. *John Roseberg, North Oaks, MN.*

The odds of a brown Christmas? Once every three or four years, the Twin Cities experience a brown Christmas, with little or no snow on the ground. Since 1895 there have been twenty-six brown Christmases, the most recent ones in 1976, 1977, 1982, 1986, and 1988. As you head farther north the odds of a brown Christmas decrease, dwindling to 5 percent in the Boundary Waters and International Falls area. Past records show that on a typical Christmas morning, there are about 3.2 inches of snow on the ground in the Twin Cities.

Statistics show that 75 percent of the winters following a brown Christmas tend to have less than normal snowfall.

Rating Snowstorms
"Hey Paul, how many inches of snow will fall?"

My favorite college professor would often complain that Americans tend to be too preoccupied with inches. He used to say, "There are some situations where you just can't pin a snowstorm down to the exact inch." He proposed an alternative, a simple yet effective way of classifying snowstorms. Here it is:

- Nuisance snowstorm: enough to coat the ground, whiten lawns, and grease up the highways with ice. Traffic is forced to slow down, with a spattering of fender benders (mostly new arrivals to Minnesota), but getting from point A to point B is generally not a big problem. Out of town visitors are visibly distressed, but to native Minnesotans, a nuisance snowstorm is little more than a reminder of winter.
- Plowable snowstorm: usually more than two or three inches, enough to shovel and plow. Some cars go into the ditch, and bridge ramps and decks become treacherous. Travel is difficult, at times stop and go. A few schools are an hour or two late, but life goes on, just a bit slower than usual.
- Crippling snowstorm: may strike Minnesota once every year or two. Everything comes to a screeching, grinding halt as more than a foot of

snow combines with high winds to produce impassable highways. Even in Minnesota, many schools and businesses are closed. Only the brave and foolish attempt to venture outdoors.

"It's too cold to snow. . . . "

Not entirely true. Theoretically, it can snow at any temperature below thirty-two degrees. However, if it's colder than ten or fifteen degrees, that usually means an arctic outbreak has pushed the main storm track well south of Minnesota. Remember, the heaviest snow tends to fall just to the north and west of the storm track. Our heaviest snows tend to come when the temperature is between twenty and thirty degrees.

Big snowflakes? Watch out! When temperatures are near freezing in the lowest mile of the atmosphere, snowflakes begin to stick together. We've all seen these monster snowflakes that resemble small snowballs. This is usually a sign that the atmosphere is what meteorologists call "critical," and a changeover to ice or even rain is possible. Small snowflakes imply that temperatures are still well below thirty-two degrees aloft, and the snow will probably not change over within the next four to eight hours.

Beware of Thin Ice!

Just because a lake or stream is frozen does not mean that the ice is safe. Here are some recommendations based on research done by the U.S. Army Cold Regions Research Laboratory in New Hampshire:

- Check the appearance. Estimate the strength by first testing the edges. Snow cover can adversely affect the strength of ice, with springtime being the most dangerous time to venture out on an ice-covered body of water.
- Generally, new ice is much stronger than old ice. Several inches of new ice may support your weight. A foot or more of old, rotten ice may not be strong enough because the ice's natural crystalline structure is changed by constant freezing and thawing.

- Ice does not freeze at a uniform rate. It may be a foot thick in one spot, and just an inch thick only ten feet away.
- A layer of snow can insulate the ice underneath, slowing down the ice-forming process, making a stroll across the lake potentially dangerous.
- Ice near the shore is weaker. Buckling action of the lakes or streams constantly breaks and refreezes the ice near the shore.
- Ice forming over flowing water is most dangerous, especially rivers, streams, or spring-fed lakes.
- Use common sense. A few minutes taken to observe the ice can make the difference between an enjoyable outdoor experience, and a disaster.

Wintertime Dictionary
These are the kinds of terms that make snow-lovers jump (on skis and skates, of course) for joy.

Alberta clippers: When upper-level jet stream winds are howling from the northwest, be on the lookout for these fickle, fast-moving storms. Alberta clippers were named after the clipper sailing ships, which at one time were the fastest vessels on the seas. The storms zip along at forty miles an hour, preceded by a couple of inches of light, powdery snow and followed by violent winds capable of reaching forty to sixty miles an hour! This often results in severe blowing and drifting, with blizzard conditions that can leave many roads impassable.

Snow flurries: used to describe intermittent light snow with little or no accumulation.

Snow squalls: brief, intense snowfalls accompanied by gusty winds (similar to summertime thunderstorms). They are most likely to be found along or behind a cold front, under an upper air disturbance, a puddle of unusually cold air aloft.

High wind warning: heard on radio and TV stations when sustained winds are forecast to reach at

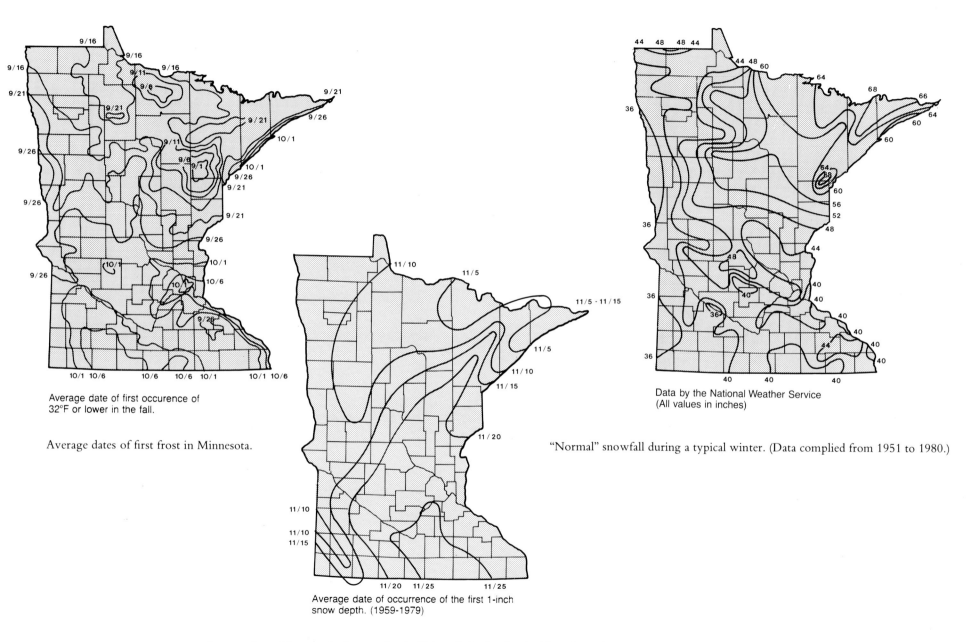

Average date of first occurence of
32°F or lower in the fall.

Average dates of first frost in Minnesota.

Average date of occurrence of the first 1-inch
snow depth. (1959-1979)

Data by the National Weather Service
(All values in inches)

"Normal" snowfall during a typical winter. (Data complied from 1951 to 1980.)

Average date of first one-inch snow depth. Although the first flurries blow through Minnesota during October, the ground typically isn't snow covered until shortly before Thanksgiving.

Trees silhouetted at sunset.

A candy coating of snow. *Connie Wanner, Willmar, MN.*

A nuisance snowfall. *Lynn and Nancy Delapp, Plymouth, MN.*

least forty miles an hour, or gusts are expected to hit fifty-seven (or more) miles per hour.

Weather advisory: issued by the local National Weather Service office when winter weather is likely to make travel difficult. When you hear an advisory on radio or TV for low windchills, snow, blowing snow, ice, or a combination of all of these, go ahead with your travel plans but stay tuned to the media and give yourself plenty of extra time to get from point A to point B.

Winter storm watch: issued when conditions are ripe for a severe winter storm, with a potential for ice, or at least six inches of snow over a twelve-hour period. Pay close attention to your local forecast, and take all necessary precautions.

Winter storm warning: When there is a high probability that a winter storm will actually strike, or if heavy snow or ice is already hampering travel nearby, a warning is issued. Weather conditions will quickly deteriorate, and travel should only be attempted with 4-wheel drive vehicles or snowmobiles.

Blizzard: the name given to a severe winter storm that produces falling or blowing snow, temperatures generally lower than twenty-five degrees, winds greater than thirty-five miles an hour, and visibilities under a quarter mile. Blizzards can approach from any direction, but are most likely to produce heavy snow when the upper level winds are blowing from Texas or New Mexico. A bitterly cold, retreating high pressure system combining with a moist wind flow from the Gulf of Mexico can set the stage for a plow-bending, shovel-busting Minnesota blizzard.

Originally, the term referred to a boxer's knockout punch. It meant a stunning blow. On March 14, 1870 an obscure Iowa newspaperman used the word to describe a severe snowstorm that had "k.o.'d" his hometown. Within ten years, the new usage had spread all the way to New York City and Canada!

Ground blizzard: This storm is most common in the Red River Valley of northwestern Minnesota, but they can strike anywhere. Every bit as dangerous as a blizzard, ground blizzards usually lack falling snow, but they make up for this with gusty, swirling, turbulent winds that can whip snow already on the ground into a flaky frenzy, and dropping visibilities to near zero, stranding motorists in a wild sea of white. The risk of a ground blizzard is greatest in hilly terrain, immediately behind an Alberta clipper, especially when the snow on the ground is light and fluffy.

Winter Driving

A few subtle reminders. Yes, I know we are all accomplished experts when it comes to winter driving, but a little review can't hurt, right?

- Allow two to three times more distance between your vehicle and the car in front of you. Panic braking on snow or ice is a potentially religious experience.
- Brake sooner than you would on dry pavement, lightly tapping or pumping your brakes to prevent your wheels from locking up. If you have a standard transmission, brake with your engine by shifting into a lower gear.
- Avoid rapid movements of the steering wheel to avoid spin-outs. Treat your accelerator pedal like it's made of egg shells to prevent fish-tailing down the highway.
- Keep your windows clean! Yes, I know this sounds stupid, but you'd be amazed at the number of accidents that result from people being unable to see out their snow-splattered windshield and side windows. They are unable to see the other guy coming. Take an extra couple of seconds and fumble with your favorite ice scraper.
- Bridges are cooled from below as well as from above, and they tend to freeze up sooner.
- The bottom line: Slow down. The threat of getting into an accident increases dramatically with speed.

Slip Sliding Away. . . .

Surprisingly, traction on our highways tends to improve as the temperature drops! When the mercury is flirting with the freezing mark, liquid water lubricates the snow pack, making highways even more slippery. However, it's worth mentioning that salt loses its ability to melt icy roads at temperatures much below ten degrees or so.

What is "black ice"? At temperatures below zero degrees, roads can become extremely slick, even if no snow is falling from the sky. At higher temperatures, hydrocarbon emissions and water evaporate after leaving your vehicle's tail pipe. But when the mercury slips into negative numbers, that water freezes directly onto roadway surfaces (a process known as deposition). Problems are most likely at intersections, especially during rush hour.

If stranded in your car during a blizzard: Stay put! Stay with the car. Do not leave your vehicle, unless you can see a house or other building nearby. Most winter fatalities are the result of people wandering off to find help. Don't try to be a hero. Wait for help to come to you. Crack your car window slightly, and use your heater sparingly to conserve fuel for as long as possible. From time to time, clear the snow away from your tail pipe to prevent carbon monoxide poisoning from entering your vehicle. Tie some sort of a flag or colorful rag to your car's antenna and keep one person awake at all times. Your chances of riding out the storm safely are much greater if you remain calm, and wait for help to reach you.

Remember your winter survival kit! If you're planning to travel, especially through the flat, open country of western Minnesota, make sure you have the following in your trunk or back seat:

- Battery jumper cables.
- A container of sand or rock salt.
- A small snow shovel.
- A flashlight.
- Matches and a candle.

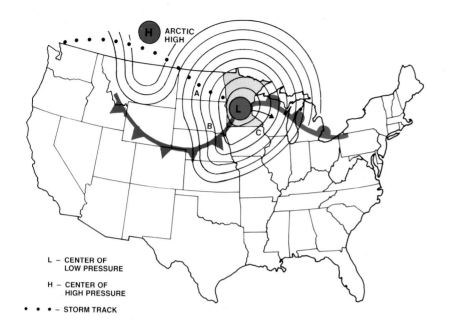

L – CENTER OF
LOW PRESSURE

H – CENTER OF
HIGH PRESSURE

• • • – STORM TRACK

A classic Alberta clipper. The weather map shows a fast-moving storm approaching from the northwest, the barometer is rising rapidly behind the arctic front, and at points A and B a tight packing of isobars (what meteorologists call a tight pressure gradient) is whipping up forty-plus-mile-per-hour winds and near-zero visibilities. Light to moderate snow would be expected at point C.

Winter wonderland. *Gerald D. Peterson, Dayton, MN.*

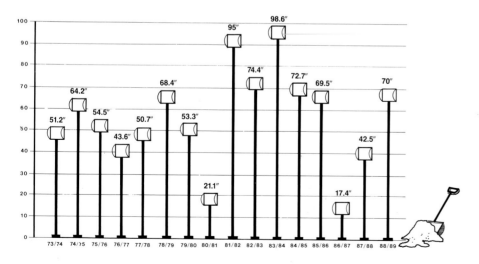

Winter snowfall in the past sixteen seasons for the Twin Cities. The winter of 1989–90 saw 35.5 inches of snow.

Hoarfrost: a fluffy, feathery deposit of ice crystals on an object that is colder than thirty-two degrees, most often found on tree branches, leaves, and fences. *Clifton J. Aichinger, North St. Paul, MN.*

Drag out your slide-rules, because you just never know what may come up in idle conversation (and on TV game shows):

$$WC(F) = 91.4 - ((0.546 V + 0.85 - 0.0365V) \times (50.8 - 0.556T))$$

To compute the windchill (WC) in degrees Fahrenheit (F), where the wind speed (V) is entered in miles an hour, and the air temperature (T) is entered in degrees Fahrenheit. Enjoy!

What's the temperature over there?
These equations are simple ways to convert Fahrenheit (F) to Celsius (C), and Celsius to Fahrenheit:

$$C = 5/9 (F - 32) \text{ and } F = 9/5C + 32$$

Weatherfact: On a cold winter day, how long should you let your vehicle's engine idle before engaging the transmission and going your way? Ten seconds. This may come as a surprise, but leading automotive experts claim that moving along slowly (in first or second gear, without racing the engine) after roughly ten seconds leads to less stress on your engine components that gunning your engine for several minutes. Some good news for type A personalities.

Trees prepare for long Minnesota winters by stopping production of new chlorophyll, the internal "engine" that produces their food. As chlorophyll breaks down, yellow-producing xanthophyll and orange-producing carotenes, which are always present within the leaves, are no longer obscured, and vivid colors begin to emerge. A combination of warm sunny days and chilly autumn nights can reveal anthocyanin, a pigment that gives leaves their reddish color, that completes the crescendo of colors!

How cold is it!? See the windchill chart on page 122.

- A tow chain or strap.
- Safety flares or reflectors.
- Blankets.
- Assorted munchies. Candy bars offer quick energy.
- A brightly colored rag or handkerchief to tie onto your car antenna should you become stranded.
- A CB radio. It's worth noting that CB radios and cellular phones have saved many lives.

The Biting Cold

What is windchill? Developed by a team of scientists researching the effects of cold weather in Antarctica shortly before World War II, the windchill formula confirms the obvious: A strong wind will make you feel even colder! Why?

If you were to take a shower, and then run out the front door and around the block, not only would you be arrested, you'd probably catch the cold of your life. Water evaporating off of your body cools your skin. That's why you feel chilled when you step out of the shower or bath. There is always a thin layer of perspiration on your skin. The stronger the wind, the greater the evaporation of sweat off of your face, hands, and toes, and the colder you feel.

A windchill of -20° means that the wind is helping to remove heat away from your body at the same rate as if it were -20° with no wind. For example, a snowmobiler moving along at sixty miles per hour on a calm day has a "wind" of sixty miles an hour and needs to dress accordingly. If the snowmobiler were going into a twenty-mile-an-hour headwind, the speed of the "wind" would bump up to eighty miles an hour.

Booze only makes you colder. Alcohol may give you a temporary feeling of warmth by triggering vasodilatation, a rapid expansion of your blood vessels. But eventually, this process exposes your blood to lower temperatures, and before long, that heartwarming tingle will wear off and you'll feel even colder than you did before you took that little nip. Becoming buzzed or down-

right inebriated when the weather is potentially life threatening outside may dull your judgment, with potentially disastrous consequences.

What Is Dangerously Cold?

Never, ever tell a Minnesotan not to go outside because it's too cold out. In all candor, when properly dressed, even a subzero wind can be invigorating and downright stimulating. Does it ever get too cold? What follows is a rough guide to remember when Canada begins to leak thumb-numbing air south of the border:

- -25° windchill: not terribly dangerous if properly dressed with multiple layers of clothing and protective headgear. Being physically active reduces the risk of frostbite even more.
- -50° windchill: exposed flesh can freeze in under a minute or two. The elderly, people with circulatory problems, and babies should remain indoors.
- -70° windchill: dangerous, even if properly dressed. Everyone should stay inside until the winds die down.

Little Consolation

Police records confirm that when the mercury goes above eighty degrees, the crime rate nearly quadruples! In sharp contrast, when backyard thermometers slip below the zero mark, the rate of theft, robbery, and violent crime drops off dramatically. It seems that even hardened criminals are capable of feeling the windchill.

Pets Feel the Chill

On those days when you can't find the mercury in your backyard thermometer, chances are your dog or cat is just as miserable as you are! Here are a few tips from the animal humane society:

- Frostbite is a very real danger. When windchills are low, keep your cat indoors to protect its ear tips; the tips can freeze very rapidly. If frostbite is suspected, warm the affected area gently and consult your veterinarian.
- After your pet has walked on streets or side-

walks where ice-melting chemicals were used, rinse its footpads to avoid sore feet.

- Make sure your dog's house is warm and dry. State law requires that you provide any dog that is outside for more than one hour with a wind- and moisture-proof house of proper size, with proper bedding, and with a door or flap to keep the cold out.
- Provide fresh water (snow is not enough). Make sure that an icy crust doesn't form on top. Feed an outdoor pet extra food to compensate for the extra calories burned up trying to stay warm.
- Remember that outdoor dogs need love and companionship during cold spells too. Pets are social animals that suffer when left alone for too long.

Does My Car Feel the Windchill?

Unless it perspires, probably not. Dogs, cats, and horses feel the windchill because they too sweat. Now it is true that a strong wind will cool your vehicle's engine down to the actual air temperature much faster than if there is no wind. Thus, on a subzero night with gusty forty-mile-per-hour winds, you may have to start up your car several times. Even so, no matter how hard the wind blows, an inanimate object can never cool down below the actual temperature. Incidentally, you have to put antifreeze in your vehicle to cover only the lowest air temperature, not the windchill temperature.

The Perils of Winter

Frostbite: Despite the warnings, impassioned pleas, and the hyperactive rantings and ravings of local TV meteorologists, scores of Minnesotans develop frostbite every winter. Extremities are most likely to be affected: toes, fingers, ears, and cheeks. Bitter cold triggers sharp pain, followed by a tingling, numbing sensation. In many cases, little pain is felt at all! The skin may become discolored, a blotchy gray, yellow, or white in appearance. In more severe cases, blisters can form, and if not treated quickly, gangrene can set in. In some extreme cases, the only way to stop infection is by amputation.

Elderly people with poor circulation are most vulnerable to frostbite, and the consumption of alcohol can blur judgment and dramatically increase the chance of getting into trouble. In addition, smoking tends to cut off blood circulation to the extremities.

Luckily, most cases are minor. Warm the affected body part in lukewarm water (holding frostbitten fingers under your armpits is one way of regaining feeling). Cover the person with warm clothes and blankets and call your doctor. Do not rub the affected area with your hands or with snow, which will only make things worse.

Hypothermia can kill! On particularly cold days, newborn babies and the elderly can have trouble generating enough internal heat to keep their body temperatures at 98.6°. Hypothermia is a dangerous drop in body temperature that can result in disorientation, shock, and eventual death. It can set in slowly, over the course of several days, so that's why it's important to check in on older friends and family members who are living alone. Is their home cold and drafty? If so, they may be headed for trouble. In colder rooms, where cribs are located near windows, newborn babies should wear warm hats to sleep.

Do cold waves trigger illness? Well, yes and no. "Can he be anymore vague?" you ask. When it's unusually cold outside, more people tend to linger indoors, around other people—coughing, sneezing, wheezing people. This increases the odds of inheriting a bug or virus. In addition, large swings in temperature—going back and forth between mild and bitter—may leave your body's natural immune system weakened, and more vulnerable to influenza and a long menu of other unpleasant microscopic visitors lurking out there.

What Is Seasonal Affective Disorder (SAD)? As many as one in three Minnesotans seem to be adversely affected by shorter daylight during the

"Red sky at morning, sailors take warning. Red sky at night, sailors delight!"
There is quite a bit of scientific proof to back up this familiar proverb, attributed first to Jesus in the book of Matthew. A red sky in the morning often implies the existence of high, thin cirrus clouds, forerunners of storms. This is especially true when the barometer happens to be falling and winds are out of the east or northeast. However, a red sunset implies that the atmosphere is quite dry, and dust in the stratosphere fifteen miles overhead is filtering out the blue wavelengths of sunlight, leaving behind the red hues.

Weatherfact: Question: If the temperature outside today is zero degrees Fahrenheit, and the forecast for tomorrow is for "twice as cold," how cold will it be? Answer: -230° F. How did we come up with that figure? Well, zero degrees Fahrenheit equals -18° C., or 255 Kelvin (it's important, in fact crucial, that you convert the temperature to an absolute scale, where zero is absolute zero). Now if the forecast calls for twice as cold, you would take half of 255, or 127.5 Kelvin. Convert back to Celsius and you have -145.5°, or -230° F.

"Sun pillar": a vertical shaft of sunlight above the rising or setting sun, caused by sunlight reflecting off of the tops and bottoms of hexagonal ice crystals suspended in a cloud layer near the ground. *Kristi Vollmer, Ortonville, MN.*

Cirrus clouds floating some twenty-five thousand feet above the ground are composed of tiny ice crystals that behave like microscopic prisms, bending white sunlight into the colors of the rainbow. Here, the rainbow is visible only in the high clouds. *Ralph George, Golden Valley, MN.*

This photo highlights three optical phenomena resulting from sunlight shining through a layer of ice crystals at twenty-five thousand feet. A twenty-two-degree halo is seen circling the setting sun. White halos are the result of sunlight reflecting off of the faces of ice crystals. Multicolored halos happen when sunlight is refracted inside these same crystals. On both sides of the sun are sun dogs, bright splashes of reddish light triggered by sunlight bent by six-sided ice crystals. *Carol Linneman, Montevideo, MN.*

Twenty- to twenty-five-foot drifts had to be cleared from the tracks near Storden, Minnesota, on February 23, 1909. *Courtesy: Minnesota Historical Society.*

winter months. Women tend to be more vulnerable to SAD than men, and many complain of anxiety and severe depression. Other symptoms include a craving for carbohydrates, a lowered sex drive and an urge to linger in bed. Scientists speculate that SAD may be a throwback to a time thousands of years ago, when our ancestors literally hibernated during the cold winter months, storing up food, and sleeping through the coldest cold fronts.

A lack of sunlight, especially during the months of December and January, seems to affect the production of a hormone in your body called melatonin, leaving some with a weak, rundown feeling. What can be done? Other than a sunny, southern vacation one remedy that seems to help is full spectrum fluorescent lights. Typical lighting gives off only one frequency. Full spectrum lights mimic the sun, giving off a wide range of frequencies. Going under the brand names Vita-light and Spectra-light and costing between $15 and $25 each, these lights seem to pull many folks out of their dark funk. Before you do anything, first consult your family physician.

But I Already Know How To Dress!

Yes, yes I know, and I am not about to insult your intelligence, but a surprising number of people seem to lack common sense from time to time. Here are a few gentle reminders:

- Numerous layers of clothing will keep you warmer than one big bulky overcoat. An undershirt, shirt, sweater, and jacket will trap your body heat more effectively, leaving you warm and toasty!
- Wear a hat, something that will cover your ears! Army studies show that 50 to 75 percent of the heat escaping your body leaves through the top of your head.
- Mittens or ski gloves will leave you warmer than ordinary gloves.
- This sounds stupid all right, but try to keep your clothes dry. Damp clothing conducts the cold much more effectively, leaving you chilled to the bone. Don't be afraid to change into another pair of warm, dry clothes. You'll stay much happier when the windchill hovers below zero.

The Tournament Blizzard

For some reason, Minnesota always seems to get smacked around by wild snowstorms during the hockey, basketball, wrestling, and swimming play-offs in late February and early March. Do large cheering crowds attract blizzards? Probably not. Here are a couple of possible explanations of increased sensitivity to "tournament blizzards":

- During tournament time, more people are on the highways, traveling from greater Minnesota into the Twin Cities. For this reason, people tend to be more sensitive to the weather and storms, more weather conscious.
- Keep in mind that March is the snowiest month of the year. On average, ten inches or more of heavy wet snow falls in the Twin Cities. Huge temperature contrasts can exist across the nation, with gulf moisture finally able to penetrate as far north as Minnesota. The result can be some memorable (and sloppy!) snowstorms.

Weatherfact: Artificial snow takes a lot of effort—and water! It takes twelve thousand gallons of water to cover one acre of ski slope with one inch of snow.

Weatherfact: On average, in the Twin Cities . . .
First frost .October 10
First flurries . . . . .October 20
First one-inch snow . . . . .November 2
Number of plowable three-inch-plus snows in a season . . . . .Five to Ten

Weatherfact: What is the only Minnesota city to make the "Top One Hundred Coldest Cities in the World" list? It's not International Falls, Embarrass, or Tower. No, it's Duluth! Because of its close proximity to Lake Superior, Duluth stays much cooler during the summer months, and that pulls down the yearly average temperature to 38.6° F. (Note: Thirty-six out of the coldest forty cities on the list are in the Soviet Union.)

Winter sunset. *Marian Beach, Mounds View, MN.*

3 Meteorology 101
Weather Forecasting from A to Z

"I can never remember whether it snowed for six days and six nights when I was twelve or whether it snowed for twelve days and twelve nights when I was six."— Dylan Thomas

So what, you ask, is meteorology? It is the study of the phenomena of the atmosphere. This includes not only the physics, chemistry, and dynamics of the atmosphere, but also many of the direct effects of the atmosphere upon the earth's surface, the oceans, and life in general. The goals often ascribed to meteorology are the complete understanding, accurate prediction, and artificial control of atmospheric phenomena.[1]

A meteorologist is usually defined as either anyone with a Bachelor of Science degree in atmospheric science, or anyone who has received formal training in the military.

ACCURACY

Here's a surprise! Nationwide, the twenty-four-hour forecast has an accuracy of about 87 percent. Unfortunately, you tend to remember the 13 percent of the time that we blow it. Strangely enough, that twenty-four-hour success rate has not improved much at all since the 1950s, despite the introduction of satellites and supercomputers.

For a long list of reasons, forecast accuracy drops off rapidly with time, reaching 56 percent by day five. Beyond six days or so, forecasts be-

come even trickier, and predicting specific temperatures or precipitation for individual cities becomes more guesswork than science. In some cases, it is possible to forecast trends as far as thirty to ninety days out (for example, the East will be wetter, the West warmer, etc.). But even here, the accuracy rate is little better than the flip of a coin, about 55 to 60 percent at best.

The greatest improvements in meteorology have come in forecasts for the three- to five-day range. Accuracy has improved dramatically since the introduction of high-speed computers. Today's four-day forecasts are as accurate as two-day forecasts used to be twenty years ago! As our understanding of the atmosphere improves, and faster supercomputers are loaded with mathematical equations that more precisely simulate how the weather really works, we can expect a gradual improvement in accuracy in the years ahead.

Why aren't the forecasts more accurate? I'm glad you asked. If you want to know how difficult it is making a five-day forecast, try this little experiment. Drop a twig in a stream, and predict exactly where that twig will be downstream five days from now. There are countless billions of variables that affect where that twig will ultimately wind up. So it goes in the atmosphere. Billions of factors determine how storms swept up in the jet stream (a fast-moving river of air aloft) will move, any handful of which may be critical. Su-

1. *Glossary of Meteorology*. Edited by Ralph E. Huschke. Boston: American Meteorological Society, 1986.

Weatherfact: As recently as the 1960s, British law decreed that if you were guilty of trying to predict the weather, you could be burned at the stake as a heretic.

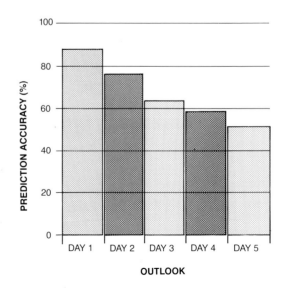

Forecast accuracy drops off rapidly with time, with less certainty for a five- or six-day forecast.

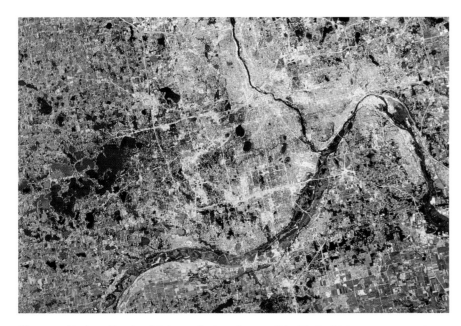

Above and below: Landsat high-resolution photos of the Twin Cities metro area, showing Lake Minnetonka on the left, with downtown Minneapolis and St. Paul just to the right of the screen center. The photo above is how it would appear from roughly two hundred miles overhead. The photo below is enhanced, with areas of vegetation showing up as a reddish color. Concrete, asphalt, and developed regions are blue-gray in appearance, with lakes taking on a black appearance. *Courtesy: Earthsat Corporation.*

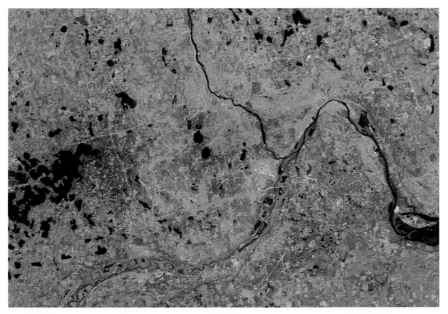

Earth from a satellite 22,300 miles above the equator. The accuracy of long-range weather forecasts is limited by a lack of weather observations, especially over oceans, and by mathematical equations that are only rough approximations of how the atmosphere really operates. *Courtesy: Environmental Satellite Data.*

49

percomputers help us manage this flood of variables, but problems remain.

Perhaps the biggest problem is a lack of reliable weather data over much of the earth. To predict tomorrow's weather, we need to know what's happening all across North America. To forecast weather a week away, we need weather observations from all over the world. You may be surprised to hear that some of our best weather information comes from China, the Soviet Union, and eastern European nations. Luckily, there exists a free exchange of weather reports among nations. Unfortunately, airport weather observations and upper-air balloon reports are rare over the oceans and third world countries. It's a little like trying to finish a jigsaw puzzle with most of the pieces missing. The bottom line: If you put incomplete current data into the supercomputer, it is just a matter of time before the forecast accuracy begins to fizzle.

But even if we had a perfect "snapshot" of current weather around the globe to feed into our computers, problems remain. Meteorologists use complex calculus equations to try to simulate how the atmosphere works, but these models are still relatively crude and inexact. We are just now beginning to realize the importance of the oceans, especially how abnormally warm or cold regions of the Pacific Ocean can affect the skies overhead. Another problem: Friction resulting from airflow over mountainous terrain is particularly difficult to describe in mathematical terms, and this can increase the "noise" in the models with time, making any forecast beyond six days an exercise in futility.

Dependable weather forecasts are essential, and accurate weather forecasts can even help to win wars. One critical weather forecast might have helped to turn the tide of World War II. In May of 1943, the Allied Invasion of France was delayed by foul, rainy weather stalled over the English Channel. General Dwight Eisenhower consulted with his best meteorologist, who assured him that there would be a break in the weather, with just enough clearing to launch the assault on Norman-

dy. Meanwhile, Hitler's meteorologists were convinced that the stormy weather would continue, with little opportunity for the Allies to launch an attack. The forecast Eisenhower heard was right on the money, and on the morning of May 30, 1943, under a partly sunny sky, the D-day drama unfolded along the coast of France.

Hitler received another bad forecast before launching his drive toward Moscow. Once again his staff of meteorologists assured him that the weather would go his way, with the Soviet Union enjoying one of the mildest, driest winters on record. As it turned out, the winter of 1941–42 was one of the snowiest and coldest of the twentieth century, and the German invaders were caught off-guard by subzero temperatures and two-story snow drifts. It is generally accepted by historians that temperatures as cold as -30° to -45° F. took a heavy toll on German troops and morale. They lacked adequate winter clothing, and their equipment malfunctioned due to the snow and bitter temperatures. After analyzing German weather records (which were classified during the war), it seems that upper-level jet stream winds were locked in a northwesterly flow for much of the winter, resulting in one arctic cold front after another. The determination of countless Russian defenders and an unusual weather pattern stopped Hitler's troops dead in their tracks.

FORECASTING THE WEATHER

How do we forecast the weather? How much time do you have? The answer could drone on forever. Put as simply as possible, to be able to predict the weather, you have to know two things: What's happening right now, and what the computers are predicting.

What's Happening Right Now

These devices enable forecasters to monitor the atmosphere, providing the much-needed information needed for short-range forecasts.

Sectional: The National Weather Service works together with the Federal Aviation Administration to monitor the weather on an hourly basis at thousands of airports nationwide. In all, more than seven hundred reports from all over America cross the weather Teletype every hour. The raw weather information is then plotted onto maps called sectionals for analysis.

In all, over one hundred thousand worldwide airport observations filter into the NMC, the National Meteorological Center, every three hours. This vital data is supplemented with forty-eight weather buoys in North American waters, each capable of radioing current conditions to a coastal receiver nearby. Thousands of reports are received from ships and planes to help to fill in the gaps. All of this raw data is fed into a $10 million supercomputer, where complex mathematical models of the atmosphere calculate future weather conditions.

Radiosonde: a weather balloon used to measure winds, humidity, and temperature from the ground to an altitude of about one hundred thousand feet. Hourly airport observations give us a sense of what is happening on the ground, but to be able to predict the weather, meteorologists need a three-dimensional picture of what is occurring overhead and upwind of their towns.

During the late 1800s and early 1900s forecasters were forced to rely on meteorographs sent aloft on tethered kites. Meteorographs automatically recorded, on a single sheet of paper, two or more meteorological parameters such as air pressure, temperature, or humidity. Unfortunately, this method had a few drawbacks. The kites usually reached an altitude of only ten thousand feet, the information could not be evaluated until the kite was brought back down to the ground, the kites could be flown only in good weather, and there was a constant danger of the kites breaking away, endangering lives and property.

From 1925 to 1937, upper-air weather information was obtained by attaching meteorographs to airplanes. But once again, this presented problems. The average altitude reached was seventeen

Midwest airports. Every airport in the Upper Midwest has a three-letter identifier. Minneapolis/St. Paul is MSP.

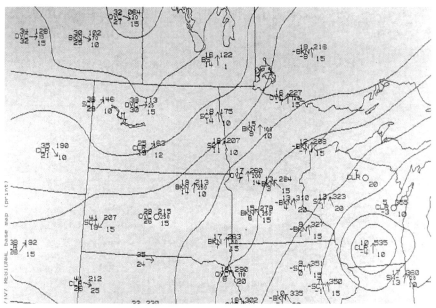

A computer-drawn sectional. Looking at this, a meteorologist would be able to find frontal systems, storms, and areas of clouds and precipitation that might affect the local forecast. Symbols are arranged around each weather station. In clockwise order (from the upper right) they indicate barometric pressure, wind direction, pressure tendency (rising or falling), dew point, current weather conditions, and temperature.

A weather balloon. *Courtesy: Ralph Nistler, National Weather Service, St. Cloud, MN.*

thousand feet, data couldn't be analyzed until after the plane had landed, and the observations couldn't be taken in stormy weather.

A radiosonde consists of a balloon, a radio transmitter, and a lightweight box containing instruments that measure air pressure, temperature, and relative humidity. The gas-filled balloon rises through the atmosphere at the rate of one thousand feet a minute. During the ninety-minute flight a ground-based tracking device follows the balloon as it ascends, allowing meteorologists to compute wind speed and direction. When winds are included in an upper-air report, it is termed a rawinsonde observation.

Some forty-five to sixty minutes after lift-off, at an altitude of ninety thousand to 120,000 feet, the balloon reaches its elastic limit and bursts. A small paper parachute slows the descent of the instruments and radio transmitter, minimizing the danger to those on the ground. Approximately one-third of all radiosondes are found and returned to be used over again by the National Weather Service.

Nagging problems. At the present time, radiosondes are still the most cost-effective way of measuring the current state of the atmosphere, but there are disadvantages to this method. If there is an isolated thunderstorm directly over the St. Cloud area but no other showers nearby and the radiosonde travels up into that thunderstorm, the sounding will be misleadingly moist. If thousands, or hundreds of thousands of balloons could be launched simultaneously, there would be less error and a more accurate "snapshot" of the current state of the skies over America. Obviously, this is prohibited by the cost.

We have some idea what is happening around breakfast time and the dinner hour, but no idea what the upper atmosphere is doing at other times of the day. Once again, spotty, infrequent measurements limit how accurately the weather computers can be initialized, or loaded with the current temperature, wind, and humidity conditions at all levels of the environment. And if the current weather analysis is off, even by just a little, that limits how accurately the computers will be able to "see" into the future.

Satellites: In order to know what is going on right now, satellites have become essential to meteorologists, especially those meteorologists forecasting for cities near oceans, with few land-based airport observations upwind (for example, the West Coast of the United States). Up until the 1950s only sporadic ship and airplane reports could be used to track a storm at sea. Today, new satellite photos are received every thirty minutes. This is essential during hurricane season, when 80 to 90 percent of the predicted hurricane track is based on satellite images.

Satellites record and transmit visible photographs and infrared images, enabling forecasters to know what the atmosphere looks like at any one moment. Visible cloud photos, taken in black and white, are transmitted during daylight, capturing the sun's light that is reflected from the earth back to the satellite sensor. Transmitted to earth roughly from sunrise to sunset, a visible picture is similar to the way the earth looks to the human eye. With visible pictures, especially close-ups with two-kilometer resolution, we are able to pinpoint overshooting tops associated with severe thunderstorms. The pictures also highlight thin cirrus clouds at twenty-five thousand feet, relatively harmless clouds that can look much more threatening on infrared images.

Infrared images become essential to track weather systems when the sun goes down. Instead of measuring reflected sunlight, the infrared or IR sensor on board the weather satellite measures the temperatures of the clouds. The coldest, thickest clouds appear as bright white with thunderstorm tops showing up as black splotches. Low clouds and fog are a dull gray color. Using IR photos, it's possible to put together a twenty-four-hour loop, an entire day's worth of weather.

Present satellite technology takes advantage of geosynchronous (geostationary) orbit. The cloud

Weatherfact: Polar-orbiting satellites keep track of ice as well as cloudiness around the earth. Images of the North Pole reveal that since 1975 the southward extent of the polar ice cap has shrunk by 6 percent. This could be another tip-off that our planet's atmosphere may be warming slightly.

Raw airport observations: Current weather information is sent from airports nationwide via satellite and Teletype at the top of each hour. Called SAs, these reports display information in the following format: three-letter station code; time; clouds or weather; visibility; pressure (millibars); temperature; dew point; wind direction and speed. In the examples below, the Twin Cities airport (MSP) is reporting scattered clouds at 4,500 and 25,000 feet; a visibility of fifteen miles; a temperature of 38°; and a dew point of 17°. Winds are "31" or from the northwest (imagine compass headings) at eleven knots. Chicago (ORD) is reporting a rain shower. Light fog is showing up in Green Bay (GRB), and snow began at thirty-six after the hour and ended forty-four after the hour at Wausau (AUW). Special weather observations between hours are called SPs and move on the Teletype when the weather is changing rapidly at a specific airport.

MSP SA 0050 45 SCT 250 SCT 15 188/38/17/3111/006

ORD SA 0050 M27 OVC 10RW- 187/41/29/1910/006/PRESFR

AUW SA 0050 25 SCT 70 SCT 250 -BKN 10 169/34/30/3505/998/SB36E44 INTMT SW

GRB RS 0050 25 SCT M45 BKN 4F 166/35/31/2807/999/ SB25E38 SWU SE

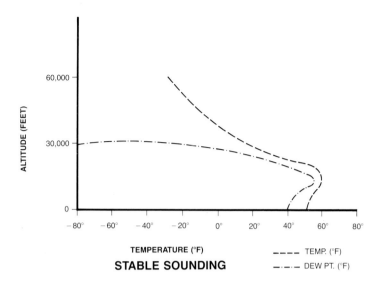

STABLE SOUNDING

TEMPERATURE (°F)

- - - - TEMP. (°F)
- · - · - DEW PT. (°F)

When temperatures increase with altitude, the atmosphere is stable. This layer of warm air aloft puts a lid on upward motion, greatly reducing the risk of convective showers, warm bubbles of upward-moving air that form as the sun heats the ground. A stable airmass is usually associated with light winds, and this can trap haze and pollutants near the earth, lowering visibilities and increasing respiratory problems. Clouds that form in a stable environment are often slow to dissipate.

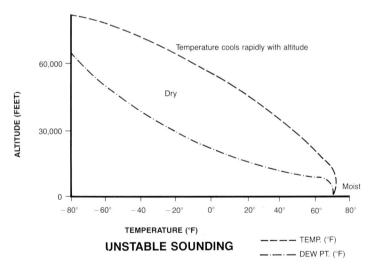

Temperature cools rapidly with altitude

Dry

Moist

UNSTABLE SOUNDING

TEMPERATURE (°F)

- - - - TEMP. (°F)
- · - · - DEW PT. (°F)

A sounding or skew-t is a graph showing the change in temperature and dew point (or moisture) with height. Looking at this, forecasters can determine the probability of cloudiness and thunderstorms, and compute the high temperature for later that day. This is an example of an unstable sounding. If it cools off too rapidly with altitude, the atmosphere may be unstable, and capable of rapid upward motion and thunderstorm growth.

Rising steam from a power plant loses its upward buoyancy as it encounters a warmer, stable layer three thousand feet overhead. The steam and smoke then spread out beneath the stable layer. This appears to be a tornado, but cumulus clouds around the "funnel" dispel that prospect. Remember, twisters do not drop out of a blue sky — you need a severe, rotating thunderstorm. *Robert N. Walker, St. Paul, MN.*

Instability. The atmosphere cools with height, at the rate of about five degrees Fahrenheit for every thousand feet. This is a typical lapse rate for a dry airmass. If the atmosphere cools more rapidly with altitude, then conditions are ripe for cottony cumulus clouds to mushroom into cumulonimbus clouds. The steeper the lapse rate curve (the faster temperatures drop with height), the greater the potential for hail, damaging winds, and tornadoes. *Sherri L. Spencer, Excelsior, MN.*

53

photographs you see on TV are taken from a satellite 22,300 miles above the equator, nicknamed GOES for Geostationary Operational Environmental Satellite. At that altitude, the satellite's speed perfectly matches the speed at which the earth rotates on its axis, so the satellite appears to hover over the same location. This permits meteorologists to loop satellite photos into a cloud "movie," showing the progression of storms and fronts with time without the angle of the picture shifting. There are other geosynchronous weather satellites in orbit over Europe, India, and Japan.

GOES satellites are also equipped with special electronic gear to receive current weather data from collection platforms on earth (weather buoys at sea, river gauges, and ships). The weather observations are beamed up to the satellite and then relayed to a central receiving station in Virginia for processing and redistribution to other meteorologists nationwide.

Most weather satellites have a life expectancy of about five years, limited by the amount of fuel on board, and the wearing out of electronic and mechanical parts. The next generation of weather satellites, called GOES Next or GOES I-M, will be launched in 1991. Improved images will be sent back to earth later that year. GOES Next will be capable of downloading more data at a much faster speed. Satellite resolution will improve to one kilometer for visible pictures and four kilometers for infrared images, which currently have an eight-kilometer resolution. The satellites should be better able to detect fog and low stratus clouds, which are often difficult to distinguish on current satellite photos.

Polar-orbiting satellites pass over the same point twice a day on average, taking ninety minutes to complete one orbit around the earth. Passing overhead at an altitude of five hundred miles, they are capable of transmitting photos with higher resolution than GOES, but the photos' usefulness is limited by their infrequency. (Minnesota is photographed roughly eight times a day by polar-orbiting satellites, compared to forty-eight GOES pictures every twenty-four hours.)

Even weather satellites burn out. Throughout most of the 1980s, the United States boasted of two geostationary weather satellites over the equator. One was positioned high above the western Atlantic Ocean, providing continuous cloud images from the Rockies eastward to the tip of Africa. The other was stationed over the Pacific, beaming back high-resolution pictures of Alaska, Hawaii, and the West Coast of the United States.

On May 3, 1986, a replacement satellite, GOES-G, had to be destroyed shortly after launch due to a faulty Delta rocket. On January 21, 1989, this failure was compounded further when the onboard imaging system of one of the two geostationary satellites, GOES-6, went black. That setback leaves us with one satellite, GOES-7, doing double-duty, scanning not only the United States but also the Pacific and Atlantic. GOES-7 was launched in February of 1987 with a life expectancy of about five years. Barring more failures, GOES-7 should remain in service until Ford Aerospace launches the next generation of weather satellites into space, tentatively scheduled for June of 1991. These new, upgraded eyes in the sky will be capable of higher resolution images. And using new instrumentation, they'll be able to send back valuable information on upper-level temperatures and winds, previously available from radiosondes (weather balloons).

Government and private meteorologists shudder when faced with the obvious question: What happens if GOES-7 burns out before the next generation can be launched? If that were to happen, we might have to borrow a bird from Europe or Japan to tide us over.

Radar. Another tool meteorologists use is radar. Radar is short for "radio detection and ranging," and the concept is a relatively simple one. A pulse of radio energy is sent out from the radar transmitter. When the pulse hits a raindrop or snowflake, some of the energy is scattered (reflected) back to the radar site. Knowing that the radar beam travels at the speed of light, it is then possible to compute how far away a target, or echo, is. And since a higher density of raindrops (associated with heavier rain) will reflect a greater percentage of the radio energy back to the radar, it's possible to determine precipitation intensity. By assigning a color or shade of gray to each intensity level, the radar can "paint" a picture onto a navigated map.

Since meteorologists (and the public) want to see where rain or snow is reaching the ground, the radar beam is nearly horizontal, usually kept one-half to one degree above the horizon. This means that the radar energy bounces off of trees, towers, and buildings near the antenna, and this reflected energy shows up as stationary blips near the radar site, called ground clutter. Ground clutter can make tracking storms directly over the radar installation difficult, although newer radars have something called clutter suppression, which eliminates ground targets altogether.

Sometimes abbreviated A.P., anomalous propagation is another false echo usually triggered by unusual temperature or moisture patterns, often in the wake of strong thunderstorms. Rapid changes in the stability of the atmosphere can paint more violent-looking cells on the radar screen, when in fact skies are sunny and dry! (Often A.P. appears like colorful spokes in a giant wheel centered over the radar site, leading some green meteorologists to issue warnings for imaginary storms.)

What the Computers are Predicting

Computers are essential to be able to forecast for more than one or two days into the future. Twice a day, current weather observations are initialized into two Control Data Cyber 205 supercomputers in Suitland, Maryland. Using advanced calculus and laws of fluid dynamics that simulate how the atmosphere should flow with time, the computer calculates how a parcel of air will behave at thousands of grid points over the northern hemisphere. The computer calculates

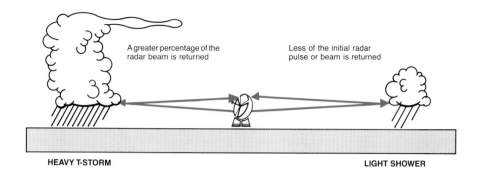

A greater percentage of the radar beam is returned

Less of the initial radar pulse or beam is returned

HEAVY T-STORM   LIGHT SHOWER

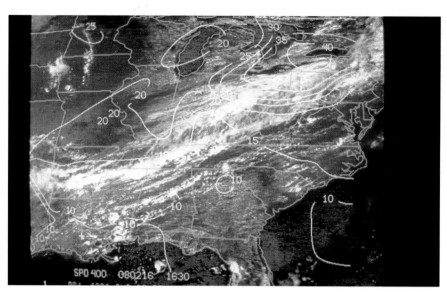

A visible picture from an eastern satellite. In this example, a computer has analyzed winds at four hundred millibars (about twenty-five thousand feet) on top of the satellite image. *Courtesy: Idetik, Inc.*

Radar is simply a slowly rotating radio transmitter. As radio waves are reflected off of precipitation, a microprocessor computes the angle of the shower (measuring from 0 to 359 degrees); the distance from the radar to the target; and the intensity (based on the amount of energy returning to the antenna). Because the radar beam travels in a straight line, the curvature of the earth will cause the pulse of energy to eventually pass over the cloud tops. Thus, radar has trouble seeing rain more than 150 to 200 miles away.

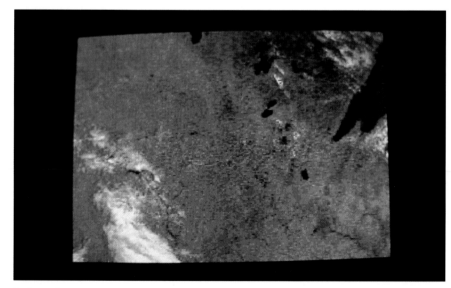

Polar-orbiting satellites photograph the earth in one hundred-mile-wide strips. This "visible shot" shows much of Minnesota, with Lake Superior in the upper-right-hand corner. If you look carefully, you can pick out Red, Leech, Cass, and Mille Lacs lakes. *Courtesy: Loren Johnson, Satellite Data Systems.*

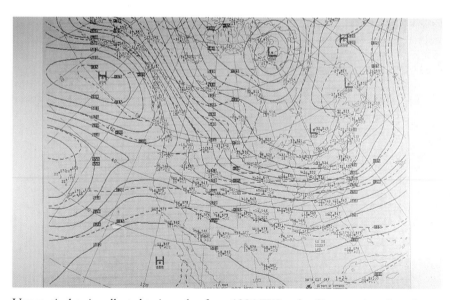

Upper-air data is collected twice a day from 129 NWS and military stations in and near the United States. This information is fed into supercomputers in Suitland, Maryland, to compute the one- to ten-day outlooks. The NWS in St. Cloud, Minnesota, launches balloons at 6:00 A.M. and 6:00 P.M. Worldwide, some seven hundred balloons are launched twice a day. This map shows wind, temperature, and moisture conditions at two hundred millibars, a pressure level that corresponds roughly to thirty thousand feet.

changes in pressure, temperature, moisture, and wind at every one of these grid points, some two hundred million calculations every second! As computers have become faster, the grid has become finer, with calculations performed on grid points closer together. Ultimately, this has led to an increase in accuracy, especially in the two- to five-day forecast.

Problems remain. Not only is it impossible to initialize the computers with one hundred percent accuracy, the advanced partial differential equations that simulate the movement of air masses are far from perfect. It has not been possible to accurately model the transfer of heat between the atmosphere and the oceans, even though we know that this is a critical factor. Friction is introduced as air passes over mountainous areas, and yet the computers have a difficult time taking this into account.

It's been estimated that an accurate twenty-four-hour forecast requires current weather data from all over the United States. For a three-day outlook, computers require current weather from Europe, South America, and Canada. For any prediction beyond five days, a complete global "snapshot" is required.

Most meteorologists can choose from four or five different computer projections of what the atmosphere "should" look like in the future. They all use different math equations to make their calculations, and sometimes they all disagree! For example, the LFM, short for Limited Fine Mesh, may suggest heavy wet snow; the NGM, or Nested Grid Model, is hinting at all rain; while the baroclinic model is leaning toward partly sunny! It's at this point that meteorologists begin to massage their ulcers and tug at their gray hairs.

Here is where the "human element" comes in. Studies show that the most accurate forecasts are those that rely on computers *and* people. We know that some computer models tend to work better in certain weather patterns than others. A forecaster may be able to look at the computer print-out and say, "Ah ha! I remember a similar storm three years ago. The LFM did a crummy job, but the NGM model handled it well. I'm going with the NGM solution." A keen memory, and even gut feeling can make a big difference. Rarely is the forecast black or white; usually, it's some nebulous, hard to distinguish shade of gray. It's worth mentioning that never are two storms or weather patterns absolutely identical. They may be similar, vaguely resembling a pattern several months or years ago, but every forecast dilemma is a new one.

A meteorologist has to look at as much current data and computer forecasts as possible, and then reason logically, picking the scenario with the highest probability of actually occurring. It's not just a matter of moving a storm from point A to point B. That's simple. The problem is that all storms change and mutate as they track eastward. Sometimes the computers have a handle on these upcoming changes, but oftentimes they don't, with embarrassing consequences for weathercasters.

Predicting the future is tough. Ask any economist, politician, or palm-reader. If you assemble ten stockbrokers in the same room and ask for a consensus on the economy, chances are good they'll come up with ten different forecasts. It all boils down to interpretation. So it goes with the atmosphere. Ten meteorologists may have ten different forecasts. The one that's most accurate probably tempered the computer solution with a good memory, common sense, and good old gut feeling (a prayer now and then can make a difference too)!

The Nested Grid Model, or NGM, is probably the most widely used computer model in the United States. Meteorologists can see displays of important information: forecast winds at five hundred millibars (or about eighteen thousand feet); forecast isobars and the predicted location of high and low pressure systems; the forecast average relative humidity in the atmosphere; and the predicted "thickness," or average temperature of the air mass, all for twelve, twenty-four, thirty-six, and forty-eight hours into the future. The

Not a Bad Investment

If you look at the federal budget allocated for the National Weather Service, you quickly realize that there are still a few bargains left out there. Measuring the atmosphere, disseminating severe weather warnings, and issuing daily forecasts costs each American about $1.25 a year!

Satellite imagery is received via satellite twenty-four hours a day. This computer sorts out the sectors, specific close-ups of North America that we want to save on disk and "loop" into movies on the air. This way, we can follow the movement of storms and fronts over time. The computer can store up to twenty-four hours of satellite photos and a day's worth of data from hundreds of airports nationwide. (It throws out the stuff we don't need to forecast for Minnesota, like the upper-level winds over the Fiji Islands, etc.)

Satellites have revolutionized the tracking and forecasting of hurricanes. Before the 1960s, meteorologists had to rely on spotty ship reports to keep tabs on these deadly storms. Today, a new photo is transmitted every thirty minutes from GOES satellites 22,300 miles above the equator to a National Weather Service ground station in Virginia where the data is processed. We can see them coming, but trying to predict where they'll go next is still more of an art than a science. The problem? A lack of upper-air data over the oceans. Thanks to continuous satellite photographs, no hurricane or tropical storm has gone undetected in the Atlantic, eastern Pacific, or Caribbean oceans since 1966.

An infrared satellite picture. In this case, the normal gray scale has been color enhanced, with the coldest clouds appearing yellow. Based on the observed temperature, the computer estimated the "top" of the thunderhead near screen center to be over forty-four thousand feet tall. *Courtesy: Idetik, Inc.*

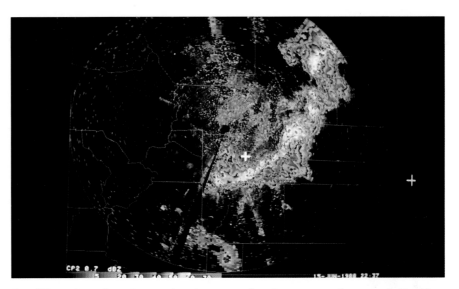

Squall line: a line of very intense thunderstorms, showing up on a radar screen in Boulder, Colorado. The bright yellow, orange, and red areas are regions of heaviest rain and hail. Radar is another means of filling in the gaps, providing current weather information between regularly reporting airports. *Courtesy: PROFS/NOAA.*

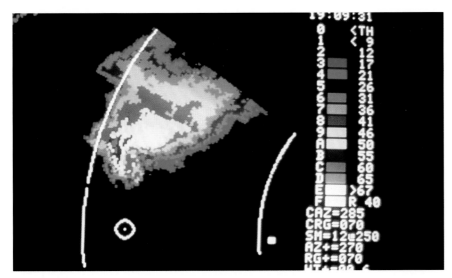

Evidence on the radar display is of a severe counterclockwise-rotating mesocyclone, a long-lasting thunderstorm capable of spinning up a tornado. Sometimes appearing like the number 6 on radar, a hook echo is an area of heavy rain or hail that is carried into surrounding dry air by intense rotation of the parent mesocyclone. The notch is called a vault or weak echo region, suggestive of an intense updraft. This radar snapshot was taken when a tornado was approaching Binger, Oklahoma, on May 22, 1981. A tornado was on the ground at point A. *Courtesy: NSSL/NOAA.*

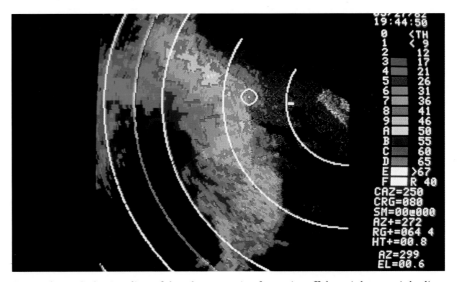

Bow echo. A bulge in a line of thunderstorms is often a tip-off that violent straight-line winds are reaching the ground. These downbursts are frequently found when upper-level jet stream winds are strong, blowing from the northwest toward the southeast. Watch the southernmost cell in a line of strong thunderstorms, or any shower that veers off to the right. These cells are most likely to become severe. *Courtesy: NSSL/NOAA.*

models are initialized with new information twice a day and calculations are performed on sixteen layers of the atmosphere. The NGM is a meshed model, which means that the computer concentrates on the western hemisphere, specifically North America. The forecasts are quite accurate out to about forty-eight hours, but since the model doesn't take current global weather into account, the forecast accuracy drops off rapidly after two to three days.

In contrast, the MRF (Medium Range Forecasting) model is a global, spectral model that takes weather over the entire northern hemisphere into account. As a result, the longer range (two- to six-day) forecasts tend to be more accurate. The only problem: The National Weather Service waits until later in the day to run this model, and most of the computer output is unavailable to TV and radio meteorologists when making up their forecasts. The NGM, since it concentrates on North America, is able to run faster on the supercomputers in Washington, D.C., and is disseminated to forecasters in time to put together their outlooks.

What is the boundary layer? The computers that use these models assume that at some level of the atmosphere, friction is no longer a factor. Air passing over hills, buildings, and other objects produces friction, or additional turbulence. This leads to noise in the computer models that eventually triggers inaccuracies in the forecasts, especially the two- and three-day forecasts.

Where are the weather forecasts most accurate? In Europe, thanks to a faster Cray-XMP supercomputer in Reading, England. Greater speed enables the computer to better simulate the way the atmosphere really works. In addition, computer programmers and mathematicians are offered diplomatic status, with higher salaries and subsidized education for their children through college. As a result, the medium-range forecast group has been able to attract some of the best minds in the world. The physics in the European model is more sophisticated, with calculations performed on some twenty-plus layers of the atmosphere. Like the MRF model in the United States, the European model looks at global wavelengths before making its prediction (it gets the big picture). European programmers spend much more time weeding out bad data and adding additional information before running the model late each afternoon. Studies show that this meticulous effort pays off, with some forecast accuracy out to seven or eight days, compared with only five or six days for the American models.

TRANSLATING THE 10:00 P.M. WEATHER REPORT

What do all those terms heard on the news mean anyway? Here's the answers!

Barometric pressure: Although it's hard to imagine, the air overhead is a fluid, with waves, troughs, and crests much like the sea. The atmosphere exerts a downward pressure or weight, capable of displacing a column of mercury to a height of about thirty inches. A drop in air pressure usually implies deteriorating weather, a rising barometer hinting at a clearing trend.

Low pressure: Commonly called a storm or cyclone, this is an area of counterclockwise-rotating winds converging to produce clouds and precipitation. As moist air spirals in toward the center of a storm, it is forced to rise and cool. As air cools, it loses its ability to hold water vapor, and the water vapor condenses into visible cloud droplets. If this upward motion continues, the microscopic cloud droplets and ice crystals stick together, and gravity pulls them to the ground as rain or snow.

Warm fronts: The atmosphere always moistens-up from top to bottom. When you see the sun getting tangled up in a thickening cobweb of milky cirrus clouds, precipitation may be less than twelve hours away, especially if the barometer is falling and winds are picking up from the east.

Those high, thin clouds will gradually lower

Weatherfact: Weather forecasts tend to be more accurate in the East than they are out in the West. This is because the farther east in the United States you live, the greater the number of balloon launches and airport observations to the west or "upwind." (This is not to say that more balloons are launched; but it is difficult to launch weather balloons west of the West—there's not much other than ocean there.) More frequent and reliable weather reports translate into more accurate computer solutions, especially for the two- to five-day forecast.

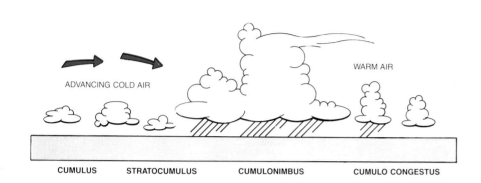

ADVANCING COLD AIR

WARM AIR

CUMULUS   STRATOCUMULUS   CUMULONIMBUS   CUMULO CONGESTUS

A cold front. *Henrietta K. Lucht, Braham, MN.*

Cold fronts are often preceded by gusty southwest winds, a rapidly falling barometer, and bloated, cottony cumulo-congestus clouds that eventually darken into cumulonimbus clouds and sputtering thunder and lightning. Following a wind shift to the northwest, showers taper, but flat, lumpy sheets of stratocumulus clouds can linger for twelve hours or more.

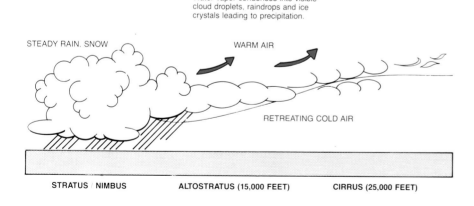

As air rises, it cools. Cool air cannot hold as much moisture. Water vapor condenses into visible cloud droplets, raindrops and ice crystals leading to precipitation.

STEADY RAIN, SNOW

WARM AIR

RETREATING COLD AIR

STRATUS / NIMBUS   ALTOSTRATUS (15,000 FEET)   CIRRUS (25,000 FEET)

A warm front.

Warm fronts tend to move very slowly, drifting to the north or east at five to fifteen miles an hour. Warm fronts are preceded by wisps of cirrus clouds at twenty-five thousand feet. The clouds gradually lower and thicken into low stratus and nimbus, producing steady rain, snow, or drizzle.

and thicken into midlevel clouds, lumpy altocumulus or flat altostratus clouds at about ten thousand feet. Then rain or snow may be less than six hours away. Warm fronts produce long-lasting, steady precipitation, the result of overrunning. As warm, moist air rises up and over a retreating dome of cooler, denser air near the ground, water vapor condenses into visible water droplets and ice crystals, eventually leading to precipitation. One note: Warm air does not just "push" cold air out of the way. The cold air has to retreat on its own, before the warm front can move through.

Warm fronts produce dull, drizzly, foggy days and nights, but they also provide the majority of our rain and snow year-round.

Cold fronts: Cold fronts mark the leading edge of colder air. Unlike warm fronts, they tend to spawn convective, showery precipitation, often accompanied by thunder, lightning, and gusty winds. Winds shift from southwest to northwest in a matter of minutes, and the barometer begins to rebound. Showers may last for several hours, but as the temperature begins to tumble, the precipitation quickly tapers to sprinkles or flurries. Most cold fronts approach from the west or northwest. Occasionally, these wedge-shaped masses of colder air approach from the northeast, from the vicinity of Lake Superior. These are called back-door cold fronts. They tend to be much more common in New England during late spring, when clammy northeast winds are capable of dropping backyard thermometers from the eighties into the fifties in a matter of minutes!

Cold fronts tend to move much faster than warm fronts, averaging about twenty miles an hour in the summer and twenty to forty miles an hour during the winter months.

Stationary fronts: These are capable of lingering for days, unloading very heavy amounts of precipitation. The result of a stalled warm or cold front, stationary fronts tend to occur during the summer months, when upper-level winds are relatively light and weather systems are slower and weaker.

Warm sector: The "no man's land" between warm and cold fronts. Here is where the highest temperatures occur, as winds pick up out of the south to southwest. If there is plenty of sun and high humidity in the air, the potential for severe thunderstorms is present.

Squall line: This is a line of severe thunderstorms that develops in the warm sector, several hundred miles ahead of the cold front. By forming in lines, thunderstorms reduce the amount of dry air that is sucked into their circulation, prolonging their life-spans and increasing their destructive potential. Here is where tornadoes, hail, and damaging winds are statistically most likely to occur.

Backlash: Found at the tail-end of a retreating storm, backlash is weather-slang for stubborn low cloudiness and very light "nuisance precipitation" triggered by warm air wrapping completely around the storm's circulation, approaching from the north of all places! Low stratocumulus clouds eventually give way to clearing skies as drier air arrives on northwest winds.

High pressure: Otherwise known as an anticyclone, this is a region of dry, clockwise-rotating air that is sinking. As air sinks, it warms up, and is able to hold more water vapor. "Highs" bring fair skies and light winds as they pass nearby. If winds become too light, they can lead to fog and to air stagnation.

Isobars: Isobars are lines drawn on weather maps that connect points at which pressure is the same and show approximately how the winds will blow. Air travels from regions of high pressure to low pressure, but as it passes over land, resulting friction or turbulence causes air to cross the isobars at a slight angle, moving toward the storm

Weatherfact: The term "front" was first used by a Norwegian meteorologist by the name of Bjerknes, who thought that these zones of "troubled, stormy weather" resembled the battle fronts scarring Europe during World War I. The term stuck, and now meteorologists the world over refer to these air mass boundaries as fronts.

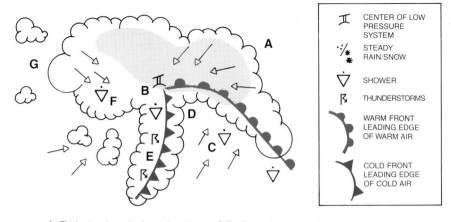

KEY:

- ♊ CENTER OF LOW PRESSURE SYSTEM
- STEADY RAIN/SNOW
- ▽ SHOWER
- ⟨ THUNDERSTORMS
- WARM FRONT LEADING EDGE OF WARM AIR
- COLD FRONT LEADING EDGE OF COLD AIR

A. Thickening cirrus clouds, northeast breeze, falling barometer
B. Steady "overrunning" precipitation, east / southeast winds, falling barometer
C. Warm sector, south / southeast winds, falling barometer
D. Increasing cumulus and cumulo-congestus clouds, south winds, rapidly falling barometer
E. Cold front, heavy showers, thunderstorms, winds shift west / northwest, rapidly rising barometer
F. "Backlash" precipitation, light showers, sprinkles, gusty northwest wind, rising barometer
G. Clearing skies, thinning cumulus clouds, north / northeast winds, rising barometer

Most fully developed low pressure systems resemble the one above. Someone traveling through the storm would encounter thickening cirrus clouds at point A; steady precipitation, a falling barometer, and an easterly wind under the warm front at point B; clearing skies and a wind shift more to the south at point C; a risk of severe thunderstorms from a squall line at point D; heavy showers and thunderstorms, gusty westerly winds, and a rapidly rising barometer as the cold front arrives at point E; low clouds, falling temperatures, and a few light sprinkles or flurries at F; and a continued rising barometer and clearing skies behind the storm at point G.

"Scud," low scrappy clouds that often form under the cloud base, often a tip-off that a slow clearing trend is setting in.

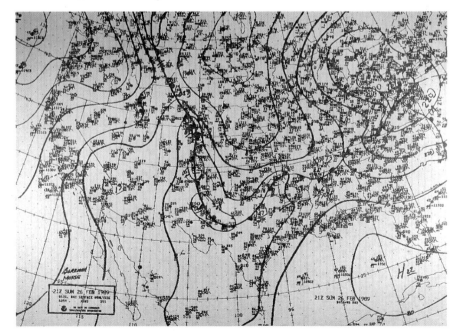

Surface map of the United States showing isobars.

61

(area of low pressure). The closer together isobars are, the faster the winds are blowing in that region. A lack of isobars nearby means light winds and little change in weather for the near future. (No, contrary to myth, an isobar is not where meteorologists hang out after a particularly devastating forecast.)

Isobars are plotted up on a national surface map, composed of data from hundreds of airports in the United States and Canada. Displaying storms, high pressure systems, and fronts, as well as individual "OBS" (hourly observations) for various airports, surface maps are transmitted to meteorologists every three hours.

Dew point: The dew point is an absolute measure of how much moisture there is in the air. If you cool the air temperature down to the dew point, the relative humidity reaches one hundred percent, and water vapor condenses into a cloud, fog, dew, or frost.

Relying on relative humidity can be misleading. For instance, a relative humidity of 90 percent on a day when the temperature is sixty degrees will still be comfortable. But a relative humidity of 40 percent on a day when the mercury is sizzling in the nineties will be oppressive! The relative humidity, as the name suggests, is truly relative to the temperature.

If you know the temperature and the dew point, it's possible to compute the relative humidity. There is no limit to how low the dew point can go, but it is impossible for the air temperature to read lower than the dew point. As a rule of thumb, the lower the dew point, the drier (and more comfortable for us) the air mass overhead.

Severe thunderstorms usually require a dew point of at least sixty degrees, and thunderstorms tend to fire up along dry lines, moisture boundaries where the dew point drops from the sixties into the forties over a short distance.

Coriolis force: The result of a rotating earth, a fictitious force called the Coriolis force appears to deflect air masses to the right of their actual movement in the Northern Hemisphere, and to the left in the Southern Hemisphere. (At the equator, there is no Coriolis force.)

Cooling degree day. A way of keeping tabs on energy consumption during the summer heat. The hotter the weather, the greater the number of cooling degree days. For instance, on a day when the high was ninety-two and the low was seventy, simply subtract sixty-five from the average temperature for the day to compute the number of cooling degree days.

$$81 \text{ (average of high and low)}$$
$$- \ 65$$
$$\overline{16 \text{ cooling degree days}}$$

Clear air turbulence: Turbulence is often encountered by high-altitude jet aircraft flying near the jet stream. Any rapid change in wind speed or direction over a short distance can lead to violent turbulence. This is known as wind shear. Over the past decade, wind shear has been one of the most dangerous weather conditions encountered by pilots, responsible for five airline accidents and some five hundred deaths, according to the Federal Aviation Administration.

The FAA is asking that all planes with thirty or more seats eventually be equipped with Doppler radar, which is capable of detecting these regions of swirling, dangerous winds.

Jet stream: A high-speed river of air some five to ten miles above the ground, most pronounced over the midlatitudes. High-flying B-29 bombers trying to reach Japan during World War II noticed that on certain days, the headwinds were so strong that they made very little forward progress. Today, with radiosonde information, jet aircraft can avoid the core of the jet stream, where winter winds can sometimes top two hundred miles an hour. Even so, a strong jet stream can lengthen a

Your Comfort Level

Dew Point	Weather
20s	Very dry
30s	Dry
40s	Crisp
50s	Comfortable
60s	Humid
70s	Oppressively humid
80s	Tropical! (Rarely seen)

Weatherfact: There are over eighty different "classes" of snow crystals, with the exact shape of a snowflake depending on the temperature and moisture conditions as the snowflake drifts earthward. Researchers estimate that there may be a million or more combinations of temperature and humidity that your typical run-of-the-mill snowflake might take. That translates into ten to the five-millionth power different sequences; each could create a crystal with a different shape. The odds of finding two identical snowflakes are very small indeed!

Weatherfact: Question: Which of these weather phenomena are classical music composers most likely to capture in their scores, snowstorms, summer heat, thunderstorms, or mist and fog? Answer: Thunderstorms, according to an article in *Weatherwise Magazine*.

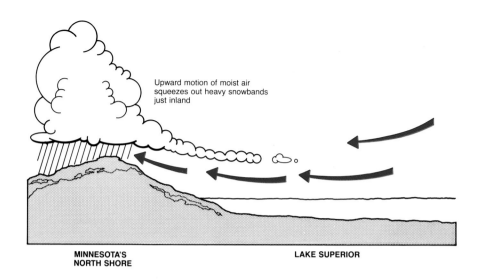

Upward motion of moist air squeezes out heavy snowbands just inland

MINNESOTA'S NORTH SHORE

LAKE SUPERIOR

Lake effect snow occurs along the hilly terrain of the North Shore. The rapid upward motion of moist east-to-northeast winds passing over Lake Superior and rising upon landfall squeezes moisture out of the air. The result: concentrated bands of heavy snow downwind of the lake. Thunder, lightning, and snowfall rates of five inches an hour are not unheard of near the North Shore. Lake effect snows are more of a problem over the Upper Peninsula of Michigan, and just to the southeast of Chicago.

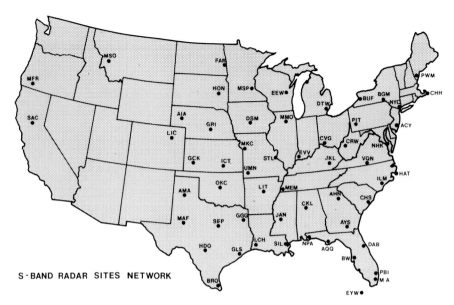

S-BAND RADAR SITES NETWORK

Radar sites around the United States. There are over one hundred National Weather Service radars in use, providing coverage to most of the nation east of the Rocky Mountains. (The Rocky Mountains, Cascades, and Sierra Nevadas drastically reduce the range that radar can "see"—limiting radar's usefulness.) *Courtesy: Kavouras, Inc.*

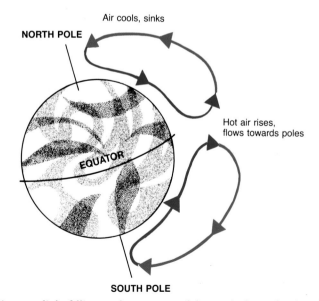

Air cools, sinks

NORTH POLE

Hot air rises, flows towards poles

EQUATOR

SOUTH POLE

Hadley cell. Direct sunlight falling on the equator and the tropics heats the air, which rises toward the poles. Since the North Pole receives only a fraction of the sun's energy, the air cools and begins to sink, flowing southward toward the tropics to be heated once more. This is one of the main "engines" that drives the world's weather.

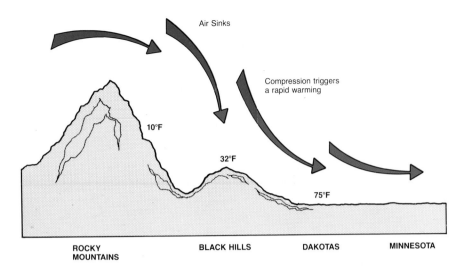

Chinook winds are named after a Native American group in Washington state that first documented their effects. As air sinks immediately downwind of a mountain range, it becomes compressed and warms up rapidly. On the eastern (leeward) side of the Black Hills, temperatures can rise ten or twenty degrees in the time it takes to brush your teeth. From time to time, this warmed air can even nudge temperatures a bit higher in Minnesota.

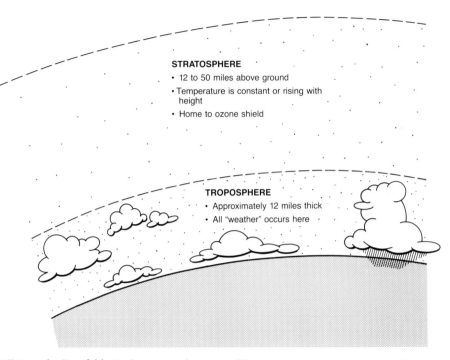

All "weather" unfolds in the troposphere, roughly the lowest twelve miles of the atmosphere, where temperatures get lower with height, reaching -40° to -60°F. At the tropopause, a boundary area between the troposhere and the stratosphere, temperatures hold nearly steady with increasing altitude. The stratosphere is home to many gases including ozone, which shields earth from harmful ultraviolet rays. Temperatures begin to rise in the upper stratosphere, reaching forty to fifty degrees above zero some thirty to fifty miles overhead.

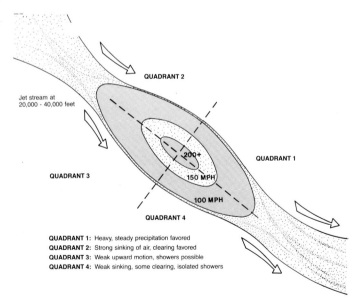

Aerial view of a jet streak, a concentrated region of maximum-speed winds imbedded within the jet stream. This surge of violent wind is usually preceded and followed by specific weather on the ground below. A rapid increase (or decrease) in the upper-level jet stream winds can help to strengthen storms, spark thunderstorms, and enhance precipitation falling out of clouds nearby.

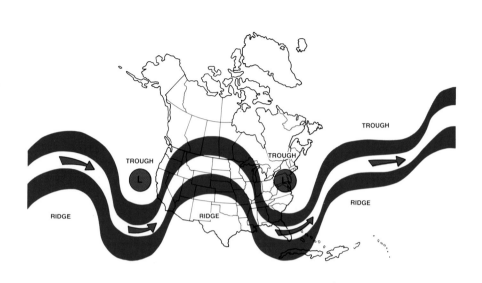

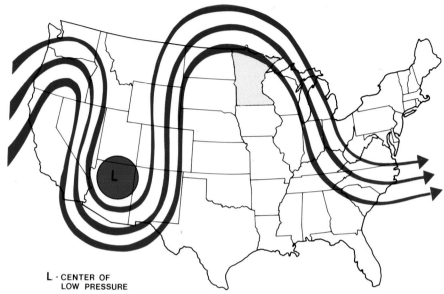

Huge "bulges" in the jet stream are called ridges; they generate high pressure and fair skies and when they stall, drought conditions. Giant "wrinkles" or "dips" in the jet stream are called troughs. Storms tend to strengthen as they pass through troughs. The approach of a trough aloft is usually a signal that the weather is about to deteriorate. By using super-computers, meteorologists attempt to predict how the jet stream will move, where it will bunch up into a ridge, where it will buckle into a trough.

High amplitude flow. When jet stream winds are too fast, the pattern is extremely unstable and the jet stream buckles, allowing cold air to race southward, and warm, moist air to surge northward. This pattern favors weather extremes, especially heavy rain and snow and record highs and lows. Cut-off lows, like the one at point A, are most likely to form over the desert Southwest. They are stalled storms in the upper atmosphere, vast regions of arctic air swirling above fifteen thousand feet, resulting in persistent clouds and precipitation. When they are finally "kicked" northeastward by an approaching storm off the Pacific Ocean, they can dump rain or snow on Minnesota. (The computers do a lousy job of forecasting when these cut-off lows will open up and move toward Minnesota.)

An icy plant. *Jack Kjos, Benson, MN.*

Zonal flow. When jet stream winds are basically west to east, Minnesota experiences a relatively mild weather pattern. Most of the Pacific moisture is squeezed out west of the Rocky Mountains, and precipitation tends to be light and showery.

Weatherfact: We all know that shoveling snow can be a strenuous and downright painful experience. But did you know that a four-inch blanket of heavy snow on a fifty-foot, two-car driveway weighs more than eighty-two hundred pounds! That's more than four tons of grunts and groans, and proof-positive that even if you're in great shape, you'll want to be careful with that snow shovel.

Weatherfact: It takes a million snow crystals (give or take a couple) to cover a two-square-foot area to a depth of ten inches!

Weatherfact: Ten percent of all the salt produced on earth is used to clear highways in North America. Scientists at the University of Minnesota are working on chemical alternatives to salt that are noncorrosive. Although initially costing more to apply to Minnesota's roads, experts estimate that these ice-melting chemicals might all but eliminate car rust and highway damage triggered by salt applications, leading to enormous savings in the long run.

flight westward, and accurate wind forecasts are essential to compute fuel consumption and maximum savings for the airline industry.

The point at which the jet stream buckles or twists determines just where high and low pressure systems are able to form and strengthen. There is a direct cause and effect—the jet stream sets the tempo for all weather.

Upper-air disturbance: A frequent alibi for surprise summertime thunderstorms, an upper-air disturbance is merely a puddle of unusually cold air in the upper atmosphere, at least four to six miles overhead. This cool-down aloft increases the instability of the air mass, and the likelihood that a bubble of warm, moist air will continue to accelerate upward, mushrooming into a cumulonimbus cloud or thunderhead. Sometimes, these patches of chilly air drifting high overhead are so small that they go undetected by National Weather Service weather balloons sent up at 6:00 A.M. and 6:00 P.M., adding to the unpleasant surprise.

Oceans: Oceans have a profound affect on the atmosphere above, including fluxes, or transfers of heat and moisture. To be able to make an accurate long-range forecast, one needs to be able to predict what the oceans will do, especially the Pacific. Oceanographers and meteorologists are realizing that the Pacific Ocean is the Achilles heel of the world's weather, with abnormalities in sea-surface temperature capable of sparking floods or even droughts thousands of miles downwind.

Sun: The "solar constant" is really a myth; in reality, the sun's energy output is far from constant. Sunspots and solar flares can cool the sun's surface, affecting the amount of energy reaching earth. The solar cycle will be peaking in 1991, with one of the strongest displays of sunspots in recent memory. These sunspot peaks have tended to coincide with periods of drought across North America, and there is mounting evidence that unusual solar ac-

tivity may lead to a strengthening of El Niño-related events Proving cause and effect is difficult, but we are discovering relationships between the sun, the oceans, and the atmosphere that may lead to a better understanding of long-term weather changes.

Moon: more than just a night-light? Hospital workers, police officers, and mental health workers have noticed a link between full moons and odd, erratic behavior on the part of some people. And now, there is a growing debate over whether the moon may help to sway weather events on earth. Specifically, the moon's orbit around the earth is elliptical, and a close pass to earth provides an extra gravitational tug, one that has a ripple effect on our atmosphere. For now, this is sheer speculation, but it's a theory that scientists will be investigating in the 1990s.

El Niño: A strange warming of the Pacific Ocean west of Ecuador and Peru that occurs on average every five to seven years is called El Niño. The name is Spanish for "the child," and its name arises from the fact that the water off the coast of South America tends to turn warm and brackish around Christmas.

El Niño is only one symptom of a much larger atmospheric abnormality called the southern oscillation. Changes in atmospheric pressure as far away as Australia can "turn off" the trade winds that blow near the equator. Less wind means less upwelling (less cold, nutrient-rich ocean water coming up to the surface). This in turn leads to sea surface temperatures some four to eight degrees warmer than normal, heating the air above.

The last severe El Niño was seen during the winter of 1983–84. It threw a monkey wrench into the jet stream over North America, triggering floods for Peru, raging storms over California, and devastating drought over Australia. El Niños tend to produce slightly warmer, wetter weather for Minnesota.

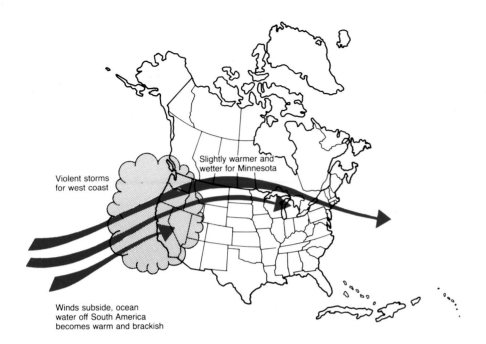

Slightly warmer and wetter for Minnesota

Violent storms for west coast

Winds subside, ocean water off South America becomes warm and brackish

El Niño.

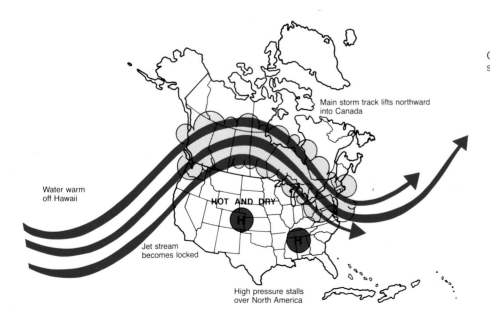

Main storm track lifts northward into Canada

Water warm off Hawaii

HOT AND DRY

Jet stream becomes locked

High pressure stalls over North America

La Niña.

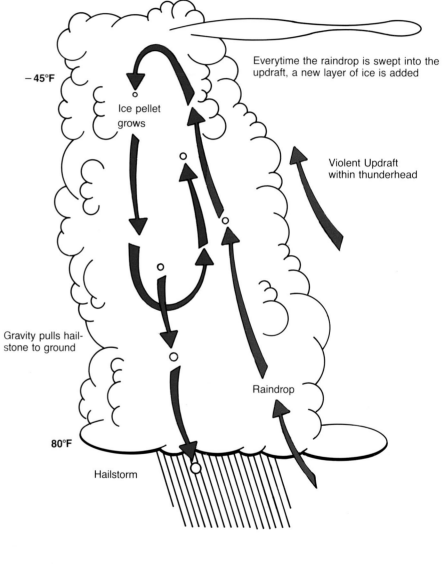

−45°F

Ice pellet grows

Everytime the raindrop is swept into the updraft, a new layer of ice is added

Violent Updraft within thunderhead

Gravity pulls hail-stone to ground

Raindrop

80°F

Hailstorm

Hail.

Severe thunderstorms are more likely when:
- Dew points are at least sixty degrees or higher.
- Winds are blowing from the south or southeast.
- The barometer is falling rapidly.
- Wispy cirrus clouds are thickening on the western horizon.
- You hear loud static on the AM band of your radio.
- A warm front has moved through within the last twelve hours.

Steady rain or snow is likely when:
- The barometer is falling.
- Winds are blowing from the east or northeast.
- The preceding day was unusually cool and dry with low humidity.
- Clouds are low and uniformly flat and gray.

La Niña: This is just the opposite of El Niño, characterized by a significant cooling of ocean water in the eastern Pacific. During the summer of 1988, the hottest and driest on record for much of America, the water off Ecuador was as much as five to ten degrees colder than normal. Once again, this affected the movement of the jet stream, carving out a persistent ridge over North America. The result was a stubborn heat-pump high-pressure system that shoved the main storm track northward into Canada.

Rain: Precipitation in the form of liquid water droplets with diameters greater than 0.5 millimeters. Heavy rain is defined as at least 0.30 inches of water (or more) in one hour.

Freezing rain or glaze ice: This is liquid rain that freezes on contact with a cold ground at a temperature under thirty-two degrees. Freezing rain can accumulate on trees and power lines, snapping branches and knocking out power if air temperatures remain below freezing for any length of time. The biggest threat is on the highways, which can be instantly transformed into deadly ice-skating rinks. Front wheel drive, or even a 4-by-4 won't help when there's a sheet of ice on the roads.

Drizzle: This is defined as water droplets with diameters of less than 0.5 millimeters, much more numerous than raindrops, and capable of producing lower visibilities than light rain.

Sleet: Sleet falls as ice pellets that form when raindrops freeze before reaching the ground. They can often be seen bouncing off objects, and they can accumulate on the ground, much like snow. Sleet is not as treacherous to drive on as is freezing rain.

Hail: Hail is lumps or balls of ice found in cumulonimbus clouds, or thunderstorms. Raindrops swept up into violent updrafts can easily freeze as temperatures dip to -40° F. or colder. Upon reaching a certain size, gravity pulls these ice pellets toward the ground, but if a nearby updraft is strong enough, the ice pellet may repeat its journey, and surrounding water droplets add another layer to the ice. This cycle can be repeated numerous times, until finally not even a severe updraft can sustain the weight of this icy chunk, and it falls to the ground.

Hail is a nightmare for agriculture, especially from the Red River valley westward to the Dakotas, Montana, and Wyoming. Nationwide, hail leaves behind nearly one billion dollars' worth of flattened crops every year. Crops most often damaged include wheat, cotton, corn, soybeans, and tobacco, with losses estimated to be enough to feed two million people for a year, according to a study done by the Illinois State Water Survey. Damaging hail is most likely in Wyoming, where an average of ten destructive storms strike every year. Iowa has the most hail-related insurance claims.

The all-time record in the United States for the biggest hailstone? Kansas, 1970, when a 1.7-pound chunk of ice fell from the sky!

Snow: Snow is precipitation composed of white or translucent ice crystals that stick together and form hexagonal shapes—some strikingly beautiful. A typical snowflake takes about an hour to travel from the cloud base to the ground (depending on the size of the flake, the air temperature, and the wind speed).

Snow forms as supercooled water drops (still liquid at temperatures well below thirty-two degrees) freeze onto microscopic condensation nuclei, tiny particles of dust, salt, or pollutants. The temperature and humidity profile of the atmosphere will determine the type of crystalline structure the snowflake takes on. Heavy snow is defined as snow falling with a visibility of five-sixteenths of a mile or less.

Meteorologists use the hourly visibility observed at local airports to pinpoint regions of heavier snow. A visibility of one mile or less can be a tip-off that snow is falling at the rate of an inch every two or three hours. When visibilities drop below a quarter mile, snow may be piling up at the rate of one to three inches an hour. There's only one problem: Fog can complicate this process, and often it's difficult to determine if a low visibility at an airport is the result of heavy snow or dense fog (or both).

Snow-rain ratio: Predicting how much snow a storm will produce is more of an art than a science, but one of the first indicators is the snow-rain ratio. Generally, the colder the air temperature, the less moisture needed to generate an inch of snow. A rough rule of thumb is ten inches of snow for every one inch of liquid water predicted by the computers. This holds true when temperatures are in the twenty- to thirty-degree range. When the temperature is near or above the freezing mark, the ratio can be closer to six to one (six inches of snow for every inch of rain). These are heavy, wet, slushy snowstorms. In contrast, an air temperature less than fifteen degrees can whip up a light, fluffy, powdery snow, with more air between the snowflakes. Here, snow-rain ratios can be as high as twenty to one, even forty to one. These snows are particularly vulnerable to blowing and drifting.

Heavy snow is favored when:
- The air temperature is between fifteen and thirty degrees.
- Winds are blowing from the east or northeast.
- The barometer is falling rapidly.
- The predicted storm track is just to the south and east of your town. A difference of just fifty miles in the storm track can mean the difference between an inch of rain, or a foot of snow (especially during November and March, when the atmosphere is still "critical" with temperatures near thirty-two degrees close to the ground). Pinning down the exact storm track is essential before predicting how many inches will fall.
- The air is dry. Evaporative cooling (remember wind chill?) will often change rain over to snow if the dew points are low, especially if precipitation is heavy.
- The month is November or March, as we are heading into and out of winter. Too much cold air in December and January can push the storm track too far south of Minnesota, lowering the chance of heavy snow.
- An arctic high pressure system is centered over, or just to the north of Minnesota.
- Temperatures in the lowest mile of the atmosphere are below thirty-two degrees. Even a thin layer of warmer air near the ground can lead to sleet or rain.

Clearing can be expected when:
- The barometer is rising.
- Winds have shifted from southwest to northwest.
- Clouds are lumpy (stratocumulus).

Old-fashioned mushroom cloud. *Diane Dingley, Eden Prairie, MN.*

Cloud-to-ground lightning. Since 1955, nearly six thousand Americans have been killed by lightning. Every year, lightning claims more lives than tornadoes, hurricanes, and floods! *Russel Dorn, Minnetonka, MN.*

Toasted marshmallow sky. Cumulo-congestus clouds are a tip-off that the sky is very unstable, and capable of thunderstorms. Updrafts within these mushrooming, cauliflower-like clouds can exceed one hundred miles an hour! *Don and Jan Carlson, New Hope, MN.*

71

4 The Perils and Pitfalls of TV Meteorology

"Hard work got me where I am. Where am I?"
"When in doubt, mumble."

THE TELEVISION METEOROLOGIST

Let's be honest with each other. A television meteorologist is a strange video mutation: part scientist, part soothsayer, part court jester. After a string of accidents, crimes, wars, scandals, and gloomy economic statistics on the 10:00 P.M. news, it's his or her duty to prance across the screen, point at obscure rectangular states, utter a little meteorological mumbo-jumbo, and by smiling sincerely in between assorted weather disasters, prevent you from jumping off the nearest bridge. It's a tall task, and I sometimes wish the theme from "Mission Impossible" were playing faintly in the background as I do the "backyard shuffle."

I'll be the first to admit that we click through too many maps. A few folks who have strayed too close to their TV sets at 10:15 have actually complained of nosebleeds from all the colorful, flashing, blinking "weather thingies" on their TV sets. Only ten years ago, meteorologists were still playing with magnetic maps and Magic Markers. We continue to be mesmerized by those newfangled weather computers that can jam ten maps into the same time it took to babble about one map in years gone by.

I'll also level with you by admitting that all meteorologists are a little sadistic. Hey, we like a good storm! It makes us feel important, wanted, needed. It gives us something to point to!

Hey, You Look Different!

Rule number one: Television adds ten years and ten pounds. Chances are *you* would look ten years older and ten pounds heavier on the tube. We also have to smear our faces with bronze-colored goo, so we don't look white and shiny and scare small children.

A few years ago, a young woman came running up to me at the Minnesota State Fair, stopped, looked me over from top to bottom and said, "Mr. Douglas, you look better on TV." Needless to say, that was a real day-brightener. Yes, we are shorter in real life, although I'm still a good four inches taller than Ted Koppel.

We even wear blue jeans! There's a rule of thumb: When you look the worst (you know, unshaven, a porcupine hair-do, breath that could start a neighborhood scuffle), that's when you're recognized the most!

I enjoy talking about the weather with strangers, especially when someone has taken the time to think up a creative question. But I want to hug people who ask me about politics, or current events, or the Twins. Yes, we like to talk about things other than the weather too!

New on the Set

Meteorologists are still a relatively recent fad on the local TV newscast. In the 1960s, TV stations hired professorial types, with smoking jackets and graying hair, mumbling their way through incomprehensible sentences, trying to impress the viewers with their vast knowledge of the weather.

The 70s brought "weather girls." (Yes, I know this sounds sexist. It *was* sexist!) Those poor women knew absolutely nothing about the weather, but they looked great on camera, and people would watch them coo and jiggle their way across the weather map.

Comedians and personalities can still be found doing the weather at many stations, especially in larger cities. But in areas where weather frequently made the news, the 70s saw a growing trend of putting credible, degreed meteorologists on the air to talk about the weather.

Today, fewer than 30 percent of the people talking about the weather on television have had any formal education in the field of meteorology. Most TV meteorologists are employed in the Midwest and on the plains, where tornadoes and blizzards can quickly reveal who knows what they're talking about, and who doesn't.

Just how many meteorologists are there out there? About ten thousand, give or take a couple. Approximately three thousand work for the National Weather Service, and another two thousand or so have careers with the armed services (with a large percentage of those in the air force or navy). To call yourself a meteorologist, you generally

Difax weather maps, fed via satellite from the National Meteorological Center in Suitland, Maryland. Over 250 maps can be received daily, displaying everything from ocean water temperatures to upper-air soundings. These are the maps we study when putting a forecast together. *Chris Grajczyk, Minneapolis, MN.*

need a four-year college degree in meteorology, or formal training from the military.

The meteorologists you see on television are just the tip of the iceberg when it comes to weather-related careers and opportunities. Meteorologists can be found working in everything from research, air pollution modeling, river forecasting (hydrology), and agricultural applications to forensic meteorology. Lawyers frequently call on meteorologists to testify whether a storm had a physical or financial impact on a client.

The Twin Cities area is one of the two or three areas you hope to someday work in if you are a meteorologist. This may be the only large metro area in the nation where all of the weekday and weekend weathercasters are meteorologists. Television stations in the Twin Cities have invested in the technology to be able to predict the weather. The meteorologist gets more than sixty seconds to go through the forecast, and you can assume that the viewing public is extremely weatherwise. Try talking about dew points or squall lines in New York City or Los Angeles. You'll be run out of town in a U-haul! Boston, Kansas City, Tulsa, and Oklahoma City are a few other cities that take the weather seriously enough to hire meteorologists, but in many other cities, the guy or gal that's doing the weather is an ex-sportscaster or booth announcer who is bribed into "ripping and reading" the National Weather Service forecast on the air (and usually pretending they came up with it themselves).

A city with no weather? Honolulu, Hawaii, may be the only city on earth where there is no regular weather broadcast on the local evening newscast, although you may get a surf report if you're patient. Locals tell me this is so because "The weather never changes—it's the same!" I doubt that will ever be a problem in Minnesota.

THE WEATHER AT KARE 11 NEWS

What is a chroma key? So that you can see our weather maps, we use a special effects system called a chroma key. We pretend to point at a weather map, when in reality all that is behind us is a large board—a piece of plywood painted a special shade of blue. A computerized switcher in the television control room automatically inserts the weather map whenever it "sees" that specific blue. I have to look at a TV monitor out of the corner of my eyes to see what I'm pointing at. It takes some getting used to—and should not be attempted immediately after waking up. Visitors are always a little baffled too. ("Why is that weatherguy pointing to a blue board? There's nothing there! Is he stupid or something? Shouldn't someone tell him?") I've heard it all.

But why the backyard? I received a phone call a few years ago from an obviously distraught gentleman. "What have you done wrong," he asked. "Why do they make you stand out there?" Good question. I find myself asking the same thing when the windchill is -50° and my lips are starting to freeze together.

When I arrived at WTCN-TV (now KARE-TV) in 1983, very few people were watching the Channel 11 newscast. Once, during a midday speaking engagement, somebody actually asked if Channel 11 was a Twin Cities TV station! That pretty much summed up our dilemma. At 10:00 P.M., more people were watching "Leave it to Beaver" than our news. We had nothing to lose. I suggested (half tongue-in-cheek) that we could have the weather report outside, in the weather I predicted (or didn't predict). In reality, all I really wanted was a window! Despite the computers, Doppler radars, and high-resolution satellite pictures, it's somewhat reassuring to be able to see the sky, to get a better sense of what Mother Nature is up to.

Management liked the idea. They tore down one of the walls in studio A, where the news is broadcast, and constructed a greenhouse for the transition from inside to outside. They erected massive lights, did some landscaping around the patio decking, hung a few bird feeders, and threw in a vegetable garden for good measure.

We knew we had to offer an alternative to some

The KARE 11 News Team

How much of the chit-chat and laughter is real? All of it. Every evening I get down on my knees and thank God that I'm working with people I like and respect. The simple fact is you can't force chemistry on the set. It's awfully hard to smile while gritting your teeth. If you don't like somebody, you may be able to hide it for a week, or a month, or maybe even a few months, but eventually the friction will come out on the air. I'm always amazed at how easily viewers can sense when two anchors are getting on each other's nerves.

What you see on Channel 11 is not canned, or rehearsed, or forced. I sincerely enjoy the company of the people in studio A, those on the air, and the small army of engineers, camera operators, directors, and producers who make us look good. Paul Magers is one of my best friends, and that friendship shows up on TV. I hope people can sense that it is not contrived, just for the camera.

What about all the fluff? What fluff? Do you mean some of the good news we include from time to time? Where is it etched in stone that the

10:00 P.M. news has to be thirty-five minutes of wars, crimes, scandals, accidents, and creeps? Why isn't good news newsworthy? There are plenty of good people in Minnesota, plenty of positive role models. Why can't we include a few of them on the air? If you watch KARE 11 News, you'll certainly get the big local and national news stories of the day—a quick, visual recap of what's going on and who's news. And when there's "breaking" or "spot" news, you'll get all the details you need to know.

I could list the awards we've won for journalistic excellence. I'll spare you though, and suffice to add one big disclaimer. There is no substitute for reading a newspaper in the morning. If you aren't reading that newspaper, you are doing yourself a terrible injustice. There is simply no way we can pack as much news into a twenty-two- or twenty-four-minute "news hole." The print and TV media complement each other quite nicely. The morning newspaper can give you depth and insight into various stories of interest. We can update those stories and reassure you that the world hasn't blown up in the meantime.

The team at KARE 11 News. *Chris Grajczyk, Minneapolis, MN.*

very solid weather reporting at WCCO and KSTP, two legendary television stations in the industry. I mean, it was downright intimidating! At one time KSTP had thirteen meteorologists and an airborne radar! Channel 11 had to come up with a "secret weapon."

There is nothing more annoying than hearing a "30 percent probability of precipitation" when it's raining cats, dogs, and canaries outside your window. The news director was confident that "if you stand out there, at least you'll get the current weather right!" Quite a vote of confidence, don't you think?

Our goal was to dress up the weather format, take it out of its generic black-and-white wrapper, and try to turn it into something colorful and visual. I can ramble on and on about a blizzard until I'm blue in the face (literally), but to point a camera outside and see giant snowflakes bonking me on the head gives the forecast more impact.

I've swallowed my share of bugs during the summer months; during the dead of winter, some nights are so cold that my cheeks are numb and my speech slurred by the bitter winds—a warm front and a frozen backside! By the way, during the invigorating days of winter, my camera operator stays inside, shooting me through the glass windows from the posh Channel 11 cafeteria. But on the first day the mercury reaches sixty degrees, the camera magically turns up outside. I'm convinced that this is not a coincidence.

A backyard bodyguard? Yes, we've had some folks try to get on television the hard way, by driving across the lawn in 4-wheel drive vehicles and motorcycles. Try pointing to Nebraska on the weather map while snowballs are being hurled your way! In the summer, it's water balloons, some fired from sling shots on the back of pickup trucks. The backyard can be quite an adventure.

We didn't want the backyard to look like a prison compound with a barbed-wire fence and guard dogs. We wanted it to look like someone's backyard. So, every night at 5:00, 6:00, and 10:00, a trained Chase security guard stands outside, searching for trouble.

The ultimate public service announcement? From time to time, we have special guests in the backyard, promoting their nonprofit, charitable events on the air. I've had the pleasure of introducing string quartets, ballet dancers, fire-eaters, drunken ten-foot brown bears, even a twenty-foot python snake. Not only does this extra twist make my job more interesting, it gives Channel 11 an opportunity to show off some of Minnesota's special people and organizations. (And let me assure you, there are plenty of them!)

So you think the backyard is odd—and let's be honest, it is. But there are even stranger weather presentations at other TV stations around the nation. Milwaukee had a weatherman who used a puppet to help him deliver the forecast. The public loved it! New York City is home to a weathercaster who has been known to stand on his head while reading off the current conditions, pointing to the maps with spoons, even a loaf of French bread! Phoenix once boasted Fluffy the weather dog. Based on a forecast of wet weather, a French poodle was dressed in a doggy raincoat. On chilly days (what, maybe sixty-five degrees?), the poor dog would be seen sniffing around the set in a hand-knit sweater. Strange, but true.

Four years ago we launched a special contest called "Weatherspies." We encouraged amateur photographers to send in their best weather-related photos, and every night we select one photo for use on the 10:00 P.M. news, acknowledging the name and hometown of the viewer who sent it in. The response has been phenomenal, with countless thousands of prints and slides flooding the weather office. What we consider to be the "Best of the Best" can be found in *Prairie Skies*.

A typical day for me begins at 5:00 A.M. I won't tell you what's going through my head when that alarm clock goes off. Using a Macintosh computer at home, I'm able to tap into a weather database, grabbing the raw information I need to make a forecast for Minnesota. From the comfort and privacy of my study, decked out in my favorite robe, unshaven, with not even a hint of studio make-up, I feed weather forecasts via high-quality phone lines and a satellite uplink to sixty-six radio stations making up the Minnesota News Network and WLOL, 99.5 FM in the Twin Cities. It sounds like I'm in the studio, but I'm really home nursing a cup of coffee, decked out in my most distinguished "jammies."

I try to grab a catnap at 9:00 A.M., but several days a week I'm up before noon to talk to a school or nursing home or service club. I'm at KARE-TV by 2:00 P.M. The next couple of hours is spent analyzing current weather around the Midwest and the nation, and trying to figure out which computer forecast we'll hang our hats on. Much of the time is spent on the phone, trying to answer weather-related questions. (A few favorites: "Paul, my little daughter is getting married—outdoors—a summer wedding—in 1993. Can you give me any idea what the weather will be?" Long pause. And, "Paul, the wife, kids, and I are heading down to the Caribbean. Can you tell me if it's going to be eighty or eighty-five degrees?" "Can I interest you in a small tropical storm?" I ask.)

When do I sleep? Well, power-napping is a favorite hobby. I am able to nod off for fifteen or twenty minutes and wake up refreshed—and for that (and many other things) I thank the good Lord! The trick is trying to juggle professional life, speaking appearances, and personal life without short-changing any of them. Walking that high-wire can be tricky indeed. And I quickly discovered that working in television news, I am "always on." At the Supervalu store or the mall people expect me to be "Paul Douglas, chatting about the weather." And that's okay. It's my job.

We put together our forecast at 4:00 P.M. and hand a copy to the Vidifont operator, who types the forecast into a souped-up graphics computer that resembles a typewriter. The forecast is saved on the computer disk and displayed live over a video background during the news.

Computer graphics have revolutionized TV

The original backyard. I wish I could take credit for the idea, but I can't. I inherited "the backyard" at Channel 16, serving the Twin Cities of Wilkes-Barre/Scranton, Pennsylvania, where I worked after graduating. We didn't have three cameras, or a greenhouse, just one camera aimed out a garage window. After some initial skepticism, viewers realized that the weather presentation could be fun without sacrificing content. But sometimes I wonder if I'll ever get an indoor gig.

A chroma key in the backyard. *Chris Grajczyk, Minneapolis, MN.*

Frank Watson preparing the computer graphics. *Chris Grajczyk, Minneapolis, MN.*

weather reports, permitting a fast-paced assortment of colorful, informative maps to be displayed. Today, current conditions and forecast maps can be drawn up on base maps using an electronic pen and tablet, choosing from hundreds of thousands of colors.

When the weather is tame, I can sneak home to have dinner with my wife and son between 7:00 and 8:00 P.M. But on nights when potentially severe thunderstorms are rumbling across the state, I'm on call just in case they "go severe," and warnings are issued. At about 8:00, preparation begins for the 10:00 P.M. news, with a special emphasis on "pre-pack," special effects that are too complex to go on the air live. These visual snippets of video and computer graphics are the only things that are put on to tape before the news. Everything else is live.

Meteorologist Frank Watson is in charge of the graphic look of our weekday weathercasts, spending roughly fifteen to twenty minutes on each map, then storing it into memory. Using a remote control, an on-air meteorologist can then cycle through a pre-assigned "menu" of maps on the air, specifying not only the order of the graphics, but the transitions too (wipes, dissolves, or simple "takes" or cuts). The computers tend to be geared more to artists than to meteorologists, but thankfully, most of them are user-friendly.

Do I use a Teleprompter? No. Most meteorologists do not use a prompter, a series of mirrors that can display a script in front of the camera lens, making it possible to read your copy while staring right at the camera. I outline the show in my head, and while clicking through the maps ahead of time, I think up what I'm going to say for each map. The weathercasts are ad-libbed and spontaneous, not memorized word for word.

Weatherspeak: Interpreting the KARE-TV Weathercast

What is "probability of precipitation?" Confusing. Do you know what a 30 percent probability of precipitation means? Think a second. Does it

mean that 30 percent of the area will get rain or snow? No. Does it mean it'll precipitate 30 percent of the time? No. Does it mean 30 percent of the viewing area will get rained on 30 percent of the time. Nice try, but no.

A 30 percent probability of precipitation means that on three days out of ten with a similar weather pattern, one point within the area will receive 0.01 inch of rain. Gulp! Okay, what does that mean? Well, a statement such as "30 percent probability of rain" is a statistical tool, but many days it can be misleading. That's why we don't use it on the air. We acknowledge that it's impossible to predict exactly where summertime showers will bubble up, but we prefer to use the following terminology:

- Isolated: Showers will be few and far between, with less than 10 percent of the area getting wet.
- Scattered: About 10 to 50 percent of the region will see precipitation. The odds are still at least fifty-fifty that you'll miss out on puddles.
- Numerous: The odds are no longer in your favor. Fifty to 80 percent of us will have to postpone our picnics.
- Widespread: usually associated with steady rain or snow falling ahead of a warm front. There's little chance you'll escape the precipitation.

What is partly cloudy? Is the glass half full or half empty? Are you an optimist or a pessimist? Actually, there is a difference. Partly cloudy implies that less than 50 percent of the sky will be cloud covered. It's often used at night, for obvious reasons. Partly sunny implies more clouds than sun, and frankly, is similar in meaning to mostly cloudy.

Part of the problem we face is one of communication. After looking at all of the maps, flipping our coins and saying a quick prayer, we make a forecast, choosing words that we hope will convey our mental image to you as accurately as possible. But this assumes that we are all on the same wavelength when it comes to weather terminology. For the record:

- Overcast: One hundred percent of the sky is covered with a solid deck of clouds. No blue sky,

sunshine, or star shine is visible.
- Mostly cloudy: Eighty to 99 percent of the sky is decorated with clouds. The sun or moon occasionally peeks through.
- Considerable cloudiness: The sky is 50 to 80 percent gray, but there will be periods of sunshine lasting a few minutes at a time.
- Partly sunny: There is a 50 to 80 percent cloud-cluttered sky, but the forecaster wants to emphasize that there will be some sun. (But the sun will be overshadowed by clouds.)
- Variable cloudiness: Go ahead, flip a coin. Fifty-fifty clouds and sun, an even mixture of the two. With planning and a little luck, it's still possible to get a memorable sunburn.
- Partly cloudy: Only 20 to 50 percent of the sky will be cloudy. Sunshine will be the rule.
- Mostly sunny: Similar to partly cloudy. Most of the day will be splattered with sunshine.
- Sunny: The sun will be out nearly the entire day, with clouds looming overhead less than 10 percent of the time. Take number fifteen sunscreen.

Growing up in the east, it was always fun listening to the forecasters hedge a forecast, giving several different scenarios of what might happen, to the point where you had no idea what the forecast for tomorrow was. My favorite expression was "changeable skies." Hey, that's pinning it down, isn't it? Can you be any more vague?

Our biggest nightmares? We have plenty: discovering your fly is down after you've been flapping your arms in front of the chroma key board for three minutes; having the battery in your remote control run out of juice, leaving you unable to switch to the next map, meaning you have to talk about the cloud cover in Iowa for two minutes; sneaking home for a quick dinner, only to get a call from the news director saying, "Hey Paul, get in here fast. A tornado has just touched down in St. Cloud!" Primal scream time.

Perhaps our biggest terror arises during the winter months, after forecasting a partly cloudy day and waking up to "fourteen inches of partly cloudy." Studies show that as a profession, meteorologists tend to overpredict snow, probably out of fear of getting caught with their snow shovels down.

One note: The viewing public does remind you when you're wrong. They are not shy by nature. God forbid if you're wrong on a weekend. And God have mercy on your pathetic little soul if you're wrong on a holiday weekend or the fishing opener. They'll never forgive you! I am still reminded of a forecast I made for July 4, 1978. I predicted partly sunny and mild, with highs in the seventies. Well, a tiny upper-air disturbance that was too small to show up on the computer guidance drifted directly overhead—and hour after hour it poured, and temperatures were in the fifties. That crummy forecast still comes up in conversation to this day when I return home to visit friends and family in Pennsylvania.

Meteorology is a fickle business. When you are right, it's a great feeling, but people never come up and say, "Hey, Paul, great forecast. Right on the money!" When you're wrong, it's a feeling similar to getting punched in the stomach, and everyone you know will rub it in. I guess that comes with the turf.

Painful Lessons

There is no such thing as bad weather. A couple of summers ago I went on the air and complained about a rainy weekend outlook. I had some outdoor activities planned, and I guess I was visibly disappointed that it was going to rain. After the weathercast I returned to the weather office. The phone was ringing. On the line was a farmer from Willmar. "Mr. Douglas?" "Yes," I answered. "I make my living farming out here in Willmar. If it wasn't for that rain, you'd be even skinnier than you are. . . . " I was speechless. He was right!

Rain can be great news for farmers, but a disaster for construction companies and outdoor resorts, like Valleyfair, that depend on dry weather to make money.

In the winter, a forecast of heavy snow is greeted with a chorus of boos from store owners, con-

Good weather or bad? I guess it depends on your point of view, whether you're planning a picnic, or planting a crop! The bottom line: It's impossible to keep everyone happy. *Shari Arhart, Winthrop, MN.*

A nighttime CB. *Mike Maricle, Minneapolis, MN.*

vinced that a flaky sky will scare away business. But don't groan about the snow, or a small army of snow lovers, skiers, ski operators, and hardy souls with plows on their 4-by-4s will call up and read you the riot act.

Be careful where you stand! This is an ongoing dilemma. Where do we stand to point to our nifty little maps? If we stand in front of California, folks visiting from Los Angeles call up and squawk. But if you huddle in front of the East Coast, native New Yorkers jam the switchboard and demand that you "Get the heck out of the way!" I'm trying to get the station to spring for a special crane and harness so I can be suspended at the very top of the screen and point with impunity. (But I'll bet folks flying to Winnipeg or Calgary would give me an earful.) I'm convinced that it's a no-win situation.

You can't please all of the people all of the time. Don't even try. Farmers want soil moisture maps. Boaters want wind speeds. Vacationers want weather in the Virgin Islands, Mexico, and Hawaii. Every year I get a tongue-lashing for not having Alaska on tomorrow's weather map.

In a three-minute weather window it's impossible to display worldwide weather. As a rule, we do try to include as much information as we can, and even if we don't mention it verbally, there's a good chance what you need to know will be displayed on one of the computer graphics.

Assorted Pet Peeves

How dare you interrupt my "soap"! It never fails. Every year, a small, vocal minority of viewers call to complain when we interrupt afternoon soap operas with tornado warnings. We run "crawls" (moving text) at the bottom of the screen for watches, and all warnings outside of the Twin Cities metropolitan area.

When we interrupt live programming for a warning, that means a tornado is on the ground, or winds in excess of seventy-five miles an hour are chewing up part of the cities. And still, some folks think we are crying wolf, or they just don't care about severe weather across town. At this point,

public relations becomes a difficult "art," and I'm grateful that these viewers are in a very small minority.

But I was right! Often, meteorologists are blamed for "busted forecasts" that their competitors across the street issued. Even when we get it right, people still give us grief! I am convinced that some folks hear only what they want to hear.

Oh, you guys are never right. Sheer bunk. Once again, some folks just seem to have selective recall, remembering the times we are wrong, and not the majority of the forecasts that are right on the money. I still say that we are right more often than your favorite stockbroker!

The "Competition"

Are you competing with the National Weather Service? No. In fact we have a very good relationship with the men and women who work at the weather service. We have one of the best local weather service offices in the nation, with timely, reliable forecasts issued at least four times a day for nineteen different zones around the state of Minnesota. In addition, they issue special agricultural forecasts, weather summaries, flood forecasts for Minnesota's streams and rivers, and hourly current conditions, which are fed via Teletype to radio and TV stations statewide.

We in the media are free to look at raw meteorological data and come up with our own forecasts, predictions that at times differ from the official National Weather Service forecast. We believe that on some days it is possible to improve on the weather service outlook. On other days, they have an edge. The viewer or listener is free to compare accuracy over the long run and make a selection based on who they perceive is most reliable.

When severe weather strikes, all of the television and radio stations need to band together and issue the official National Weather Service watches and warnings. Now this may sound like a contradiction, but it's not.

Research shows that if the public receives conflicting forecasts for tornadoes or severe

weather, they will be more likely not to take action and seek shelter. If viewers tune to Channel 5 and hear a tornado warning for Hennepin County, and then tune over to Channel 11 only to hear a tornado warning for Ramsey County, chances are they'll sit on their hands and do nothing.

I have 340 or so days a year to try to come up with a more accurate forecast than the "guys and gals across the street." But on days when the sky turns potentially violent, approximately twenty to twenty-five days a year, the media needs to speak with one voice, thus avoiding potential confusion and apathy.

The United States is unique when it comes to freedom of speech and the ability to disagree with the official government's forecast. In Europe, Japan, most of Asia, and almost every Third World country, it is illegal to go on radio or television and issue your own interpretation of what the weather should do. Departing from the government outlook can literally get you thrown into jail! In the end, the consensus is that the public tends to be better served by competition, even among weather forecasts. This provides incentive to go the extra mile, look at more data, spend more time poring over the maps, trying to get a better handle on the weather pattern than your competitor across the street. Usually, the "hungrier" forecaster will come up with the more accurate forecasts over the long term.

Making It Big in TV Meteorology

Some encouraging trends. The local television news philosophy used to be "have blow-drier, will travel." During the 1970s, newscasters, sportscasters, and weathercasters ricochetted across the nation like corn kernels in some monstrous popcorn machine. Every two years you were expected to make a move, upward and onward, take another step on the ladder toward Chicago, Los Angeles, and New York. It got to the point where local anchors couldn't pronounce the names of towns within their markets. A few never bothered to unpack their furniture, confident that a better offer was just a phone call away.

Well, somewhere along the way, local television viewers got smart. They didn't like this ongoing edition of musical anchor chairs. They opted for the veterans, the old-timers, the men and women who had been around for a long time.

Finally, news directors are realizing that the key to success in ratings is stability. Keep the same faces on the air for a while and give the audience time to warm up to them! Don't keep making changes. Viewers want to know that when they turn on the tube they'll know who will greet them at the other end. They don't like surprises.

Dave Moore and Bud Kraehling at WCCO-TV are perfect examples of what stability can do for a television station. Hopefully, this trend will continue to take hold at other stations in other cities around the country.

Make your hobby your job. I know it sounds bizarre, but it is possible. In junior high school I told my friends that someday, I would be on TV doing the weather. They laughed and laughed. "C'mon Paul, you have a paper route! Who are you trying to kid?" I worked for several years at McDonald's, washed dishes at a Sheraton Hotel, and made subs and pizzas at an Italian restaurant. But I kept reading about the weather, grabbing every book I could find at the school library and the corner bookstore. I watched all the TV forecasters I could, driving my poor folks mad with the TV remote control. (It is possible to view nine different weather forecasts in the Philadelphia-Baltimore area.) And I watched the sky, making my own forecasts, trying to out-predict the local weathercasters. I tinkered with a computer in high school, coming up with my own crude model for predicting the weather. And I asked lots of questions.

In college I started my own private weather forecasting service, Total Weather. Out of my Penn State dorm room (and later, the attic of an apartment off campus), I forecasted the weather on eleven radio stations around the state of Pennsylvania.

During my senior year, I called a TV station in northeastern Pennsylvania and told their weatherman (who was not a meteorologist) what to predict, and where to put the symbols on the evening weather map. One day the news director called. He was frantic. Both on-air weathercasters were out of the country on vacation, a huge scheduling mistake. Could I drive up and do the weather on-air for just one evening? "I don't know what you look like," he said. "Frankly, I don't even care what you look like. Just help us out this once—please!"

I drove for two and a half hours. Numb with fear, I squeaked my way through the weather. Looking at the tape afterwards, I saw I was stiff and awkward. It looked like rigor mortis was setting in on the air! I remember driving back to school, thankful that I was on radio. Who needs this TV stuff?

The next day I received a call from the news director, thanking me for helping out. "Would you like to do weekend weather for us full time?" he asked. There was a long pause at the other end of the phone. Gulp—well, why not. "Sure," I said, not convinced I knew what I was getting myself into.

So, every Saturday, after the Penn State Nitanny Lion football game in Happy Valley, I drove 120 miles each way to do the weekend weather on WNEP-TV. They paid me $50 a weekend, and put me up Saturday nights at the Luxury Budget Inn. You can just imagine what this place looked like —a room and an oil change for $29.95 a night. I certainly wasn't getting rich, but it was my break into the business.

If you're thinking about getting into television news, it's vital that you just get your foot in the door. Once you're in, you can send out tapes to consultants who will try to get you work in a larger city (they get a fee from the TV station that's looking). Too many aspiring anchors wait by the telephone after graduating and expect to be fielding offers from Chicago and San Francisco. Unless your daddy is the news director, it's just not going to happen.

But if you truly have a perfectionist mentality, if you are always critiquing your own work, if you're never quite satisfied with your on-air presentation, then you will slowly improve over time and you will move into higher paying jobs in larger towns.

Yes, major market anchors can make a lot of money, but like sports stars, there is little stability —they are living from contract to contract, knowing darn well that there are hundreds of new recruits in smaller markets who would jump at the opportunity to grab their jobs.

Even today, weather is still a hobby, something I'd be infatuated with even if I weren't talking about it on radio and TV. (Although when a blizzard or tornado is approaching, and the phones are ringing off the hook, and a tour of hyperactive kids is squirming through the newsroom, and the news director wants to discuss a new project—on those days I have to gently remind myself that weather is a hobby.) It's not a bad deal though. Every Wednesday they hand me a paycheck for doing something I enjoy. They pay me to play with the weather gadgets, and peer into the future. I'm not complaining.

Read! My boss might not like to hear me say this, but the only way you can expand your vocabulary, spark your creativity, and exercise your "brain muscle" is by reading. When you watch television, the TV does all the work for you! All you have to do is sit there and stare at the screen, absorbing this colorful electronic "drizzle." But reading forces you to visualize a story in your mind, transforming you from an observer into a participant.

There are a few good shows on television. But there is plenty of junk, "cotton candy for the eyes," as I've heard it described. By being selective in what you watch on the tube, and reading about topics that interest you (like that hobby that someday will earn you some money), you will avoid contracting a "flabby" brain.

I have some friends who are brilliant forecasters, but they will never land a job on radio or television. They didn't take speech or English seriously, and today they can't put two sentences back to back without "uuhs" or "likes" or "ya-knows." People think they're stupid, even though they are some of the brightest people on the planet. The sad fact is that any potential employer will judge you on how you present yourself, and how well you communicate. Take your language skills very seriously.

Future meteorologists, there's still time to find legitimate work. If you're sure you want to point to big blue sheets of plywood for a living, there are a few things you can do to improve your chances of getting into television.

In high school, make sure you excel in science and math. You'll have to take calculus to receive a degree in meteorology, so a firm foundation in trigonometry will help, and if you can take an introduction to calculus course your senior year of high school, you'll be ahead of the gang. Try to take at least one computer science course. You should feel somewhat comfortable with computers since we rely on them to forecast and display the weather. But don't neglect your English. It's vitally important to fine-tune your communication skills. Talking in front of others, possibly on a debate team, will help out tremendously.

I have always been shy and introverted. Being on television and talking to countless hundreds of Lions Clubs and fourth graders has helped me to loosen up and feel more comfortable in front of others. Any time you can stand up in front of a crowd and talk about the weather (or any other subject for that matter), your comfort level will increase, so when you do get that lucky first break in Austin or Alexandria or Eau Claire you won't freeze up and turn to quivering jelly!

Women are very much in demand as TV meteorologists. For some reason, twenty to thirty years ago young women were not encouraged to be meteorologists. As a result, you can count the number of female meteorologists nationwide on two hands. The opportunities are incredible, especially if you have "presence," a spark of personality that sets you apart from others, and a degree.

In general, while the government is slowly phasing out jobs at the National Weather Service, the prospects for employment at television stations continue to improve. News directors want credibility. That's why they hire attorneys as legal correspondents, doctors as medical correspondents, and yes, meteorologists to talk about the weather.

The only college in Minnesota to offer a four-year meteorology degree is St. Cloud State University, which boasts a well-staffed department with some state-of-the-art weather hardware. Otherwise, the nearest schools with a full-fledged meteorology program are the University of North Dakota at Grand Forks, or the University of Wisconsin at Madison.

Bob Cocker, Eagan, MN.

5 The Cutting Edge

The Future of Meteorology as We Approach the Year 2000

"Challenge and excitement will characterize the field of meteorology in the 1990s. Doppler radar, automated surface observations, and advanced computer systems will provide weather forecasters the ability to examine the atmosphere in fine detail. The result: better warnings and forecasts for the nation."—Jim Campbell, meteorologist in charge, Twin Cities National Weather Service

What is the future of meteorology? How will the science evolve and improve during the 1990s and beyond? There is much speculation and debate within the profession, but several trends are already emerging: computer technology and other advances.

COMPUTERS

Supercomputers will become faster, permitting more calculations at more layers of the atmosphere. Currently, the most elaborate computer model running in the United States analyzes the sky above us in eighteen layers, from the ground up to an altitude of ten to twelve miles. The European model computes changes at more than twenty levels, permitting finer detail and resolution, and ultimately leading to more accurate forecasts.

Quicker computers will also lead to a greater number of grid points in each model. A grid point is a spot on the map where the computer forecasts future changes in weather in fifteen-minute incre-

ments throughout the entire troposphere. Currently, the points these grid points represent are spaced some fifty miles apart (at sixty degrees north latitude). Hurricane forecasters in Miami can use a higher-resolution grid to help them predict just where a hurricane will go next. Theoretically, the closer together the grid points that calculations are performed on, the more accurately the computers will approximate the way the atmosphere really works. And the supercomputers will have to get bigger and faster to accommodate the mounting flood of new data. It's estimated that enhanced information from a new generation of satellites, Nexrad radars, and Automated Surface Observing System sites will produce one hundred times more data for the year 1995.

Oceans have a profound effect on weather. To be able to predict the weather beyond a week or so, one needs to be able to forecast abnormalities in sea-surface temperatures in the Pacific, which is a science in itself. Improving the seven- to thirty-day forecast will require more knowledge on how underwater volcanic eruptions and fluctuations in water temperatures influence air masses and the jet stream high overhead.

By the twenty-first century, meteorologists may be able to offer some "skill" (better than a fifty-fifty flip of a coin) out to ten to fourteen days. Beyond that, accuracy for the thirty- to ninety-day outlook may improve from 55 to 65 percent or so. It is extremely doubtful that in our lifetime

the guy or gal on the evening TV weathercast will be able to say with certainty that "fourteen days from now rain is likely with a high of 60°." That is wishful thinking. Our understanding of the weather is still incomplete and the atmosphere is too complex, having too many unknown variables. Even the most sophisticated high-speed computer is unable to predict an underwater volcanic eruption in the Pacific Ocean that may warm the waters off Peru and lead to strange contortions in the jet stream over North America days later.

OTHER ADVANCES

What follows is a list of some of the most promising breakthroughs in the science of meteorology, technological leaps that will lead to gains in accuracy during our lifetime. Please don't be scared by the fancy abbreviations, acronyms, and clever nicknames for these programs, many of which are government funded.

AFOS, Automated Forecast and Observing System: a computerized communications system that permits display of high-resolution graphics and alphanumeric Teletype products on the same terminal. Reducing the need for conventional paper weather charts, AFOS has been in use at nearly three hundred National Weather Service offices since the late '70s. By typing in a simple command, forecasters can call up current temperature, wind, or moisture maps from any level of the at-

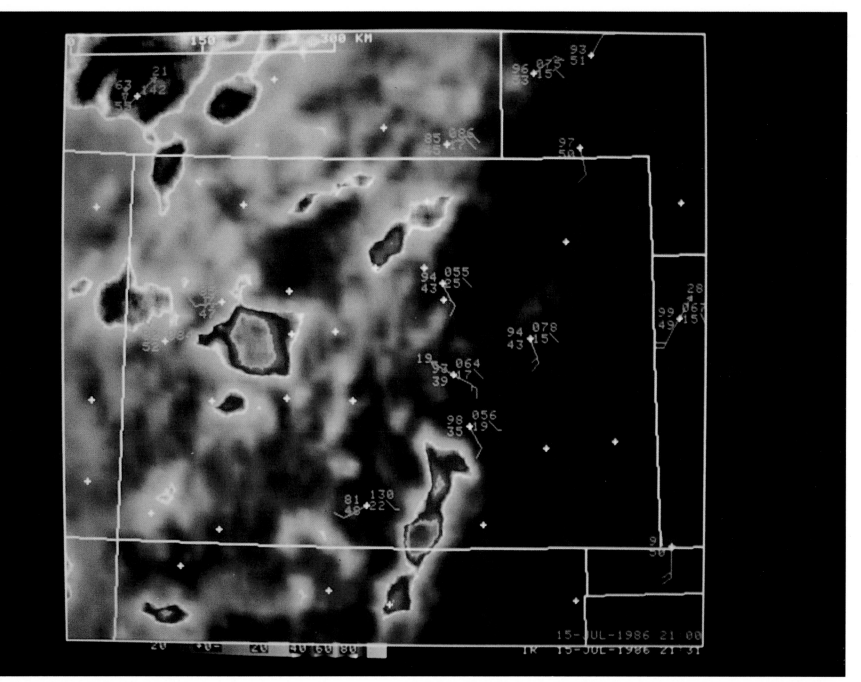

A PROFS computer screen in Boulder, Colorado, displaying current weather at airports and live radar on the same screen, with the goal of pinpointing the arrival time and severity of thunderstorms. *Courtesy: PROFS/NOAA.*

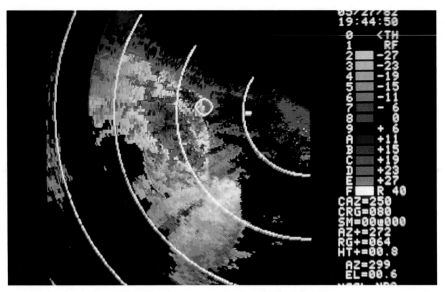

Nexrad radars will display Doppler shifts, measuring the movement of raindrops and helping to zero in on rotating thunderstorms. This is a conventional display of reflectivity, showing the location of rain and hail. This boomerang-shaped line, known as a bow echo, went on to produce damaging straight-line winds. *Courtesy: NSSL/NOAA.*

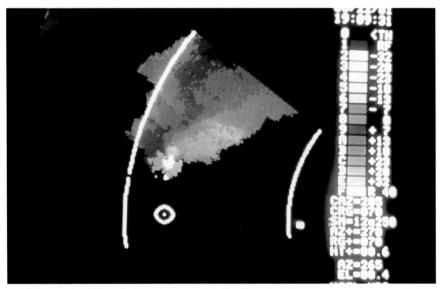

Doppler radar with a radial velocity display can pinpoint rotating mesocyclones, which often spawn tornadoes. The red area is highlighting air moving away from the radar site in Oklahoma City. The yellow and blue areas are regions of winds blowing toward the site. In between, where the air is spinning violently, a tornado is occurring. *Courtesy: NSSL/NOAA.*

The Binger tornado of May 22, 1981 was on the ground at the same time radar operators were watching the Doppler display above, proving that the technology can save lives! *Courtesy: NSSL/NOAA.*

mosphere and display that information on a local or national map. By comparing current conditions with previous computer forecasts, the meteorologist on duty can assess just how the computers are performing, and modify the forecast accordingly.

ASOS, Automated Surface Observing System

a cooperative venture between the National Weather Service and the Federal Aviation Administration. ASOS is a fully automated weather sensing instrument that permits hourly weather observations in towns where there are no staffed airports. ASOS sites are capable of measuring current temperature, dew point, wind, barometric pressure, even cloud height. Some sites are even capable of measuring horizontal visibility. A ceilometer determines cloud height by projecting a focused beam of light on the cloud deck overhead. Using a light-sensitive detection device and simple trigonometry, it's possible to compute the altitude of clouds, night or day. Generally speaking, automated weather observations are not as reliable as those readings taken by trained FAA or National Weather Service observers, but ASOS sites are an important weather supplement, helping to fill in the gaps by providing essential real-time weather measurements as often as every five minutes.

In Minnesota, automated hourly readings using ASOS technology have begun in Roseau, Crane Lake, Willmar, Fergus Falls, Faribault, and Albert Lea. Raw data will be available to TV and radio stations. By using a telephone or home computer, anyone will be able to access raw weather information from these new observation sites.

AWOS, Automated Weather Observing System

similar to ASOS, but operated entirely by the FAA at scores of airports around the nation.

AWIPS-90, Advanced Weather Interactive Processing System

a state-of-the-art computer system that can combine and display vast amounts of real-time meteorological data at once. Coming on-line at National Weather Service offices during the 1990s, AWIPS may help to dramatically improve short-range severe thunderstorm forecasts.

Nexrad, short for Next Generation Radar

Developed and funded by the Department of Transportation, Defense and Commerce (of which the National Weather Service is one agency), Nexrad is an ambitious program that may lead to the installation of as many as one hundred high-powered Doppler radars by the mid-1990s at a projected cost of $2 million per radar. Forming a protective network virtually from coast to coast, these state-of-the-art radars will automatically compute some seventy or more special products, helping meteorologists to pinpoint the location of severe local storms, including tornadoes, hailstorms, and flash floods.

The first operational Nexrad unit is scheduled to be deployed in early 1990, but the Twin Cities National Weather Service won't have Nexrad radar capabilities until late 1992 or early 1993. To escape the problems of "ground clutter" and false radar echoes, the local Twin Cities National Weather Service is planning to move its office from the airport in Richfield to a site in the far western or southwestern suburbs. Moving this far away from the "urban heat island" may have some interesting effects on the official hourly temperature. (Expect colder official readings each hour and more record lows if the National Weather Service goes through with its plan to move.)

Most of the research into a prototype Nexrad system is being performed in Norman, Oklahoma, on a powerful ten-centimeter Doppler radar unit. Current Dopplers being used by television stations nationwide send out a five-centimeter pulse of energy and, although useful, are subject to attenuation and are essentially useless beyond fifty miles of the radar site.

Unlike conventional radars that detect only the location and intensity of precipitation, Doppler radar is so advanced that it can also detect movement of precipitation. Like any radar, Doppler radar searches for regions of precipitation within severe thunderstorms by sending out pulses of radar. These pulses reflect off of precipitation and other particles in the atmosphere (actually anything that the radar pulse hits). Doppler radar is sensitive to the Doppler shift, making it more accurate than other radars. Because of the Doppler effect, Doppler radar can measure minuscule shifts in the wavelengths of reflected radar pulses. The increases or decreases in the wavelengths of the pulses tell a built-in computer that the regions are moving toward or away from the radar site. Doppler radar can be adapted to display rain and turbulence on regular TV sets. Mesocyclones, severe, counterclockwise-rotating thunderheads, almost always produce deadly winds or hail. By using Doppler radar, mesocyclones can be easily identified and monitored.

Since a tornado touchdown is almost always preceded by a rotating mesocyclone aloft, Nexrad Doppler radar sites may be able to give as much as twenty minutes' warning that a particular cell is likely to turn tornadic, increasing the warning time to the public. By the year 2000 it may be possible to pinpoint city blocks that are threatened, rather than having to warn entire counties. Nexrad will be able to compute one- and three-hour rainfall totals, as well as total precipitation from a storm, helping forecasters issue timely flash-flood warnings. Nexrad radar will highlight regions of dangerous wind shear, of particular interest to pilots and air-traffic controllers at our nation's airports. In short, Nexrad will help to take some of the guesswork out of short-range severe storm forecasting, providing a flood of information for government and private meteorologists to analyze.

NSSL, the National Severe Storms Laboratory

Located in Norman, Oklahoma, NSSL has as its sole mission the study of severe local storms. Here, scientists are developing a prototype Nexrad radar, perfecting the ten-centimeter Dopplers that will scan America's skies during the 1990s and the twenty-first century. Here, meteorologists are wrestling with questions like: Why do some mesocyclones spawn tornadoes, while others don't; and, since the tornado first forms several miles overhead, what physically pulls the funnel down to the ground? (Regarding the second question, research points to something called a rear-flank downdraft, a sudden downward gust near the trailing southwestern edge of a mesocyclone, as the culprit.) Eventually, tornadoes occlude: Rain-cooled air is sucked into the storm's circulation and chokes off the warm updraft, causing the twister to become thin and ropelike before dissipating altogether. But what permits some tornadoes to go on being destructive for hours, while most garden-variety tornadoes last only five to ten minutes?

For more than ten years, a tornado-intercept program has been operating out of NSSL. Scientists and meteorology students at the University of Oklahoma nearby routinely chase mesocyclones that are capable of dropping tornadoes, gathering firsthand information out in the field! Using two specially equipped vans complete with rooftop mounted video cameras, sensitive barometers, and wind measurement devices, the chase teams are guided to "ripe cells" using two-way radios. In constant communication with Doppler radar specialists at Norman, the chase teams attempt to get as close to a tornado as possible, without risking life and limb. Their goal is to place a large, reinforced metal barrel full of weather instruments (appropriately nicknamed Toto!) in the direct path of a twister. In the past, wind instruments struck by tornadoes have blown away. Using Toto, it may someday be possible to find out precise wind speeds and barometric pressures within the core of the funnel.

In 1985, photographer Bob Durland and I spent two weeks at the NSSL in Norman, Oklahoma, traveling thousands of miles in search of an atmospheric needle in a haystack—towering cumulonimbus clouds. We witnessed spectacular lightning displays and hail as large as softballs.

At the end of the second week we were convinced that we would return to Minnesota empty-handed, without witnessing the birth of a tornado. Near the town of Ardmore, Oklahoma, the chasers received news of "explosive anvil growth" showing up on satellite photos just twenty miles up the road. We hopped into our vans and chase vehicles and fifteen minutes later documented the formation of a rotating wall cloud. Toto was unloaded from the back of a pickup truck, its onboard barometer and wind instruments clicked on. As we were pulling away from the scene, a tornado funnel dropped down less than a mile away.

It was a wild, almost surrealistic moment. I can still remember racing down a muddy Oklahoma road, hanging onto Bob's legs as he dangled out the car window to get a clear shot of the twister chasing us less than a quarter mile away! I was yelling, Bob was screaming, and in the background we could hear the muffled roar of the tornado.

Minutes later we returned to the original site where Toto had been deployed. For the first time ever, Toto had been sideswiped by a small tornado. We found it covered with mud in a ditch nearby. Later analysis would show that the winds had topped eighty miles an hour with a sharp downward spike in barometric pressure. The meteorologists present were ecstatic, and we had been very lucky to be in the right place at the right time to capture this close encounter with nature's most evil wind.

Profiler: an experimental Doppler radar that measures wind speed, wind direction, and turbulence, providing a three-dimensional view of the atmosphere on a real-time basis. A network of thirty sites should be operational by the year 1995. Unlike radiosonde weather balloon observations that are made only twice a day, profiler data can be obtained around the clock, taking the guesswork out of what's happening aloft. Operating on a lower frequency than conventional five- or ten-centimeter Doppler radars, profilers can peer as high as sixteen kilometers, or ten miles into the sky

overhead, the radar beam penetrating through clouds, and even precipitation. A small percentage of the radar energy is scattered back to earth by refraction, the result of minor variations in temperature and humidity. Profilers may be especially useful in detecting clear-air turbulence, violent shifts in wind direction and speed that can lead to injuries and even damage aboard high-flying airplanes.

Wind profiler data will be available to a meteorologist every six minutes, and this should be most helpful during severe weather outbreaks over the plains states.

PROFS, Program for Regional Observing and Forecasting Services: Operating in Boulder, Colorado, since 1980, PROFS is an attempt to synthesize and streamline the vast amounts of incoming weather data into colorful graphics that can be quickly analyzed by meteorologists, with the goal of improving the short-range five-minute to six-hour forecast, or "nowcast."

Working with the National Weather Service, the FAA, and the United States Air Force, much of the technology and experience gained from PROFS will be transferred to AWIPS-90 computer systems at National Weather Service offices nationwide during the 1990s.

The PROFS computer network utilizes GOES geostationary as well as Tiros polar-orbiting satellite images, and can display live radar from various sites simultaneously. In addition, real-time data from FAA-manned airports and a supplemental network of observing stations can be displayed and various meteorological parameters plotted and contoured. Live ten-centimeter Doppler radar, lightning strikes, hydrology reports from river gauges, and even current weather from Delta and United aircraft high overhead can all be ingested into the computer display system, giving PROFS unique forecasting abilities.

On several occasions, meteorologists using the PROFS workstation were able to issue severe thunderstorm or heavy snow warnings well be-

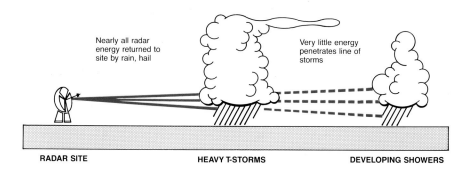

Nearly all radar energy returned to site by rain, hail

Very little energy penetrates line of storms

RADAR SITE   HEAVY T-STORMS   DEVELOPING SHOWERS

Five-centimeter Doppler radars used by television stations nationwide are capable of detecting mesocyclones but are prone to attenuation. A shorter radio wavelength means that more of the radar pulse is reflected back to the radar site, and if rain nearby is especially heavy, a five-centimeter Doppler radar may be unable to see a second line of approaching thunderstorms farther away. Ten-centimeter Nexrad Dopplers will be much less susceptible to attenuation and will be able to penetrate nearby cells and display other threatening storms hundreds of miles away.

A profiler antenna. *Courtesy: Tycho Technology, Inc.*

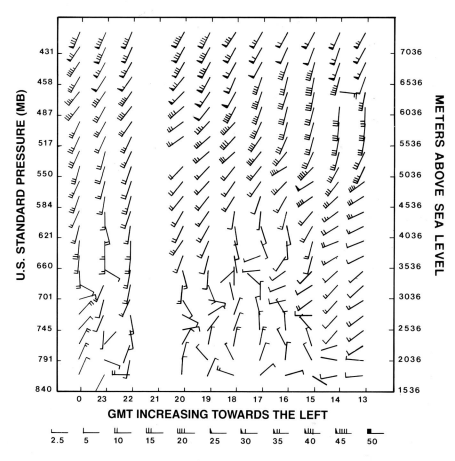

GMT INCREASING TOWARDS THE LEFT

2.5 5 10 15 20 25 30 35 40 45 50

Profiler print-out. Profilers are of much more use to meteorologists than are radiosondes, or weather balloons, which are launched only twice a day. This is a twelve-hour plot of upper-level winds. The most recent observation is on the left, and using this tool, a meteorologist can predict what the winds will be doing high overhead in the near future with much greater confidence. (Each "barb" represents ten knots, or twelve miles an hour. The direction can be found by remembering that a compass goes from 0 to 359 degrees. In this case, winds near the ground are blowing lightly from the north, while stronger jet stream winds aloft are blowing from the southwest.)

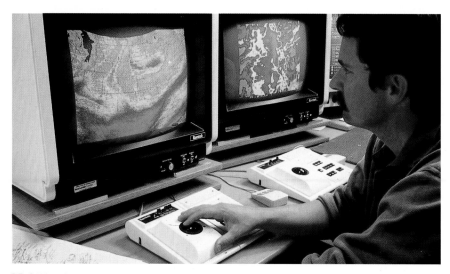

PROFS is being used at the National Weather Service in Denver to try to improve the accuracy of short-range forecasts. A menu screen, which gives the forecaster access to a wide range of meteorological data, is behind his head on the right. *Courtesy: PROFS/NOAA.*

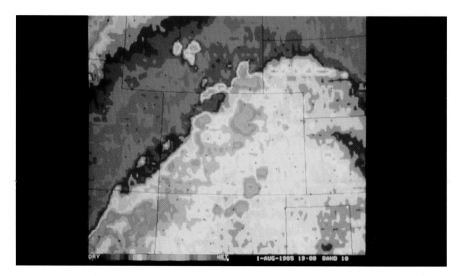

A water vapor image or "VAS" covering the central Rocky Mountains, taken by the GOES satellite. The measurements are sensitive to the presence of water vapor in the upper atmosphere near four hundred millibars (about twenty thousand to twenty-five thousand feet overhead). The color bar at the bottom of the screen shows the amount of water vapor sensed, red for dry air, green and blue for moisture and clouds. *Courtesy: PROFS/NOAA.*

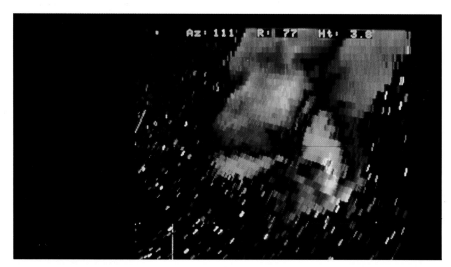

This is a radial velocity display, showing the approaching or receding wind along a radial and the wind's speed. The top color bar (blue shades) refers to air approaching the radar. The bottom scale refers to air receding from the radar. The center of the rotating mesocyclone shown is to the right of the picture center. Both approaching and receding wind velocities are "folded"; that is, they are so strong they are off the scale, in this case in excess of 25.6 meters per second. This rotation is concentrated in a small area, probably indicative of a tornado. *Courtesy: PROFS/NOAA.*

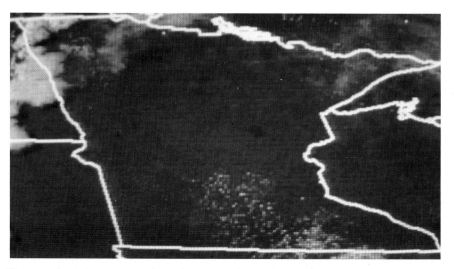

Kavouras is a private meteorological company based at the Twin Cities international airport. Specializing in sophisticated computer hardware and software for television stations, Kavouras is also the leading source of weather data for airlines and airports from coast to coast. In this photo, you can see Mille Lacs, Cass, and Red lakes, as well as a line of thunderstorms rumbling into the Red River valley. *Courtesy: Kavouras, Inc.*

fore the rest of the meteorological community could (including the National Weather Service and local TV and radio forecasters). In all, some twenty-six different forms of data are ingested into the system, with some colorful and impressive results.

Remote sensing: Government agencies aren't the only organizations on the cutting edge of meteorology. Many for-profit companies and consultants are analyzing National Weather Service data, which falls under the public domain, and reselling it to weather-sensitive industries ranging from construction companies to farmers to NASA. These services that take raw data and adapt the data to specific uses often develop their own computer hardware and software to help them interpret the raw weather service data.

Nationwide, hundreds of meteorologists take advantage of remote-sensing technology, receiving real-time lightning strike data, current weather from automated weather instruments nearby, and a glut of images from the GOES, Tiros, and high-resolution Landsat satellites. By interpreting this data and issuing reliable, timely warnings businesses can save thousands, even millions of dollars. In some cases, just one accurate forecast can result in savings that more than pay for a year's worth of tailor-made weather forecasts from the private meteorologist.

Lightning detection can be a matter of fiscal survival for businesses ranging from utilities to telephone companies to golf courses. All can be brought to their knees by one untimely cloud-to-ground lightning strike. Knowing which cells on radar are producing dangerous lightning can permit these industries to bring emergency backup systems on line, and dispatch repair crews to vulnerable areas before the storm actually strikes.

Other companies are extremely lightning sensitive as well. The aviation industry gets nervous during loading and refueling operations on exposed runways. The blasting industry and the military can be disrupted as well. Loading war-heads onto submarines during a thunderstorm is just asking for trouble! Computer companies are subject to power surges that can ruin circuit boards.

R*SCAN was a private company based in Minneapolis that has a nationwide network of seventy-two lightning sensors. These specially constructed antennas, spaced some two hundred miles apart, can pinpoint the location and intensity of a cloud-to-ground lightning bolt within a few milliseconds, instantly relaying that information back to a central command post where the information is redistributed to subscribing customers around the nation. Each antenna "listens" for lightning in the two hundred to five hundred kilohertz band, just below the AM radio frequencies. (In essence, the static that you hear on AM radio during a thunderstorm is what the lightning network is trying to detect.) A log of each lightning strike can be printed out, permitting a blow-by-blow recap of the storm, essential in matters of litigation (where lightning triggered a death, fire, or accident). Used together with radar, lightning detection systems can provide businesses, television stations, and the general public with an extra safety tool.

Weather modification: Over the centuries, weather-weary folks have tried tinkering with the skies overhead, with generally disappointing results. Such attempts have included firing cannons into thunderstorms, animal sacrifices, setting out pots of water, clashing armor, ringing church bells, and dancing. Lots of dancing.

On November 13, 1946, a scientist by the name of Vincent Schaeffer sprinkled three pounds of ground dry ice into a cloud over upstate New York. Minutes later, a burst of snow was observed and a hole appeared in the cloud.

Since then, meteorologists working for the National Weather Service and the private sector have tried to improve the odds of 'making rain" by switching to silver iodide, a chemical that, when burned, has a geometric shape similar to a snow flake. Silver iodide fools supercooled water vapor in a cloud into forming an ice crystal, and if enough ice crystals stick together, gravity pulls this snowflake to the ground. Silver iodide is most often released from "smoking flares" on airplanes flying between ten thousand and twenty thousand feet. In California, because of the state's greater need for water in reservoirs, silver iodide is sometimes released by burning the chemical in a large Bunsen burner-like device on the ground, and letting the smoke drift up into "ripe" clouds, clouds on the verge of making precipitation. On occasion, we can give Mother Nature a gentle nudge, increasing rainfall by as much as 5 to 10 percent. Cloud seeding increases the efficiency of a cloud, making more rain fall from the sky.

But weather modification technology is still relatively crude and unreliable. Our efforts now tend to work best in the enhancement of snow over mountainous terrain, snow that will eventually provide precious water for reservoirs dotting the western states. The federal government has slashed funding for research, but several dozen private companies offer weather modification services. Nevada and Illinois have ongoing weather modification programs. Officials in Utah estimate that cloud seeding results in a 15 percent increase in rainfall. And North Dakota has an ambitious program to reduce hail, spending half a million dollars annually. The meteorologist in charge of the program, based at the University of North Dakota at Grand Forks, believes cloud seeding results in an extra inch of rain every year, enough to reap thirty times the program's costs in bigger grain harvests. Potential hail-producing thunderstorms are seeded with silver iodide, in the hope that this will trigger rain, leaving fewer raindrops behind that can grow into damaging hailstones.

Although it's doubtful that anyone will ever attempt to tamper with a tornado, scientists have had some limited success reducing wind speeds within hurricanes. In the 1960s, the National Oceanic and Atmospheric Administration teamed up with the U.S. Navy in project Stormfury. Silver iodide was dropped into hurricanes to try to widen the storms' eyes, weakening the destructive thunderstorms swirling around the eye-walls, and thus diminishing the most severe winds near the centers of the storms. In 1963, one day after seeding, hurricane Beulah showed a 30 percent decrease in intensity. The program was halted because of legal ramifications and a storm of protest from some Caribbean and Pacific nations who were convinced that hurricane modification by the United States was robbing their countries of precious rains.

The potential legal, political, and ethical problems arising from weather modification are enormous. Who has a right to play God? Some farmers living in the Red River valley of Minnesota remain convinced that cloud seeding over North Dakota increased flooding on their land in the mid-80s. During dry spells, farmers love additional rainfall, but resorts and construction companies will probably opt for dry weather. Who decides?

It's doubtful whether cloud seeding can alter a drought, when few clouds are available to begin with. Perhaps the greatest success has come at our nation's airports. When temperatures are below freezing, cloud seeding can punch holes into ice fogs, permitting planes to take-off and land. The Soviets are quick to point out their weather modification triumphs. They begin seeding clouds west of Moscow in late March and on into April, to ensure a dry, snowless May Day military parade!

The Soviets may be more aggressive in terms of weather modification, but they are lagging far behind the United States in computer firepower. It's estimated that the Soviets are ten to twenty years behind the United States when it comes to operational computer forecasts.

On a daily basis, we are inadvertently changing the weather. For instance, contrails from high altitude jet aircraft can spread out into thin cirrus clouds, which can keep temperatures one to three degrees lower during the day and two to four degrees higher at night.

More fog has been observed downwind of power plant cooling towers, capable of releasing enormous amounts of waste-steam into the atmosphere. During the coldest days of winter, when winds are light, normal car exhaust can help to seed the clouds, enhancing snowfall slightly over busy freeways, increasing the threat of icing-over. Whether we realize it or not, we are modifying the weather everyday!

Golf course effect: Weather records kept in Palm Springs, California, show that temperatures there have lowered as much as two to three degrees over the last twenty years. This cooling trend has been linked to the "greening" of Palm Springs, the addition of more than sixty golf courses, which are thousands of acres of well-watered turf. The result has been higher relative humidities and more evaporative cooling, leading to cooler thermometers.

Humans can impact local climate. Phoenix has seen a warm-up of as much as two to four degrees over the same period that Palm Springs cooled down, the result of rapid development—more asphalt and more concrete, materials that retain the sun's heat well into the nighttime hours. Changes in land use, especially over the desert Southwest, can "taint" local weather, with uncertain long-term results.

Cropcasting

Crop forecasting by satellite — in this photo, for Argentina. Using satellite data, private companies like Earthsat, Inc. in Washington, D.C., are able to estimate how weather will affect crop yields around the world. Wheat, corn, coffee, sugar, cocoa, and a multitude of other crops are extremely weather sensitive. Too much or too little rainfall can make the difference between a bountiful harvest and financial disaster.

Foreign buyers purchase nearly two-thirds of some American crops. A better knowledge of food production and predicted harvests can help farmers make better decisions. Commodities brokers need to know if drought, floods, or excessive heat will affect production, and thus demand for a specific crop.

Earthsat divides up the world into forty-eight-square-kilometer units that are about the size of an average midwestern county. Daily weather data is collected from each unit in the worldwide grid, with satellite data filling in some of the gaps where rainfall information is sparse or nonexistent. A high-speed computer processes all of this information — temperature, rainfall, humidity, and winds — into a crop-growth simulation model that estimates how the weather will affect the crop in that specific unit. The result is a reliable assessment of current crop conditions, from which a more accurate crop forecast or "cropcast" can be made.

VERY DRY
DRY
MARGINAL
ADEQUATE
WET

SO. AMERICAN SOYBEANS
FEBRUARY 20, 1989
TOPSOIL MOISTURE

Cropcast soil moisture from an Earthsat satellite. *Courtesy: Earthsat Corporation.*

Virga: snow that evaporates before reaching the ground. Cloud seeding can increase snowfall by as much as 5 to 10 percent, especially over hilly terrain. *Paul Grover, Cottage Grove, MN.*

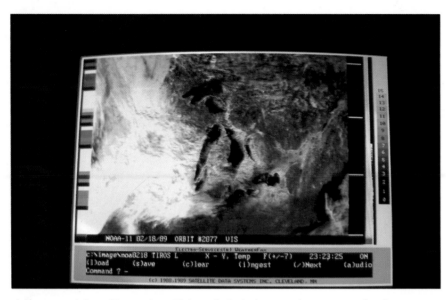

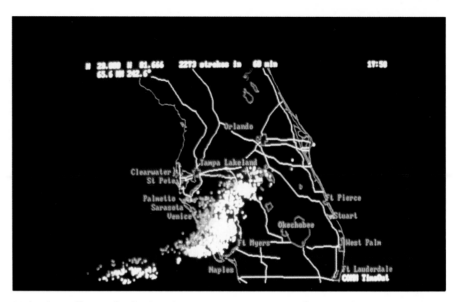

A "homemade" satellite receiver. Using relatively inexpensive computer hardware, a modified computer card, simple software, and a crude satellite dish, anyone can pick up GOES, polar-orbiting, and even Russian satellite images at home! The photos arrive via Wefax, a continuous (and free) radio signal bouncing off of the GOES satellite. Visible and infrared photos are available, and the pictures can be archived, even looped into movies. The satellite photo above is a visible, polar-orbiting image, which arrives from four to eight times daily. The photo shows the outline of the Great Lakes and a huge stripe of fresh snow over much of the Midwest. *Courtesy: Satellite Data Systems.*

Lightning strikes can be displayed on any computer using software and a simple telephone modem. In this example, a squall line is generating intense lightning in a band from Orlando to Fort Meyers, Florida. The most recent cloud-to-ground lightning strikes show up as white, and the older strikes purple and blue. In this manner, it's possible to track the precise movement of dangerous lightning. *Courtesy: R*SCAN.*

Multiple lightning strikes.

Hurricane Gilbert—the aftermath. *Patti Evens, Sauk Rapids, MN.*

A distant grumble. *Philip Cina, Centuria, WI.*

6 Forecast 2000

Environmental Concerns Facing Minnesota, America, and the Planet

"Where forests grow, what regions can grow what kind of crop, what the lake levels are in the great lakes . . . these kinds of things should change. . . . "—Dr. Stephen Schneider, a scientist specializing in climate, National Center for Atmospheric Research, Boulder, Colorado

Our pure and pristine prairie skies are in grave danger. Minnesota has always prided itself as being a clean state, a refuge for countless thousands of plant and animal species that thrive in our lakes, woods, and wetlands. We are blessed with clean water, and a lack of heavy industry "upwind" in the Dakotas prevents episodes of smog that seem to grip so much of America. Air pollution is almost a foreign word in our vocabulary. The spectacular photos sprinkled throughout this book are proof positive that there is indeed something right with Minnesota's skies.

But the rest of the world is using the atmosphere as a convenient dump, an endless sewer in the sky. That legacy is now coming back to haunt us, and much to our horror, we are discovering that we may be causing permanent harm to the thin protective shell surrounding our planet. That twelve-mile-thick marriage of life-giving gases, relatively thinner than the skin on an apple, took billions of years to evolve. In the course of a century we have spoiled this envelope of air.

The leap from an agriculture-based economy to a nation of commuters, rampant development, and

"smoke-stack" industries is largely to blame for the mess we find ourselves in today. Some call this progress, but what we are now realizing is that, truly, there is no free lunch. Exponential growth in standards of living has taken a heavy toll on the environment. The greenhouse effect and depletion of stratospheric ozone know no state or international boundaries. These are threats to our quality of life, far-reaching global dilemmas that will not be fixed with a quick painless shot of technology. They will demand changes in lifestyle, political activism on a scale not seen since the Vietnam War — and money. In the coming years we will all have to reach deeper into our pockets to fund cleaner, more efficient sources of energy. There is simply no other alternative.

ENVIRONMENTAL THREATS

"I feel that nothing we do will actually prevent (the greenhouse effect) from happening the way it looks like it's going to happen. But slowing it down will give us all time to adjust. . . . "—Dr. Kerry Emanuel, atmospheric scientist at M.I.T.

Smog: a term originally coined in 1905 to describe a fog contaminated with industrial pollutants. Today this term applies to urban pollution, with or without "natural" fog.

Photochemical smogs of nitrogen oxides, hydrocarbons, and ozone are the result of automobile exhaust reacting with sunlight. This leads to

"In recent years, there is a justifiable perception that the weather is more variable and is causing more problems than it did in the 1960s and 1950s, but that's because the 60s and 50s were abnormally calm. . . . "
—Dr. Murray Mitchell

Toxic Emissions

The Environmental Protection Agency estimates that waste gases are emitted from industry nationwide at the rate of 2.4 billion tons a year. That is an astoundingly high figure, perhaps as much as ten times greater than previously thought. More than three hundred toxins have been monitored, some thought to be associated with respiratory problems, cancer, birth defects, neurological disorders, and mutations. Of these, only seven gases are regulated by federal agencies.

During an average year, Minnesota residents and industries spew twenty-nine million tons of toxins into the air, ranking twenty-seventh worst in the nation. The most severe air pollution is concentrated around the Great Lakes, which seem to act like a giant whirlpool of sorts, sucking pollutants into the Midwest from all parts of the nation. Congressman Jerry Sikorski estimates that 80 percent of the pollution in Lake Superior comes from the atmosphere.

Nationwide, some seventeen thousand industrial plants have been monitored for air pollution. By far the biggest offender is the chemical industry, producing four times more toxins than other sources. It's estimated that more than one hundred million Americans, including residents of the Twin Cities, live in areas where pollution exceeds government guidelines.

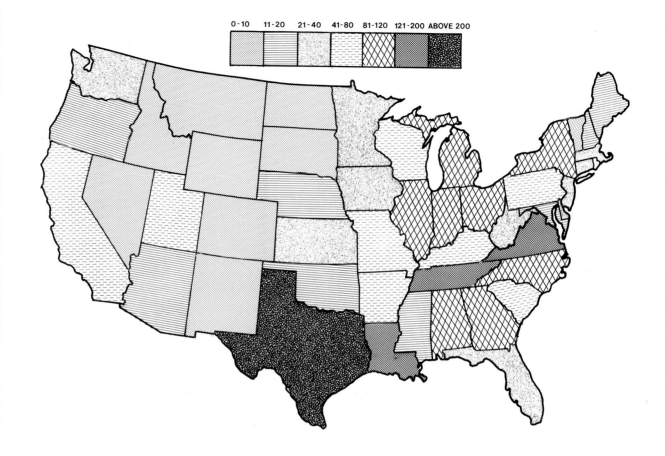

0-10 11-20 21-40 41-80 81-120 121-200 ABOVE 200

Toxic emissions. State-by-state comparison of emissions of toxic waste materials based on figures for 1987. (Millions of pounds annually.)

a dirty blanket of brown, hazy air often seen over cities like Denver, Phoenix, and Los Angeles. Ozone is naturally found in the stratosphere, some twelve to fifteen miles above the earth, where it screens out harmful ultraviolet rays. But near the ground it can lead to a long list of respiratory ailments, posing the greatest threat to the elderly.

Sulfur-laden smogs are produced by the large-scale combustion of fuel-oil and coal. This form of smog is more of a problem from the Ohio Valley into the Great Lakes, home to a greater concentration of dirty "smoke-stack" industries.

Urban heat island: Cities give off heat. Industries, homes, and cars generate excess heat that has nowhere to go but into the atmosphere. In addition, asphalt and concrete retain heat, keeping large metro areas as much as five to ten degrees warmer at night. The growing season in the Twin Cities metro area is about two weeks longer than the surrounding suburbs (great news for farmers in downtown Minneapolis and St. Paul).

Since "official" National Weather Service hourly temperatures are taken at airports in urban areas, a definite bias is seen for city temperatures. With the greenhouse effect making news, some scientists are concerned that the urban heat island may be skewing temperatures toward the warm side. Several studies suggest that man-made heat in and near large- and even medium-sized cities may be responsible for a half- to a one-and-a-half-degree warm-up seen on temperature records this century. How much of this is true greenhouse warming triggered by CO_2, and how much is a by-product of development and "urban sprawl" is still a hot topic of debate within the meteorological community.

The urban heat island creates another dilemma for forecasters. Do you forecast the high or low temperature for the airport (where the "official" temperature reading is taken), or for the suburbs where most of the viewers live, communities that can be as much as ten degrees cooler especially on clear, calm winter nights. That's why we give a

temperature range during the weather forecast — to try to take this disparity between city and country into account.

Acid rain: formed when airborne moisture combines with two pollutants, sulfur dioxide and nitrogen oxides, both produced during the combustion of fossil fuels such as coal and oil. Power plants and cars are the biggest sources of these air pollutants, which form sulfuric and nitric acid within clouds. These acids fall with rain, or in other forms of wet deposition such as snow, hail, dew, fog, or frost. Acids can also fall in dust or particles as dry deposition.

Minnesota's lakes are threatened by acid rain, which can interfere with the reproductive cycle of fish. Of Minnesota's three thousand "fishing lakes," over seven hundred lakes, many still brimming with walleye, smallmouth bass, and lake trout, may be susceptible to acidification, where key organisms in the fish food chain can be killed off by acidic water. Tourism is Minnesota's third largest industry, and the Minnesota Pollution Control Agency estimates that the economic value of the resources at risk is $78 million to $260 million a year.

In northeastern Minnesota one of every three fishing lakes is sensitive to acid rain. As a result of the last Ice Age much of northeastern and north central Minnesota has thin soil and exposed bedrock. This means that there is little natural alkalinity in the soil to neutralize the acid fallout. This makes these lakes more vulnerable to acid damage (unlike lakes in southern and southwestern Minnesota, where thick soil and leaves can buffer or weaken the acid). In addition, rain falling on northern Minnesota seems to be more acidic, with an average pH of 4.7, almost ten times more acidic than "pure rain" with a pH of 5.6. Rain falling on farmland in southern and western Minnesota shows close-to-normal pH. This may be due in part to the alkaline prairie soils in these areas, which are blown into the atmosphere by the wind.

About twenty-two hundred of Minnesota's

Metromex Project
Meteorologists have long suspected that large cities can modify the weather downwind, over neighboring suburbs. In 1977, this phenomenon was researched in detail over St. Louis and its surrounding neighborhoods, with surprising results.

A lack of soil moisture means that cities tend to be warmer and drier. But scientists discovered that pollution, everything from dust to particulates, can provide condensation nuclei by the billions, fooling the atmosphere into forming raindrops. Scientists were surprised to find a 10 to 30 percent increase in flash floods, hail, and severe thunderstorms just downwind of St. Louis.

The legal implications are profound. Will Stillwater or Red Wing someday sue the Twin Cities for helping to spawn a damaging flood over their town? The premise sounds pretty far-fetched, but the scenario is not as absurd as you might think.

Our cars emit more than 1.5 billion tons of carbon dioxide every day.

Earth has lost roughly 25 percent of its forests, and one hundred plant and animal species become extinct each day.

Since Earth Day 1970, the United States has spent approximately one trillion dollars trying to control air and water pollution.

Water may become our most precious natural resource during the 1990s and beyond. Already, western states are fighting over water supplies, and although Minnesota is blessed with over three thousand "fishing lakes" our fresh-water supply is in danger.

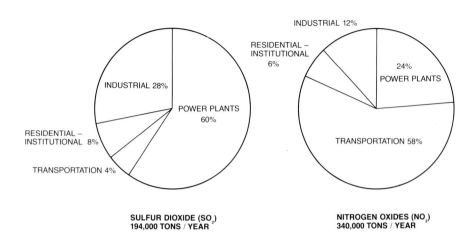

SULFUR DIOXIDE (SO$_2$)
194,000 TONS / YEAR

NITROGEN OXIDES (NO$_2$)
340,000 TONS / YEAR

Minnesota produces roughly 1 percent of the annual emission of sulfur dioxide and nitrogen oxide in the United States. Currently, individual power plants in Kentucky and Ohio emit more sulfur dioxide every year than does industry in the entire state of Minnesota.

The urban heat island. *Louis D. Haas, St. Paul, MN.*

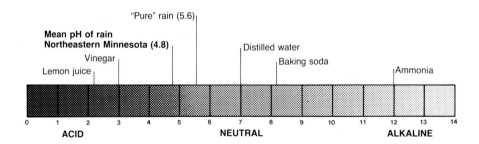

The pH scale is used to measure acidity. The pH scale ranges from 0.0 to 14.0, where less than 7.0 is acidic, 7.0 is neutral, and greater than 7.0 is alkaline. A logarithmic scale, each drop of one point in pH implies a ten-fold increase in acidity. For example, vinegar, with a pH of 3.0, is ten thousand times more acidic than distilled water, which is neutral at pH 7.0. A lake with a pH of 5.0 is ten times more acidic than a lake at pH 6.0. Normal rainwater is naturally acidic, with a pH of 5.6. This is due to carbon in the atmosphere, which combines with moisture in the air to form carbonic acid.

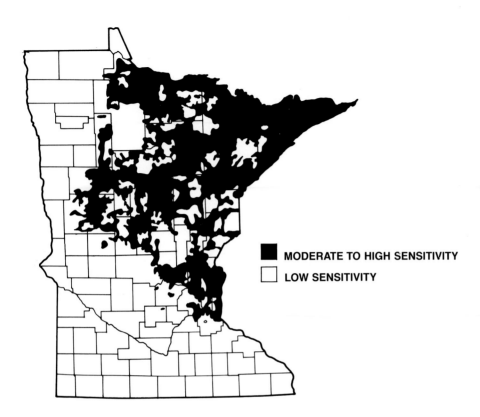

Acid-sensitive areas of Minnesota.

MODERATE TO HIGH SENSITIVITY

LOW SENSITIVITY

Michael O'Keefe, White Bear Lake, MN.

A calm Minnesota lake.

"We also believe, and with increasing strength in that belief, that the temperature the world over has increased by about 1.5 degrees over the last hundred years."—Dr. Gordon Macdonald, atmospheric scientist, Mitre Corporation

"The drought that we had in 1988 probably will probably become more frequent as we move into the greenhouse"—Dr. Gordon Macdonald, atmospheric scientist, Mitre Corporation

"The global warming phenomenon is the most significant economic, political, environmental and human challenge of the next decade and well into the next century for all of us."—Colorado senator Timothy Wirth

"It's an opportunity for us to make our energy systems more efficient which can actually save us money in the long-run, make our products more competitive, reduce acid rain, and reduce the health effect of air pollution in cities . . . we have to make ourselves less vulnerable to climate changes of all kinds. That means developing crops that work better with more CO2 and drier conditions. . . . "—Dr. Stephen Schneider, atmospheric scientist, NCAR, Boulder, Colorado

"A lot of these problems are only going to get solved by bright people . . . and we need more of them. I certainly wish there were more bright kids going into science. . . . "—Dr. Kerry Emanuel, M.I.T., Cambridge, Mass.

twelve thousand lakes are potentially susceptible to acidification. Of these, about two hundred are extremely sensitive to acid rain. Even though no lakes have acidified yet, the acidity of the rain and the rate of acid deposition in northeastern Minnesota is now at or above the level that caused lake acidification in Scandinavia, which is geologically similar to Minnesota. Recent research suggests that some lakes in northern Minnesota may be experiencing the initial effects of acidification, a process that has left thousands of lakes in New England and Canada "sterile" and lifeless.

Forestry, Minnesota's second largest industry, may be vulnerable as well, with an estimated 3.5 million acres of forestland at risk of long-term acidification.

Is there a link between acid rain and drought? Recent research suggests that widespread drought conditions may influence acid rain-causing chemicals in the air by increasing certain kinds of dust. NOAA scientists believe that dry winds during a drought can whip up dust into the atmosphere, helping to release dangerous toxic metals into lakes and streams downwind of the fields.

What can be done? There are things we can all do to protect our lakes and forests from the ravages of acidification.

- Write to your state and federal elected officials in support of strong controls on air pollution and acid rain.
- Installing "scrubbers" to remove many of the acidic gases is expensive for utilities and other industries, and it may eventually show up as a higher energy bill. But do we have any other choice?
- You can reduce unnecessary driving. When possible, use alternatives: walk, bike, ride the bus, or form car pools.
- Keep your car well-tuned. You'll save money and energy, as well as reducing pollution.
- Conserve energy. Utilities remain the largest single source of sulfur dioxide. By cutting down on energy use, we can cut down on the need for new, potentially polluting power plants. Turn off lights; avoid peak-time (8:00 A.M. to 6:00 P.M.) energy use; try opening a window instead of flicking on the air conditioner; weatherproof your house to save fuel; plan meals to use the oven heat wisely; and use the stairs instead of the elevator.
- Remain informed, and try to learn more about the problem. The DNR and the MPCA have printed and audiovisual materials available for public education.

The greenhouse effect: There is a growing consensus among atmospheric scientists worldwide that the long-range outlook calls for an unavoidable warming trend, a slow upward spiral in temperature that may affect global food production, sea levels, even the strength of hurricanes as we head into the twenty-first century.

The culprit is carbon dioxide. CO_2 is a colorless, odorless gas released every time we burn gas, oil, or coal. It's estimated that since the dawn of the Industrial Revolution, we've increased the carbon dioxide content of the atmosphere overhead by 25 percent, dumping some 140 billion tons into the sky at the astounding rate of three billion tons a year. Now that's a bigger CO_2 increase than anything in the previous two hundred millennia on earth, a truly mind-boggling number! The United States, with only one-twentieth of the world's population, produces nearly a quarter of the annual global CO_2 from burning fossil fuels.

Carbon dioxide acts like a blanket, trapping warmth near the ground, allowing sunlight in, but preventing warmth from escaping, much like a greenhouse. The process is somewhat more complicated than that, with CO_2 re-radiating longwave, infrared radiation toward the ground. It's worth pointing out that a total lack of carbon dioxide will make our planet inhospitable, some fifty-three degrees centigrade colder, with a climate similar to that found on Mars. On the other hand, a runaway greenhouse effect will leave us baking near the boiling point of water, just like the planet Venus. It's logical to assume that more CO_2

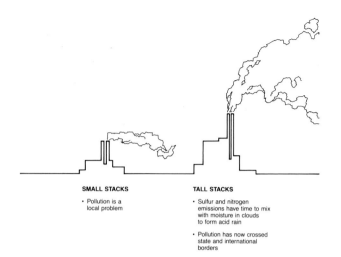

SMALL STACKS

- Pollution is a local problem

TALL STACKS

- Sulfur and nitrogen emissions have time to mix with moisture in clouds to form acid rain

- Pollution has now crossed state and international borders

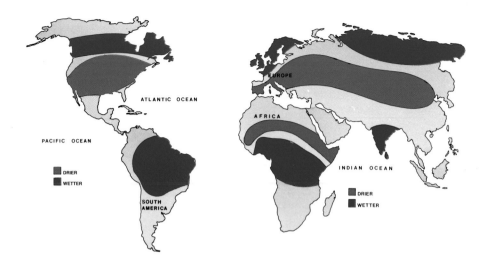

DRIER
WETTER

DRIER
WETTER

Tall smokestacks have transformed air pollution from a local problem into a global dilemma. These taller stacks have helped to clear the air in some towns. But because sulfur and nitrogen are pumped higher into the atmosphere, they travel hundreds, even thousands of miles downwind, giving these gases more time to combine with moisture and fall as acid rain. Minnesota produces about 10 percent of its own acid rain; the rest is "imported" from industrial areas to the south and west, primarily Texas, Missouri, Iowa, and Canada. Acid rain does not respect state or international boundaries.

Greenhouse warming as predicted by a climatic computer model for the twenty-first century. Five out of six computer simulations predicted drier weather for the Midwest, in fact, for much of the American Midwest and plains. A large portion of southern Europe could be drier, with an increase in rainfall for parts of Canada, northern Europe, South America, central Africa, India, southern Australia, and Siberia. Unfortunately, soil in these regions tends to be poor, unable to support the record grain, wheat, and corn harvests that feed much of the world's mushrooming population.

Polluting our skies.

A threatening sky. *Bob Hoffman, Eagan, MN.*

will result in a net warming of the earth's troposphere over time, and that seems to be what we are witnessing.

Here's what we know: A number of exhaustive studies, some utilizing samples of as many as sixty-five million temperature observations, show a one- to two-degree Fahrenheit warm-up, worldwide, since 1900. The warming seems to be most pronounced near the poles, with some north slope oil wells in Alaska registering a four- to five-degree Fahrenheit thaw this century. There seems to be a much greater seasonal fluctuation in CO_2 at high latitudes, with CO_2 peaking in February and dropping off to a minimum in September. This is due to plant and tree growth because the trees' green leaves are able to absorb CO_2 in the photosynthesis process, thus removing some excess carbon dioxide from the air. Carbon dioxide is responsible for roughly 50 percent of the greenhouse warming. Other "greenhouse gases" include methane, released by decaying matter, nitrous oxide, and CFCs, chlorofluorocarbons, which also contribute to a thinning of ozone in the stratosphere.

"A large fraction of the scientific community would guess that the world will continue to warm up . . . perhaps as much as three or four degrees Fahrenheit in the next thirty years," warns Gordon Macdonald. Some worst-case scenarios project earth's atmosphere warming up by as much as four to nine degrees by the year 2050, with disastrous consequences. Warming ocean water expands, and already this century coastal towns have witnessed a six-inch rise in sea levels. A rapid warming into the next century would also melt glaciers and vast sections of polar and Antarctic ice, where 90 percent of the earth's ice is stored, causing water levels to rise by as much as two to five feet and partially submerging cities like Los Angeles, Boston, Miami, and New York under hip-deep salt water. Building dikes and levees to keep the water out could be expensive, possibly running into the billions of dollars.

Of even greater concern is that a warmer atmosphere might tend to shift the main storm track, or jet stream, to the north into Canada leaving America's fertile farm belt hotter and drier. This would ultimately lead to drastically smaller harvests and the specter of worldwide famine.

Will we be able to adapt to a warmer, and in many cases drier home? Will we be able to afford to adapt? The Central Intelligence Agency is studying the ramifications of the greenhouse warming, concerned that a warming could heighten political tensions and increase the threat of war in weather-sensitive regions of the earth. It is well known that more than half of the world's population depends on rice to survive. But a recent heat wave in China confirmed that when the mercury goes above ninety to ninety-five degrees, rice yields drop by 20 to 50 percent.

Although the greenhouse effect probably was not to blame for the drought of '88, there is concern that a gradual increase in the earth's background temperature could provide a riper environment for droughts to develop. Instead of coming once every twenty years, drought conditions might arise every three to five years. Dr. Stephen Schneider of NCAR, the National Center for Atmospheric Research in Boulder, Colorado, was asked to speculate on Minnesota's climate beyond the year 2000. "It'll be several degrees warmer. The kind of heat intensity that you saw (in 1988) would probably recur with increasing frequency. . . . That doesn't mean every year will be hot, but you'd have a lot more of the extremes. Our models suggest that it would be substantially drier. There would probably be lots of arguments about who has irrigation water to make up for it, and what kinds of crops are going to be grown. Prices may be higher. . . . "

Jim Campbell, meteorologist in charge of the Twin Cities National Weather Service office, warns, "We ought to be concerned about it because the drought might be a forerunner of what may happen in thirty or forty years. . . . Maybe we'd be having summers like this all the time if the greenhouse continues." Farmers and folks with lake-front property won't be the only ones affected. "If you get a degree or two warmer, then the probability of having some extreme heat wave that really affects not only their heating bill and their air conditioning, but their health, and their grandmother's health . . . is quite significant," warns Dr. Schneider.

Nineteen eighty-eight went into the record books as the warmest year, globally, and those records date back to the middle and late 1800s. Four of the five warmest years of the twentieth century have occurred during the 1980s. Is this all sheer coincidence, or is this the start of an ominous trend?

Deforestation: Growing trees absorb excess carbon dioxide from the air and convert it into oxygen, helping to offset the greenhouse effect. But rapid development and a desire to exploit precious natural resources have led to the wholesale clearing of forests, trees that in turn remove vast amounts of CO_2 from the atmosphere through the natural photosynthesis cycle. The "slashing and burning" of trees, especially in Brazil and many Third World countries, releases an enormous amount of carbon that has been stored inside of these trees, carbon that adds to the greenhouse effect. Scientists estimate that as much as 20 percent of the greenhouse warming may be due to deforestation.

And the trends are anything but encouraging. Forests worldwide are disappearing at the rate of one football field every second. This year, twenty-eight million acres of forestland, an area roughly the size of Tennessee, will be cut down in the name of progress. It's estimated that half of the world's virgin timberland is in the Amazon rain forest of Brazil, where there is intense pressure to clear land for cattle grazing and agriculture. Recently, the United States and other western nations have attempted to pressure the Brazilian government into setting aside large parts of the Amazon in a natural setting. The Brazilians have denounced what they call "foreign meddling" and claim that they will proceed with their own environmental plan to protect the Amazon.

Ozone depletion: All life on earth is protected by the sun's harmful ultraviolet rays by the ozone layer, a paper-thin layer of gas some ten to thirty miles above the ground. Produced when UV rays collide with oxygen molecules, ozone prevents 99 percent of these deadly rays from ever reaching the ground.

But there's a problem. Ozone molecules high overhead in the stratosphere are being destroyed by synthetic chemicals—chlorofluorocarbons, otherwise known as CFCs. First synthesized in the 1920s, CFCs are used as coolants in refrigerators and air conditioners. They are also found in solvents, foam insulation and containers, halon fire extinguishers, and they serve as propellants in spray cans used in many industrialized nations.

Within the last decade, scientists have discovered that synthetic CFCs are capable of drifting up into the stratosphere, where they can linger for more than a century. In a complex chemical reaction involving frigid ice clouds at temperatures as low as -117° F., chlorine atoms are broken off from CFC molecules, and these chlorine atoms attack ozone molecules, producing oxygen (which doesn't screen out UV rays) and another chlorine atom. The process can continue almost endlessly, with one chlorine atom capable of destroying tens of thousands of ozone molecules. CFCs are inert, extremely stable and long-lasting. They almost never break down, and that's why the problem is so difficult to deal with.

In 1982 satellites and high-flying aircraft first detected an "ozone hole" over Antarctica, a 30 to 50 percent drop in ozone over the South Pole. Recently, scientists have discovered some thinning of the ozone layer over the North Pole as well. Weather balloons and sensitive satellites detected a 10 to 20 percent drop in ozone, lasting for one to two weeks at a time. The Minnesota Pollution Control Agency predicts that the ozone layer over the northern tier states, including Minnesota, has

been depleted by 3 percent in the last decade, resulting in a noticeable increase in melanoma, skin cancer, which, if not detected early, can be fatal. Worldwide, a 3 percent thinning of stratospheric ozone has been observed since 1969, meaning that 6 percent more UV radiation is reaching our beaches and lakes. This could mean an increase of forty thousand cases of skin cancer each year in just the United States alone.

Medical records suggest that this is not just science-fiction hype. Nationwide, there has been a 93 percent increase in skin cancer since 1980. "Binge sunbathing" is to blame for many of these cases. A person with a blistering sunburn is twenty times more likely to develop a life-threatening melanoma.

Skin cancer is not the only threat posed by CFCs. An increase in ultraviolet radiation will lead to more eye cataracts (the leading cause of blindness), and a weakening of our immune systems, making it more difficult to fight off disease. Much of the algae and plankton found in the oceans might not survive, threatening food chains that support fish and ultimately humans. Numerous trees are sensitive to UV radiation, and might not be able to adapt quickly enough to survive. Food crops will be affected, especially rice, which feeds half of the world's population.

Ironically, less ozone aloft will allow more UV rays to reach the ground, where they will react with oxygen to produce more ozone in our larger cities, adding to the air pollution and choking cities like Denver, Phoenix, and Los Angeles. Ozone near the ground is twenty thousand times more effective at trapping heat than carbon dioxide, and this could worsen the greenhouse effect. (Remember how I said that all the environmental problems are interrelated? That is why a comprehensive, global solution is needed.)

It is a cruel twist of fate: not enough ozone in the stratosphere, but much too much near the ground, especially near urban centers. Surface ozone pollution may severely reduce grain crop yields, and EPA scientists predict that this low-level smog

The six warmest years of the twentieth century: 1988, 1987, 1983, 1981, 1985 (in that order). Is this all a coincidence?

The Great Minnesota Desert? According to University of Arizona data, a "typical" drought in the Upper Midwest lasts for about thirteen years. This conclusion is based on tree rings, which leave a permanent record of moisture availability from year to year. The average period between droughts is twenty and one-half years.

We hear much about the Dustbowl days of the 1930s, but the tree stumps' concentric growth rings suggest that droughts in the 1860s and 1870s were far worse, and during the mid-1500s large expanses of the northern and western plains resembled deserts, having little or no vegetation.

Blame the Cows
Methane is one of the greenhouse gases, and a large source of methane is the world's termite and cow population. Methane is a by-product of fermentation in the stomachs of cows, and do they ever produce a lot of it! The International Food and Agricultural Organization estimates that there are over a billion cows grazing on good ol' terra firma, each capable of belching four hundred liters of methane a day!

Methane levels are up 100 percent from a century ago, and when it comes to trapping heat, chlorofluorocarbons outdo carbon dioxide five thousand times over.

Deadly Sunblock?

Smog, low-level ozone produced when ultraviolet rays strike oxygen molecules near the ground, may actually help to protect city dwellers from skin cancer, cataracts, and severe sunburn that excess ultraviolet radiation can trigger. The downside is that city residents are breathing in foul air in the process—getting back to the old notion that indeed there is no free lunch.

Minnesota companies release some thirty-two hundred metric tons of chlorofluorocarbons into our skies every year. Among the biggest offenders: electronic firms, hospitals, and biomedical industries. Currently, there are no state programs to reduce CFC emissions.

Weatherfact: Who suffers from the worst air pollution on earth? Although residents of Los Angeles and Denver might argue, it is generally accepted that the world's worst air can be found in the Soviet Union and its Warsaw Pact neighbors. Unlike the United States, Canada, and western Europe, there are virtually no emission controls for cars, trucks, or industrial plants in countries from Poland and East Germany south to Yugoslavia. The burning of brown coal has fouled thousands of lakes and streams, has killed off countless acres of timber, and has left much of eastern Europe shrouded under a sooty blanket of dirty air. Cleaning up the atmosphere, and the environment, will be expensive—and slow.

may be to blame for a 30 percent drop in harvests, costing American farmers $3 billion a year.

What can be done? In 1985, twenty-four nations (including the United States and the Soviet Union) signed the Montreal Protocol. It called for a 35 percent reduction in global CFC use by the year 2000. But as new evidence of ozone thinning comes in each year, there is more of a sense of urgency, and many leading scientists are now advocating the complete worldwide elimination of CFC production by the mid-90s. Why can't we have a total CFC ban today? Because an estimated 140 billion dollars' worth of American industry and business still relies on CFCs. And even though CFC alternatives do exist, they are still considerably more expensive to produce. Other than an outright ban on CFCs, there are other things we can do:

- Recycle CFCs. Cars, air conditioners, and refrigerators release CFCs into the atmosphere when they are discarded or destroyed. By transferring CFCs from old products to new purchases, you are helping to protect the ozone layer.
- Reduce the number of air-conditioner joints, and tightening valves and seals. Car air conditioners lose about 30 percent of their CFCs through leakage and another half in servicing.
- CFCs escape from Styrofoam packaging when it is broken. By properly disposing of foam packaging, and serving "fast-food" in alternative containers, fewer CFCs will become airborne.
- The price of CFCs has been so low that manufacturers have not had any incentive to come up with alternatives. Whether it be through federal legislation or tax incentives, the world's large chemical companies need to accelerate the production of other substitutes. If that means higher prices for some consumer products, the long-term price will be modest indeed.
- Until more evidence of global ozone thinning is received, treat the sun with respect. Using a

sunblock with a rating of fifteen or higher is wise, as is limiting the time you spend tanning, especially during the midday hours.

Safeguarding our water: The greenhouse effect may increase the frequency and severity of droughts in the years ahead, drying up shallow lakes and wetlands. Surface water supplies are threatened by fertilizer and pesticide run-off, and the dumping of industrial waste fluids and untreated sewage. In a 1987 study, the Minnesota Health Department found that 37 percent of the wells in the state were contaminated with pesticides. Underground aquifers, some thirty to four hundred feet below our feet, are capable of providing an immense amount of clean water. It's estimated that enough ground water lies under Minnesota to fill up an eighteen-foot-deep lake the size of the state! But seepage from landfills, chemical-waste dumps, and septic tanks may taint these vast supplies of water. And once an underground aquifer is contaminated, it takes centuries to clean itself up again. When you consider that three-quarters of all Minnesotans rely on ground water for drinking and other household uses, you can understand why there is growing concern.

Things can be done to safeguard our water supply. Requiring modifications in soil tillage, planting, and pesticide application will help. The proper disposal of old pesticides and pesticide containers, and the sealing up of abandoned wells, will help to preserve our water supply into the twenty-first century.

Over the years, we've all used water as if it was some endless commodity, almost too cheap to meter. That mind-set will probably have to change if we are to avoid critical water shortages in the coming years.

Possible Consequences of Global Warming

Everyone is talking about the planet's average temperature on the rise, but the averages themselves won't hurt you. Severe storms, droughts, and stronger hurricanes will, and climatologists worry that extreme events such as these may become more frequent as we put more heat into the system. Indeed, weather records show much more variability in America's weather since 1978, this coming after a period of relatively few extremes from 1956 to 1978.

Category 5 hurricanes similar to Gilbert, which slammed into Cancun, Mexico, in 1988, may pack even more destructive power in the years ahead, according to Dr. Kerry Emanuel of the Massachusetts Institute of Technology. "The Gilberts of the year 2030 may be somewhat more intense than the Gilberts of today," he predicts. Hurricanes get their energy from warm ocean water. Generally, the top two hundred feet of ocean water, closest to the surface, needs to be warm. Emanuel is concerned that the greenhouse effect may heat up the oceans even more, resulting in more violent hurricanes. "What we do know is that if you warm up the tropical oceans by a few degrees you fairly dramatically increase this maximum possible intensity. There are some models that suggest that the Gulf of Mexico, for example, will warm up three or four degrees, which could increase the destructive potential on the order of 50 percent." Currently, the maximum upper limit of wind speeds in a hurricane is close to two hundred miles an hour. Dr. Emanuel foresees a possibility of category 5 storms with winds of 250 mph or more, capable of unthinkable damage. And higher sea levels resulting from the expansion of ocean water and melting of polar ice will leave coastal communities more vulnerable to flooding caused by these mega-hurricanes. "Today's 100-year storm might come every fifteen to twenty years if the sea level is one to two feet higher over the next thirty years," he adds.

Emanuel's theory is controversial, and much-debated within the meteorological community, but it's becoming all too clear that a warmer earth (and ocean) might have far-reaching consequences.

Before you run screaming for the basement, remember that we are dealing with theories here, and there are still a number of respected scientists who are convinced that all the hype and hoopla surrounding the greenhouse effect amounts to a lot of hot air. Their rebuttals include:

- The warming seems to have started before the Industrial Revolution began in the mid-1800s, when you would have expected to see a sharp increase in CO_2.
- You would expect to see an acceleration in the warming of the earth as we dump ever more CO_2 into the air, but the warm-up has been pretty constant with time.
- The oceans are a big unknown. They may act as a "sink," with countless trillions of microscopic plankton and other microorganisms able to absorb excess carbon dioxide, preventing an ecological disaster. According to Dr. Gordon Macdonald, last year 5.4 billion tons of CO_2 were released through the burning of fossil fuels, and yet "only" three billion tons made its way into the atmosphere. Where did the rest go?
- A scientist by the name of Ray Bradley predicts that a warmer earth will lead to more evaporation of ocean water, triggering more cloudiness, which will ultimately cool the planet. He claims that this cooling effect is four times larger than any warming caused by the predicted doubling of CO_2! His records show that the "average global temperature" may be trending upward, but that this is misleading. Winters over middle- and high-latitudes have been getting snowier over the last thirty years, while summer droughts have been on the increase in southern, tropical latitudes.
- Scientific evidence showing a greenhouse warming this century may be tainted by the urban heat island effect. Most of the temperature records examined have been from National Weather Service offices, usually located at airports within built-up urban areas (that tend to be warmer than the surrounding countryside). How much of the rise in temperatures is the greenhouse effect, and how much is excess city heat drifting over the airport?

Weatherfact: Air pollution from motor vehicles in the United States may be responsible for $40 to $50 billion in annual health-care expenditures and as many as 120,000 unnecessary or premature deaths, according to a series of studies released by the American Lung Association.

We are already paying for air pollution at the grocery check-out. A recent study suggests that air pollution may be responsible for as much as three billion dollars' worth of crop damage every year. According to the Izaak Walton League, pollution may be trimming wheat yields by 37 percent and soybean yields by 18 percent by inhibiting photosynthesis, the process by which green plants use sunlight, water, and carbon dioxide to produce food.

The biggest offender: ground-level ozone, triggered primarily by auto and truck emissions. Although essential in the stratosphere, where it shields earth from harmful ultraviolet radiation, ground-level ozone can combine with sunlight and stagnant "inversions" in the atmosphere to produce smog, a threat to infants, the elderly, and people with respiratory disorders.

Although not as great a threat in Minnesota as in the Great Lakes area and Northeast, this ozone pollution in rural Minnesota may be significant enough to affect many varieties of plants, according to the EPA.

What happened to the quality of life? Research done by the Minnesota Pollution Control Agency shows that in 1988, 351 of Minnesota's largest industrial firms reported releasing seventy-six million pounds of toxic chemicals. Of these chemicals, roughly two-thirds were emitted into the air; the remainder found its way into bodies of water, disposal sites, and other locations.

"A temperature increase of four degrees Fahrenheit has never occurred before in written human history. . . . "—Dr. Irving Mintzer, director, Worldwatch Institute

"There is no statistically significant evidence of an overall increase in annual temperature or change in annual precipitation in the contiguous United States from 1895 to 1987."—Thomas Karl, climatologist, National Oceanographic and Atmospheric Administration.

Many scientists argue that with all of these unknowns and contradictions, we should wait until more evidence comes in on the state of our atmosphere. But critics of this "do nothing philosophy" charge that if we wait until all of the incriminating temperature evidence comes in, it'll be too late to do anything about the greenhouse warming. They maintain that we need a global insurance policy of sorts, spending some money now to avoid an ecological disaster as we head into the twenty-first century.

Greenhouse Hype?

Although there is a growing consensus among scientists worldwide that a global warming will indeed accelerate as we move into the twenty-first century, there is some evidence to the contrary. Temperature measurements of earth's atmosphere taken by Tiros-N series weather satellites suggest that there has been no detectable warming. The measurements were collected between 1979 and 1988. According to Roy W. Spencer, of the Marshall Space Flight Center in Huntsville, Alabama, " . . . we found that the Earth's atmosphere goes through fairly large year-to-year changes in temperature, and over that 10-year period we saw no long-term warming or cooling trend."

The study, released in early 1990, concluded that despite some dramatic temperature swings both hot and cold, the northern hemisphere warmed up slightly and the southern hemisphere cooled, but the net effect for the entire globe was basically zero.

However, these scientists did not rule out the possibility of the greenhouse effect showing up in future satellite and ground-based observations. And according to one of Spencer's coinvestigators, John R. Christy from the University of Alabama in Huntsville, " . . . by the turn of the century we should see a trend."

Perhaps the bigger question is: If we do detect an indisputable upward trend in global temperature, will it be too late to do anything about it?

More That We Can Do

Coping with the greenhouse effect will require dramatic changes in lifestyle, in the way we commute, and in the way we consume energy. Some of the brightest minds within government and private industry will need to grapple with possible solutions. There are things that can be accomplished gradually and relatively painlessly, and can be phased in during the 1990s to reduce the chances of rising oceans and expanding droughts. Among them:

- Encourage energy efficiency on a scale not seen before in the United States, even during the oil embargo of the 70s.
- Gradually phase out the use of coal as a power source, and encourage alternatives to coal in Warsaw Pact and Third World countries (possibly tie this to United States aid).
- Continue to increase the mileage standards for U.S. cars and trucks to greater than thirty-five miles a gallon by the year 2000. Recently, falling oil prices have removed some of the sense of urgency in coming up with more fuel-efficient cars. The Office of Technology Assessment estimates that the nation's new passenger cars could achieve an average fuel efficiency of thirty-three miles per gallon by 1995 using existing technology. (That's about 5 mpg higher than the current average.) Greater reliance on front-wheel drive, 4-speed automatic transmissions and 4-cylinder, 4-valve engines will improve energy efficiency.
- Reduce deforestation by regulating the pace of development and urban sprawl. Make developers plant two or three new trees for every existing tree that needs to be cut down. The "Global Re-leaf" program of the American Forestry Association estimates that planting one hundred million trees around homes and businesses in the United States could reduce atmospheric carbon dioxide emissions from energy production by some eighteen million tons a year, saving American consumers $4 billion each year in energy costs!

 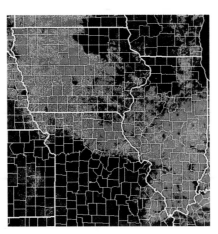

August, 1987. Normal crop conditions.　　　August, 1988. Drought conditions.

Droughts as they appeared from a low-orbiting Landsat satellite. Regions showing up as red had sufficient soil moisture. Blue areas were experiencing drought conditions during the summer of 1988. Crop condition: Red = excellent; Yellow = good; Green = fair; Blue = poor; Black = background, not classified. *Courtesy: Earthsat Corporation.*

Thunder shadows, towering thunderheads casting shadows on a deck of high cirrus clouds.

Sunset on the lake. *Mary Robideau, New Hope, MN.*

- Encourage wise use of timberland resources in developing Third World countries, possibly linking aid and debt-restructuring to efforts at conservation.
- Increase energy efficiency in existing products. Fluorescent lights consume roughly half the energy that regular incandescent bulbs require. New, high-efficiency turbines are available for the generation of electricity. Utilities and private industries need to be encouraged to embrace these new, energy-saving technologies.
- Private industry will quickly ask, "What will this cost us?" Offering tax credits for companies that invest in new high-efficiency technology may be the "ultimate carrot."
- Consider a fuel tax. Americans still pay considerably less for gasoline than every other western nation on earth. Cheap gas does not encourage frugality and energy conservation. A few pennies of each dollar could go toward research into the greenhouse effect, and the search for energy alternatives.
- Electric utilities are responsible for an estimated 33 percent of carbon dioxide generation in this country, and additional efforts can and should be made to clean up the waste gasses leaving their tall stacks. Many of the environmental problems facing us today are interwoven. For example, new "scrubbers" used to reduce sulfur emissions and the scourge of acid rain downwind were found to increase the release of CO_2 into the air, a classic example of "robbing Peter to pay Paul."
- Eliminate CFCs, chlorofluorocarbons, altogether by the year 1995. In addition to destroying the ozone layer, which shields earth from harmful ultraviolet rays, CFCs are a major contributor to the greenhouse effect.

Kristopher Strait, Foley, MN.

7 Weather Trivia

Just How Weatherwise Are You?

"Some are weatherwise, some are otherwise."
—Benjamin Franklin

Just how weatherwise are you? If you're a Minnesota native, you probably pride yourself with a keen knowledge of weather-related trivia and factoids. Frankly, it may be more than just idle chit-chat in front of the water cooler. Being weather-savvy is a matter of survival! If your head is clear, and you feel up to the challenge, try to answer the following questions. You may be surprised at the answers! (Each question may have more than one answer.)

1. What is the only Minnesota city to make the top one hundred coldest cities in the world list?
   A. Duluth
   B. Bemidji
   C. International Falls
   D. Alexandria
   E. Trick question, there are none!

2. Which of the following weather phenomena claims the most lives every year?
   A. Tornadoes
   B. Hurricanes
   C. Lightning
   D. Blizzards and snowstorms
   E. Heat waves

3. When you see lightning, you can determine how far away it is by counting the number of seconds until the thunder arrives, and dividing by:
   A. 1
   B. 5
   C. 10
   D. 20
   E. 100

4. Which of the following is true?
   A. Cars feel the windchill
   B. Pets feel the windchill
   C. A wind speed of more than 40 mph can make you feel warmer
   D. You only feel the windchill under a high pressure system
   E. None of the above

5. At home, the safest place to be during a tornado is:
   A. In the southwest corner of your basement
   B. In a mobile home
   C. Near an open window
   D. In the basement, under the stairwell
   E. Watching for TV warnings in the family room

6. If you are stuck in your car during a blizzard, you should:
   A. Stay in your car
   B. Crack the window slightly, and use the heater sparingly
   C. Clear snow away from the exhaust pipe
   D. Leave your car and try to find a shelter nearby
   E. Tie a handkerchief or cloth to your car's antenna

7. Which of the following are tip-offs that a storm is approaching?
   A. A falling barometer
   B. Kids at school are more active
   C. Birds are flying closer to the ground
   D. You can see the underside of the leaves
   E. More aches and pains, especially for arthritis sufferers

8. The ozone layer:
   A. Is roughly fifteen miles overhead
   B. Is paper-thin, only three millimeters deep
   C. Shields the earth from harmful ultraviolet rays
   D. Is being "eaten away" by carbon dioxide, an odorless, colorless gas used in aerosol cans
   E. Is thinning out near the North and South poles

9. Which of the following might imply that earth is warming up?
   A. More clouds on the satellite photos
   B. A decrease in polar ice seen on satellite photos
   C. More spectacular, reddish sunsets
   D. "Killer bees" moving northward into Mexico
   E. A six-inch rise in ocean water levels this

Bob Appert, Marine on St. Croix, MN.

Judy Odeen, Bloomington, MN.

Tom Petricka, River Falls, WI.

Normally, the atmosphere cools down with height, about five degrees Fahrenheit for every thousand feet. Occasionally, this pattern is reversed, with temperatures rising with altitude. This can result in wave clouds (all of the above), smooth, streamlined clouds that defy description!

century

10. Which of the following is a "fair weather cloud"?
    A. Nimbus
    B. Cirrus
    C. Stratocumulus
    D. Cumulus humilis
    E. Cumulonimbus

11. What is black ice?
    A. Ice that forms at night
    B. Severe icing that threatens aircraft during heavy, wet snowstorms
    C. Glaze ice that forms when liquid rain falls on ground that is colder than 32° F.
    D. Ice that develops from car exhaust, especially on subzero days, when traffic is stop and go
    E. Thin ice on area lakes, found just before the ice-out in April

12. Symptoms of SAD, Seasonal Affective Disorder, triggered by less daylight during the winter months, include:
    A. Increased appetite, especially for carbohydrates
    B. Urge to sleep much of the time
    C. Anxiety and depression, with women affected more than men
    D. Less circulation to body extremities, leading to colder fingers and toes
    E. Lowered sex-drive

13. Alberta clippers:
    A. Tend to dump heavy, wet snow on Minnesota
    B. Approach from the northwest, from western Canada
    C. Can move very quickly, as fast as forty miles an hour
    D. Drop light, powdery snow, prone to blowing and drifting
    E. Often whip up violent winds in their wake, spawning zero visibilities in ground blizzards

14. How much rain and snow falls on the earth every second? (I know this is a tough one, but go ahead and take a guess!)
    A. Twelve tons
    B. Fifty tons
    C. One hundred ninety tons
    D. Fifteen thousand tons
    E. Sixteen million tons

15. The very first weather observations were taken by:
    A. Farmers
    B. Meteorologists
    C. Logging and mining companies
    D. Telegraph operators
    E. Surgeons

16. Which of the following is a tornado tip-off?
    A. Lumpy mammatus clouds at the tail-end of a storm
    B. Vivid rainbows
    C. Nearly continuous static on AM radio bands
    D. Large hail
    E. Counterclockwise-rotating wall clouds lowering toward the ground

17. A downburst:
    A. Is a violent thunderstorm downdraft that reaches the ground
    B. Produces potentially damaging straight-line winds
    C. Leaves behind circular damage patterns in aerial photos
    D. Can whip up wind gusts in excess of one hundred miles an hour
    E. Can sometimes show up on Doppler radar

18. Most tornadoes occur:
    A. Near warm fronts
    B. Just ahead of cold fronts
    C. When upper-air jet stream winds are strong
    D. When air near the ground is moist, with dew points close to 60° F.
    E. At the southernmost point in a line of severe thunderstorms

19. Nationwide, the accuracy rate among meteorologists for the twenty-four hour forecast is (be kind):
    A. 50 percent
    B. 65 percent
    C. 80 percent
    D. 87 percent
    E. 95 percent

20. The emergency outdoor sirens are sounded for:
    A. Tornado warnings
    B. Very severe thunderstorm warnings when 75-plus-mph winds are expected
    C. For all severe thunderstorms
    D. For severe chemical spills and fires
    E. As a test, the first Wednesday of each month during severe weather season

21. Lightning:
    A. Claims more American lives every year than tornadoes and hurricanes combined
    B. Starts from the ground and goes up about 10 percent of the time
    C. Is a natural fertilizer for crops and plants
    D. Can strike during the winter, as well as spring and summer
    E. Is more likely to strike the southern suburbs of the Twin Cities because of favorable underground rock formations

22. Of the following, who began a career as a weathercaster?
    A. Pat Sajak
    B. David Letterman
    C. Suzanne Sommers

D. Danny Devito

E. Diane Sawyer

23. The energy expended by shoveling snow is roughly equivalent to:
    A. Changing a dirty diaper
    B. Playing a vigorous round of golf
    C. Brisk walking
    D. Jogging at nine miles an hour
    E. Trying out for your black belt in karate

24. Most airline cancellations and delays are the result of:
    A. Thunderstorms near the runways
    B. Gusty cross-winds
    C. Dense fog
    D. Heavy snowstorms
    E. Gross incompetence

25. Which cloud is often mistaken for a UFO?
    A. Altocumulus lenticularis
    B. Scud
    C. Shelf cloud
    D. Cumulus congestus
    E. Cap cloud, or pileus cloud

26. What percentage of the nation's TV weathercasters are meteorologists with at least four years of formal training?
    A. 20 percent
    B. 32 percent
    C. 50 percent
    D. 75 percent
    E. 95 percent

27. Which of the following forecasts heard in a weathercast imply a day when the sun is out more than 75 percent of the time?
    A. Partly sunny
    B. Partly cloudy
    C. Variable cloudiness
    D. Some sun
    E. Overcast

28. Which of the following moves the fastest?
    A. A large hailstone
    B. An F2 tornado

C. A category 4 hurricane

D. Snowflakes in a blizzard

E. A prize-winning horse at Canterbury Downs

29. Why are fish more apt to bite when a storm is approaching?
    A. Skies are sunny; easier to see bait
    B. Precipitation agitates lake water surface, throwing fish into a feeding frenzy
    C. Winds usually increase, whipping up a nice "walleye chop"
    D. Falling barometer loosens food particles from lake bottom.
    E. Just a dumb old wives' tale

30. An average sneeze produces winds of:
    A. Ten miles an hour
    B. Forty-five miles an hour
    C. Seventy-five miles an hour—hurricane force
    D. One hundred thirty miles an hour, tornado force
    E. What a sloppy way for a research scientist to make a living!

How did you do? (The answers are in Appendix 1.) The questions were by no means easy. Count up the number you got right and score yourself on the following totally arbitrary scale:

Twenty-five right: weather genius. Yes, you too could probably thumb though the farmer's almanac and point to a big, blue chroma key board for a living!

Twenty right: very commendable. You are certainly capable of making intelligent weather chit-chat at the coffee maker every morning. Tune in the weather channel on cable TV for a little after-hours tutoring.

Fifteen right: Well, at least you didn't embarrass yourself. You need to brush up on your weather trivia. Please keep this book in your favorite bathroom for reference.

Ten right: Are you from Los Angeles or Honolulu? Do you live in the Skyway system? Get outside, lift your gaze skyward and drink in the canopy of color overhead. Or better yet, spend a little time down at the community library researching clouds.

Five right: Hello, cave-dweller! Take a deep breath of fresh air!

8 The Minnesota Almanac
More Than You Ever Wanted to Know About Minnesota Weather

An inflamed sky. *Betty Adrian, Belgrade, MN.*

TWIN CITIES STATISTICS
"You can prove anything with statistics."

JANUARY

Normal Precipitation: 0.73 inches
  Maximum precipitation: 3.63 inches in 1967
  Minimum precipitation: 0.11 inches in 1959
Normal Snowfall: 9.0 inches
  Maximum snowfall: 46.4 inches in 1982
Normal High: 21.2°
Normal Low: 3.2°
Average Wind Direction/Speed: northwest, 10.5 mph

Day	Normal High	Low Low	Record High	Record Low
1	21	5	48 (1897)	-40 (1860)
2	21	4	56 (1855)	-36 (1885)
3	21	4	46 (1880)	-29 (1834)
4	20	4	42 (1839)	-32 (1834)
5	20	3	47 (1885)	-31 (1834)
6	20	3	49 (1900)	-27 (1864)
7	20	3	45 (1949)	-34 (1887)
8	20	3	46 (1885)	-32 (1856)
9	20	2	45 (1939)	-32 (1977)
10	19	2	46 (1928)	-30 (1886)
11	19	2	44 (1835)	-31 (1977)
12	19	2	48 (1987)	-35 (1868)
13	19	2	47 (1987)	-34 (1868)
14	19	2	49 (1944)	-26 (1963)
15	19	2	42 (1830)	-37 (1888)
16	19	1	46 (1834)	-29 (1888)
17	19	1	49 (1842)	-32 (1844)
18	19	1	48 (1880)	-36 (1887)
19	19	1	49 (1921)	-34 (1970)
20	19	1	52 (1908)	-32 (1888)
21	19	2	48 (1900)	-41 (1888)
22	20	2	51 (1900)	-34 (1936)
23	20	2	56 (1853)	-34 (1886)
24	20	2	59 (1846)	-37 (1840)
25	20	2	58 (1944)	-32 (1850)
26	20	2	52 (1931)	-26 (1832)
27	21	2	47 (1864)	-23 (1950)
28	21	3	50 (1846)	-29 (1873)
29	21	3	49 (1931)	-29 (1951)
30	21	3	48 (1879)	-30 (1862)
31	22	3	44 (1892)	-27 (1887)

Selected Cities	Average High	Average Low
Duluth	14.7	-4.4
Alexandria	14.5	-5.8
Bemidji	12.3	-11.1
St. Cloud	16.6	-4.8
Rochester	18.9	0.4
Windom	20.0	-0.3

FEBRUARY

Normal Precipitation: 0.84 inches
  Maximum precipitation: 2.14 inches in 1981
  Minimum precipitation: 0.06 inches in 1964
Normal Snowfall: 7.7 inches
  Maximum snowfall: 26.5 inches in 1962
Normal High: 25.9°
Normal Low: 7.1°
Average Wind Direction/Speed: northwest, 10.4 mph

Day	Normal High	Normal Low	Record High	Record Low
1	22	4	54 (1931)	-28 (1951)
2	22	4	47 (1987)	-30 (1862)
3	23	4	51 (1934)	-31 (1863)
4	23	5	50 (1834)	-28 (1886)
5	23	5	51 (1834)	-27 (1979)
6	24	5	55 (1852)	-24 (1875)
7	24	6	53 (1987)	-30 (1835)
8	24	6	46 (1834)	-29 (1899)
9	25	6	57 (1852)	-33 (1899)
10	25	7	47 (1977)	-35 (1857)
11	25	7	57 (1882)	-31 (1899)
12	26	8	56 (1882)	-30 (1875)
13	26	8	54 (1830)	-32 (1838)
14	26	8	57 (1830)	-40 (1838)
15	27	9	63 (1921)	-25 (1838)
16	27	9	60 (1981)	-26 (1936)
17	27	9	55 (1981)	-30 (1849)
18	28	10	58 (1981)	-21 (1903)
19	28	10	57 (1981)	-20 (1929)
20	28	10	57 (1981)	-21 (1862)
21	28	11	59 (1930)	-21 (1873)
22	29	11	57 (1930)	-22 (1873)
23	29	12	59 (1959)	-30 (1832)
24	29	12	59 (1880)	-26 (1840)
25	30	12	58 (1976)	-23 (1967)
26	30	13	64 (1896)	-24 (1897)
27	30	13	54 (1896)	-22 (1879)
28	31	14	57 (1932)	-26 (1962)

Selected Cities	Average High	Average Low
Duluth	21.0	1.0
Alexandria	21.8	0.8
Bemidji	20.7	-5.1
St. Cloud	23.8	1.6
Rochester	25.5	6.5
Windom	26.2	6.1

MARCH

Normal Precipitation: 1.68 inches
  Maximum precipitation: 4.75 inches in 1975
  Minimum precipitation: 0.32 inches in 1958
Normal Snowfall: 9.6 inches
  Maximum snowfall: 40 inches in 1951
Normal High: 36.9°
Normal Low: 19.6°
Average Wind Direction/Speed: northwest, 11.4 mph
Average number of days with thunder: 0.9

Day	Normal High	Normal Low	Record High	Record Low
1	31	14	56 (1878)	-32 (1962)
2	31	14	55 (1840)	-20 (1833)
3	31	15	65 (1905)	-16 (1839)
4	32	15	61 (1983)	-26 (1865)
5	32	16	62 (1846)	-15 (1836)
6	33	16	67 (1987)	-17 (1869)
7	33	16	73 (1987)	-19 (1857)
8	33	17	63 (1846)	-17 (1843)
9	34	17	61 (1846)	-16 (1856)
10	34	18	60 (1838)	-17 (1948)
11	35	18	61 (1822)	-27 (1948)
12	35	19	62 (1843)	-10 (1856)
13	35	19	69 (1851)	-22 (1867)
14	36	20	66 (1851)	-19 (1867)
15	36	20	69 (1927)	-14 (1867)
16	37	21	71 (1930)	-18 (1843)
17	37	21	76 (1894)	-17 (1867)
18	38	22	73 (1842)	-8 (1923)
19	39	22	72 (1910)	-15 (1875)
20	39	22	66 (1938)	-16 (1855)
21	40	23	76 (1938)	-15 (1855)
22	40	24	71 (1945)	-14 (1888)
23	41	24	83 (1910)	-15 (1843)
24	41	25	76 (1939)	-8 (1965)
25	42	25	78 (1939)	-8 (1967)
26	43	26	79 (1845)	-15 (1843)
27	43	26	75 (1946)	-1 (1855)
28	44	27	78 (1946)	-1 (1923)
29	45	27	76 (1910)	-5 (1969)
30	46	28	83 (1968)	-7 (1843)
31	46	28	73 (1920)	-11 (1843)

Selected Cities	Average High	Average Low
Duluth	31.0	12.6
Alexandria	32.9	13.3
Bemidji	32.1	8.0
St. Cloud	34.9	14.2
Rochester	35.8	17.9
Windom	37.2	17.7

APRIL

Normal Precipitation: 2.04 inches
  Maximum precipitation: 5.4 inches in 1975
  Minimum precipitation: 0.59 inches in 1952
Normal Snowfall: 3.1 inches
  Maximum snowfall: 9.6 inches in 1957
Normal High: 55.5°
Normal Low: 34.7°
Average Wind Direction/Speed: northwest, 12.3 mph
Average number of days with thunder: 2.7

Day	Normal High	Normal Low	Record High	Record Low
1	47	29	82 (1881)	1 (1843)
2	48	29	78 (1987)	9 (1854)
3	48	30	80 (1921)	6 (1837)
4	49	31	81 (1921)	9 (1920)
5	50	31	81 (1830)	11 (1859)
6	51	32	77 (1954)	5 (1857)
7	51	32	76 (1988)	6 (1936)
8	52	33	83 (1931)	8 (1865)
9	52	33	81 (1930)	17 (1837)
10	53	34	88 (1977)	4 (1826)
11	54	34	83 (1968)	10 (1857)
12	54	35	83 (1890)	12 (1962)
13	55	35	78 (1938)	2 (1962)
14	56	36	85 (1954)	10 (1822)
15	56	36	82 (1915)	13 (1857)
16	57	36	88 (1964)	10 (1875)
17	57	37	79 (1911)	10 (1875)
18	58	37	81 (1915)	16 (1857)
19	58	38	83 (1923)	19 (1928)
20	59	38	83 (1980)	20 (1826)
21	59	39	95 (1980)	21 (1846)
22	60	39	90 (1980)	23 (1874)
23	60	39	84 (1820)	17 (1850)
24	61	40	85 (1820)	24 (1875)
25	61	40	91 (1962)	25 (1907)
26	62	41	85 (1970)	26 (1950)
27	62	41	85 (1910)	21 (1909)
28	63	41	88 (1855)	26 (1842)
29	63	41	92 (1952)	22 (1958)
30	64	42	91 (1934)	24 (1846)

Selected Cities	Average High	Average Low
Duluth	46.2	29.4
Alexandria	50.4	32.2
Bemidji	48.7	28.1
St. Cloud	52.7	32.3
Rochester	53.5	34.8
Windom	54.6	33.9

MAY

Normal Precipitation 3.37 inches
  Maximum precipitation: 8.03 inches in 1962
  Minimum precipitation: 0.61 inches in 1967
Normal Snowfall: 0.2 inches
  Maximum snowfall: 3 inches in 1946
Normal High: 67.9°
Normal Low: 46.3°
Average Wind Direction/Speed: southeast, 11.2 mph
Average number of days with thunder: 5.3

Day	Normal High	Normal Low	Record High	Record Low
1	64	42	91 (1959)	24 (1849)
2	64	43	91 (1959)	23 (1841)
3	65	43	93 (1909)	18 (1967)
4	65	43	91 (1952)	22 (1967)
5	65	44	88 (1909)	28 (1891)
6	66	44	89 (1896)	27 (1974)
7	66	44	92 (1963)	26 (1885)
8	66	45	90 (1874)	28 (1960)
9	67	45	91 (1987)	27 (1966)
10	67	45	90 (1987)	26 (1857)
11	68	46	88 (1900)	27 (1946)
12	68	46	90 (1900)	28 (1946)
13	68	47	89 (1900)	29 (1888)
14	69	47	95 (1932)	30 (1839)
15	69	47	91 (1931)	31 (1907)
16	70	48	94 (1934)	31 (1890)
17	70	48	93 (1987)	31 (1915)
18	70	48	91 (1911)	27 (1915)
19	71	49	92 (1838)	33 (1852)
20	71	49	91 (1934)	30 (1892)
21	71	49	92 (1964)	32 (1844)
22	72	50	99 (1925)	30 (1838)
23	72	50	91 (1856)	28 (1963)
24	72	50	88 (1834)	32 (1925)
25	73	51	94 (1978)	33 (1901)
26	73	51	96 (1978)	35 (1906)
27	73	52	95 (1969)	34 (1907)
28	73	52	98 (1934)	28 (1842)
29	74	52	92 (1840)	33 (1965)
30	74	53	98 (1934)	37 (1947)
31	74	53	106 (1934)	33 (1889)

Selected Cities	Average High	Average Low
Duluth	61.0	39.7
Alexandria	66.1	44.8
Bemidji	64.5	40.1
St. Cloud	68.0	43.7
Rochester	68.0	46.0
Windom	68.8	45.8

JUNE

Normal Precipitation: 3.94 inches
  Maximum precipitation: 7.99 inches in 1975
  Minimum precipitation: 1.06 inches in 1973
Normal Snowfall: 0 inches
  Maximum snowfall: 0 inches
Normal High: 77.1°
Normal Low: 56.7°
Average Wind Direction/Speed: southeast, 10.5 mph
Average number of days with thunder: 7.6

Day	Normal High	Normal Low	Record High	Record Low
1	75	53	96 (1852)	37 (1946)
2	75	54	93 (1940)	35 (1946)
3	75	54	92 (1923)	34 (1945)
4	76	54	96 (1823)	39 (1891)
5	76	55	92 (1925)	40 (1894)
6	76	55	95 (1987)	35 (1843)
7	76	55	94 (1987)	37 (1901)
8	77	56	93 (1976)	36 (1885)
9	77	56	95 (1911)	39 (1915)
10	77	56	99 (1956)	41 (1972)
11	77	57	98 (1821)	40 (1874)
12	78	57	95 (1823)	39 (1877)
13	78	57	100 (1823)	37 (1969)
14	78	58	98 (1987)	40 (1842)
15	79	58	98 (1823)	42 (1961)
16	79	58	97 (1823)	43 (1961)
17	79	58	97 (1933)	41 (1842)
18	79	59	98 (1953)	39 (1876)
19	79	59	100 (1933)	38 (1842)
20	80	59	98 (1933)	40 (1842)
21	80	59	96 (1838)	44 (1902)
22	80	60	98 (1911)	42 (1960)
23	80	60	99 (1922)	44 (1972)
24	81	60	101 (1988)	44 (1972)
25	81	60	98 (1934)	46 (1957)
26	81	60	99 (1931)	46 (1888)
27	81	60	104 (1934)	42 (1842)
28	81	61	102 (1931)	47 (1895)
29	82	61	102 (1931)	47 (1924)
30	82	61	100 (1931)	47 (1892)

Selected Cities	Average High	Average Low
Duluth	70.0	48.7
Alexandria	75.1	54.9
Bemidji	73.6	50.9
St. Cloud	76.3	53.6
Rochester	77.0	56.0
Windom	79.1	56.4

JULY

Normal Precipitation: 3.69 inches
  Maximum precipitation: 7.1 inches in 1955
  Minimum precipitation: 0.58 inches in 1975
Normal Snowfall: 0 inches
  Maximum snowfall: 0 inches
Normal High: 82.4°
Normal Low: 61.4°
Average Wind Direction/Speed: south, 9.4 mph
Average number of days with thunder: 7.7

Day	Normal High	Normal Low	Record High	Record Low
1	82	61	100 (1883)	46 (1852)
2	82	62	96 (1911)	49 (1924)
3	82	62	100 (1949)	47 (1967)
4	82	62	100 (1949)	43 (1972)
5	82	62	100 (1982)	41 (1842)
6	83	62	104 (1936)	46 (1842)
7	83	62	101 (1936)	44 (1891)
8	83	62	101 (1936)	46 (1842)
9	83	63	99 (1976)	48 (1895)
10	83	63	106 (1936)	49 (1945)
11	83	63	106 (1936)	49 (1945)
12	83	63	106 (1936)	48 (1941)
13	83	63	105 (1936)	50 (1926)
14	83	63	108 (1936)	48 (1842)
15	84	63	102 (1988)	48 (1863)
16	84	63	102 (1926)	51 (1911)
17	84	63	99 (1936)	52 (1937)
18	84	63	101 (1940)	49 (1873)
19	84	63	100 (1940)	51 (1882)
20	84	63	102 (1901)	50 (1871)
21	84	63	105 (1934)	49 (1947)
22	84	63	105 (1934)	49 (1947)
23	84	63	105 (1934)	46 (1850)
24	84	63	104 (1941)	47 (1891)
25	84	63	99 (1941)	47 (1891)
26	84	63	100 (1894)	45 (1962)
27	84	63	104 (1931)	49 (1962)
28	84	63	100 (1955)	52 (1925)
29	84	63	98 (1933)	47 (1971)
30	84	63	100 (1933)	50 (1889)
31	84	63	105 (1988)	47 (1924)

Selected Cities	Average High	Average Low
Duluth	76.6	54.9
Alexandria	81.6	60.3
Bemidji	79.6	56.2
St. Cloud	82.0	58.3
Rochester	81.6	60.5
Windom	84.0	61.0

AUGUST

Normal Precipitation: 3.05 inches
  Maximum precipitation: 9.31 inches in 1977
  Minimum precipitation: 0.43 inches in 1946
Normal Snowfall: 0 inches
  Maximum snowfall: 0 inches
Normal High: 80.8°
Normal Low: 59.6°
Average Wind Direction/Speed: southeast, 9.2 mph
Average number of days with thunder: 6.5

Day	Normal High	Normal Low	Record High	Record Low
1	84	63	101 (1988)	46 (1842)
2	84	63	98 (1982)	46 (1971)
3	83	63	99 (1941)	46 (1971)
4	83	63	102 (1947)	48 (1978)
5	83	63	100 (1947)	48 (1870)
6	83	62	97 (1916)	48 (1977)
7	83	62	97 (1983)	45 (1972)
8	83	62	96 (1894)	47 (1888)
9	83	62	95 (1947)	46 (1888)
10	83	62	101 (1947)	46 (1904)
11	82	62	97 (1947)	47 (1968)
12	82	62	94 (1866)	45 (1961)
13	82	61	98 (1880)	48 (1860)
14	82	61	96 (1978)	43 (1964)
15	82	61	103 (1936)	47 (1960)
16	81	61	97 (1972)	47 (1962)
17	81	61	100 (1947)	42 (1962)
18	81	60	98 (1976)	38 (1870)
19	81	60	97 (1976)	39 (1967)
20	80	60	97 (1839)	40 (1950)
21	80	59	98 (1947)	45 (1836)
22	80	59	97 (1898)	43 (1890)
23	79	59	97 (1948)	42 (1891)
24	79	59	98 (1948)	41 (1891)
25	79	58	94 (1948)	41 (1887)
26	78	58	96 (1838)	44 (1844)
27	78	57	99 (1926)	42 (1887)
28	78	57	95 (1854)	40 (1891)
29	77	57	96 (1969)	39 (1863)
30	77	56	96 (1941)	44 (1871)
31	77	56	94 (1898)	34 (1832)

Selected Cities	Average High	Average Low
Duluth	76.6	53.3
Alexandria	79.0	58.2
Bemidji	76.7	53.6
St. Cloud	79.2	55.9
Rochester	79.1	58.1
Windom	81.0	58.5

SEPTEMBER

Normal Precipitation: 2.73 inches
  Maximum precipitation: 7.53 inches in 1942
  Minimum precipitation: 0.41 inches in 1940
Normal Snowfall: trace
  Maximum snowfall: 1.7 inches in 1942
Normal High: 70.7°
Normal Low: 49.3°
Average Wind Direction/Speed: south, 9.9 mph
Average number of days with thunder: 4.2

Day	Normal High	Normal Low	Record High	Record Low
1	76	56	97 (1913)	36 (1974)
2	76	55	97 (1937)	42 (1974)
3	75	55	97 (1925)	32 (1974)
4	75	54	98 (1925)	39 (1885)
5	75	54	98 (1922)	36 (1885)
6	74	54	98 (1922)	35 (1885)
7	74	53	98 (1976)	40 (1956)
8	74	53	99 (1931)	36 (1883)
9	73	52	95 (1947)	38 (1883)
10	73	52	104 (1931)	37 (1917)
11	72	52	96 (1895)	33 (1844)
12	72	51	94 (1908)	35 (1839)
13	72	51	95 (1939)	32 (1848)
14	71	51	98 (1939)	33 (1852)
15	71	50	98 (1939)	30 (1852)
16	71	50	94 (1955)	35 (1842)
17	70	50	96 (1895)	34 (1943)
18	70	49	93 (1891)	30 (1863)
19	70	49	94 (1895)	30 (1820)
20	69	48	91 (1895)	28 (1962)
21	69	48	94 (1937)	30 (1866)
22	69	48	95 (1936)	26 (1848)
23	68	47	90 (1891)	30 (1983)
24	68	47	89 (1935)	30 (1942)
25	68	47	91 (1920)	31 (1836)
26	68	47	87 (1923)	27 (1965)
27	67	46	87 (1894)	28 (1823)
28	67	46	91 (1898)	26 (1942)
29	67	46	89 (1897)	27 (1945)
30	66	45	87 (1897)	26 (1939)

Selected Cities	Average High	Average Low
Duluth	64.0	45.2
Alexandria	68.8	48.0
Bemidji	65.8	44.0
St. Cloud	69.4	46.6
Rochester	70.7	49.0
Windom	72.4	48.2

OCTOBER

Normal Precipitation: 1.78 inches
  Maximum precipitation: 5.68 inches in 1971
  Minimum precipitation: 0.01 inches in 1952
Normal Snowfall: 0.5 inches
  Maximum snowfall: 14 inches in 1873
Normal High: 60.7°
Normal Low: 39.2°
Average Wind Direction/Speed: southeast, 10.5 mph
Average number of days with thunder: 1.8

Day	Normal High	Normal Low	Record High	Record Low
1	66	45	86 (1897)	24 (1974)
2	66	45	89 (1953)	22 (1974)
3	66	44	86 (1976)	25 (1845)
4	65	44	89 (1922)	20 (1836)
5	65	44	87 (1879)	25 (1952)
6	65	44	85 (1879)	26 (1976)
7	64	43	85 (1856)	25 (1976)
8	64	43	84 (1966)	25 (1870)
9	63	42	86 (1938)	22 (1895)
10	63	42	90 (1928)	25 (1987)
11	63	42	84 (1930)	22 (1876)
12	62	41	87 (1975)	21 (1838)
13	62	41	84 (1956)	22 (1837)
14	61	40	86 (1947)	24 (1937)
15	61	40	85 (1947)	21 (1876)
16	60	40	86 (1938)	23 (1952)
17	60	39	84 (1910)	22 (1844)
18	59	39	87 (1950)	16 (1972)
19	59	38	81 (1953)	15 (1972)
20	58	38	83 (1953)	18 (1960)
21	58	38	88 (1947)	16 (1913)
22	57	37	80 (1899)	17 (1873)
23	56	37	82 (1899)	17 (1835)
24	56	36	76 (1973)	15 (1822)
25	55	36	80 (1830)	7 (1853)
26	55	35	83 (1955)	8 (1853)
27	54	35	75 (1823)	16 (1976)
28	53	34	75 (1948)	17 (1905)
29	52	34	78 (1922)	11 (1843)
30	52	33	83 (1950)	10 (1843)
31	51	33	83 (1950)	15 (1878)

Selected Cities	Average High	Average Low
Duluth	53.3	35.7
Alexandria	57.1	36.6
Bemidji	65.8	44.0
St. Cloud	58.3	35.8
Rochester	59.5	38.4
Windom	61.4	37.0

NOVEMBER

Normal Precipitation: 1.2 inches
  Maximum precipitation: 5.15 inches in 1940
  Minimum precipitation: 0.02 inches in 1939
Normal Snowfall: 5.1 inches
  Maximum snowfall: 30.4 inches in 1983
Normal High: 40.6°
Normal Low: 24.2°
Average Wind Direction/Speed: northwest, 10.9 mph
Average number of days with thunder: 0.6

Day	Normal High	Normal Low	Record High	Record Low
1	50	32	77 (1933)	10 (1951)
2	50	32	72 (1978)	9 (1951)
3	49	31	74 (1978)	8 (1853)
4	48	31	74 (1975)	2 (1951)
5	47	30	70 (1975)	3 (1951)
6	47	30	73 (1893)	3 (1853)
7	46	29	72 (1874)	10 (1925)
8	45	29	68 (1931)	5 (1856)
9	45	28	67 (1931)	-1 (1848)
10	44	28	67 (1930)	3 (1986)
11	43	27	62 (1961)	-1 (1986)
12	43	27	62 (1952)	-4 (1966)
13	42	26	68 (1930)	0 (1986)
14	42	26	65 (1953)	0 (1919)
15	41	25	69 (1953)	1 (1911)
16	40	25	68 (1931)	-4 (1842)
17	40	25	71 (1953)	-5 (1880)
18	39	24	68 (1904)	-4 (1891)
19	39	24	65 (1930)	-5 (1932)
20	38	23	64 (1834)	-3 (1921)
21	38	23	64 (1913)	-4 (1880)
22	37	22	60 (1867)	-10 (1835)
23	37	22	55 (1905)	-11 (1857)
24	36	21	57 (1890)	-10 (1890)
25	36	21	62 (1914)	-18 (1880)
26	35	20	62 (1914)	-16 (1977)
27	35	20	61 (1909)	-13 (1872)
28	34	20	58 (1941)	-20 (1887)
29	34	19	69 (1825)	-14 (1872)
30	33	19	62 (1922)	-23 (1822)

Selected Cities	Average High	Average Low
Duluth	35.4	20.9
Alexandria	37.4	20.7
Bemidji	34.8	17.1
St. Cloud	39.0	20.5
Rochester	41.3	21.8
Windom	43.1	22.3

DECEMBER

Normal Precipitation: 0.89 inches
  Maximum precipitation: 4.27 inches in 1982
  Minimum precipitation: trace in 1943
Normal Snowfall: 7.3 inches
  Maximum snowfall: 33.2 inches in 1969
Normal High: 26.6°
Normal Low: 10.6°
Average Wind Direction/Speed: northwest, 10.4 mph

Day	Normal High	Normal Low	Record High	Record Low
1	33	18	57 (1969)	-15 (1898)
2	32	18	56 (1969)	-25 (1891)
3	32	17	56 (1941)	-21 (1871)
4	31	17	51 (1960)	-20 (1821)
5	31	16	51 (1900)	-20 (1821)
6	31	16	63 (1939)	-20 (1831)
7	30	16	54 (1938)	-20 (1821)
8	30	15	60 (1939)	-22 (1849)
9	29	15	58 (1939)	-27 (1876)
10	29	14	54 (1979)	-18 (1977)
11	28	14	56 (1913)	-22 (1831)
12	28	13	53 (1968)	-21 (1891)
13	28	13	53 (1891)	-21 (1917)
14	27	13	52 (1884)	-27 (1901)
15	27	12	50 (1874)	-25 (1965)
16	27	12	58 (1939)	-22 (1851)
17	26	11	53 (1939)	-19 (1849)
18	26	11	55 (1923)	-24 (1983)
19	25	10	52 (1923)	-29 (1983)
20	25	10	51 (1890)	-24 (1916)
21	25	10	55 (1877)	-25 (1830)
22	24	9	54 (1889)	-23 (1865)
23	24	9	58 (1889)	-29 (1821)
24	24	8	46 (1957)	-33 (1855)
25	23	8	51 (1922)	-39 (1873)
26	23	7	51 (1986)	-25 (1855)
27	23	7	48 (1828)	-24 (1872)
28	22	7	52 (1879)	-27 (1880)
29	22	6	46 (1829)	-24 (1917)
30	22	6	47 (1890)	-28 (1820)
31	21	5	50 (1904)	-24 (1973)

Selected Cities	Average High	Average Low
Duluth	21.8	5.6
Alexandria	22.7	5.4
Bemidji	20.1	-0.1
St. Cloud	24.2	6.0
Rochester	26.3	10.5
Windom	27.8	9.5

Appendix 1
Weather Trivia Answers

1. A. Duluth ranked eighty-third out of the top one hundred coldest cities on earth. Because of close proximity to the chilly waters of Lake Superior, Duluth's average temperature came in at 38.6° F. (Incidentally, you may be interested to know that thirty-six out of the top forty coldest cities on the list were found in the Soviet Union!)

2. E. The drought and heat wave of 1988 might have directly and indirectly claimed as many as ten thousand lives nationwide.

3. B

4. B and C. At wind speeds greater than forty miles an hour, friction can actually begin to reverse the windchill effect, making you feel warmer!

5. D

6. A, B, C, E

7. A, B, C, D, E. Teachers report that kids tend to act up before a storm. Birds have extremely sensitive ears, capable of sensing even tiny changes in atmospheric pressure. When the barometer is falling they fly closer to the ground to try to relieve some of this air pressure. Also, an approaching storm usually implies winds blowing from the east, allowing one to see the underside of leaves. A falling barometer can allow fluids in joints to expand, exerting more pressure and triggering more pain, especially among arthritis and bursitis sufferers.

8. A, B, C, E. (Chlorofluorocarbons are the big chemical offenders.)

9. A, B. Recent research suggests complicated "feedback" from the greenhouse warming, possibly resulting in more evaporation of ocean water and more cloudcover. In addition, over the last fifteen years, polar-orbiting satellites have taken photos that suggest that the southward extent of the polar ice cap has shrunk by 6 percent, possibly another tip-off of global warming.

10. D

11. D

12. A, B, C, E

13. B, C, D, E

14. E

15. E

16. A, C, D, E

17. A, B, D, E

18. A, C, D, E

19. D

20. A, B, D, E

21. A, B, C, D

22. A, B, C, E

23. D

24. C

25. A

26. A

27. B

28. A. A large hailstone can hit the earth traveling at about forty miles an hour or more!

29. C, D

30. D

Appendix 2
Twin Cities Sunrise and Sunset Table

DAY	JAN. Rise A.M.	JAN. Set P.M.	FEB. Rise A.M.	FEB. Set P.M.	MAR. Rise A.M.	MAR. Set P.M.	APR. Rise A.M.	APR. Set P.M.	MAY Rise A.M.	MAY Set P.M.	JUNE Rise A.M.	JUNE Set P.M.	JULY Rise A.M.	JULY Set P.M.	AUG. Rise A.M.	AUG. Set P.M.	SEPT. Rise A.M.	SEPT. Set P.M.	OCT. Rise A.M.	OCT. Set P.M.	NOV. Rise A.M.	NOV. Set P.M.	DEC. Rise A.M.	DEC. Set P.M.
1	7:52	4:42	7:33	5:21	6:52	6:00	5:55	6:41	5:03	7:18	4:30	7:52	4:30	8:04	4:58	7:40	5:35	6:51	6:11	5:54	6:51	5:02	7:31	4:33
2	7:52	4:43	7:32	5:22	6:50	6:02	5:53	6:42	5:02	7:20	4:29	7:53	4:31	8:03	4:59	7:39	5:36	6:49	6:12	5:52	6:53	5:00	7:32	4:33
3	7:52	4:44	7:31	5:24	6:48	6:03	5:51	6:43	5:00	7:21	4:29	7:54	4:31	8:03	5:00	7:38	5:37	6:47	6:13	5:51	6:54	4:59	7:33	4:33
4	7:52	4:45	7:30	5:25	6:46	6:04	5:49	6:44	4:59	7:22	4:28	7:55	4:32	8:03	5:01	7:36	5:38	6:45	6:14	5:49	6:55	4:58	7:34	4:32
5	7:51	4:46	7:29	5:27	6:45	6:06	5:47	6:46	4:57	7:23	4:28	7:56	4:32	8:02	5:03	7:35	5:39	6:44	6:16	5:47	6:57	4:56	7:35	4:32
6	7:51	4:47	7:27	5:28	6:43	6:07	5:45	6:47	4:56	7:24	4:28	7:56	4:33	8:02	5:04	7:34	5:41	6:42	6:17	5:45	6:58	4:55	7:36	4:32
7	7:51	4:48	7:26	5:29	6:41	6:08	5:43	6:48	4:55	7:26	4:27	7:57	4:34	8:02	5:05	7:32	5:42	6:40	6:18	5:43	6:59	4:54	7:37	4:32
8	7:51	4:49	7:25	5:31	6:39	6:10	5:42	6:49	4:53	7:27	4:27	7:58	4:35	8:01	5:06	7:31	5:43	6:38	6:19	5:41	7:01	4:53	7:38	4:32
9	7:51	4:50	7:23	5:32	6:37	6:11	5:40	6:51	4:52	7:28	4:27	7:58	4:35	8:01	5:07	7:29	5:44	6:36	6:21	5:40	7:02	4:51	7:39	4:32
10	7:50	4:52	7:22	5:34	6:36	6:12	5:38	6:52	4:51	7:29	4:26	7:59	4:36	8:00	5:08	7:28	5:45	6:34	6:22	5:38	7:04	4:50	7:40	4:32
11	7:50	4:53	7:20	5:35	6:34	6:14	5:36	6:53	4:49	7:30	4:26	7:59	4:37	8:00	5:10	7:26	5:47	6:32	6:23	5:36	7:05	4:49	7:41	4:32
12	7:50	4:54	7:19	5:37	6:32	6:15	5:34	6:54	4:48	7:32	4:26	8:00	4:38	7:59	5:11	7:25	5:48	6:30	6:25	5:34	7:06	4:48	7:42	4:32
13	7:49	4:55	7:18	5:38	6:30	6:16	5:33	6:56	4:47	7:33	4:26	8:01	4:39	7:59	5:12	7:23	5:49	6:28	6:26	5:32	7:08	4:47	7:43	4:32
14	7:49	4:56	7:16	5:39	6:28	6:18	5:31	6:57	4:46	7:34	4:26	8:01	4:39	7:58	5:13	7:22	5:50	6:27	6:27	5:31	7:09	4:46	7:44	4:32
15	7:48	4:58	7:15	5:41	6:26	6:19	5:29	6:58	4:45	7:35	4:26	8:01	4:40	7:57	5:14	7:20	5:51	6:25	6:28	5:29	7:10	4:45	7:44	4:32
16	7:48	4:59	7:13	5:42	6:25	6:20	5:27	6:59	4:43	7:36	4:26	8:02	4:41	7:56	5:16	7:18	5:53	6:23	6:30	5:27	7:12	4:44	7:45	4:32
17	7:47	5:00	7:12	5:44	6:23	6:21	5:26	7:01	4:42	7:37	4:26	8:02	4:42	7:56	5:17	7:17	5:54	6:21	6:31	5:25	7:13	4:43	7:46	4:33
18	7:46	5:01	7:10	5:45	6:21	6:23	5:24	7:02	4:41	7:38	4:26	8:03	4:43	7:55	5:18	7:15	5:55	6:19	6:32	5:24	7:14	4:42	7:46	4:33
19	7:46	5:03	7:08	5:46	6:19	6:24	5:22	7:03	4:40	7:40	4:26	8:03	4:44	7:54	5:19	7:14	5:56	6:17	6:34	5:22	7:16	4:41	7:47	4:33
20	7:45	5:04	7:07	5:48	6:17	6:25	5:21	7:05	4:39	7:41	4:26	8:03	4:45	7:53	5:20	7:12	5:57	6:15	6:35	5:20	7:17	4:40	7:48	4:34
21	7:44	5:05	7:05	5:49	6:15	6:27	5:19	7:06	4:38	7:42	4:26	8:03	4:46	7:52	5:22	7:10	5:59	6:13	6:36	5:19	7:18	4:39	7:48	4:34
22	7:43	5:07	7:04	5:51	6:13	6:28	5:17	7:07	4:37	7:43	4:27	8:04	4:47	7:51	5:23	7:09	6:00	6:11	6:38	5:17	7:20	4:39	7:49	4:35
23	7:42	5:08	7:02	5:52	6:11	6:29	5:16	7:08	4:36	7:44	4:27	8:04	4:48	7:50	5:24	7:07	6:01	6:09	6:39	5:16	7:21	4:38	7:49	4:35
24	7:42	5:10	7:00	5:53	6:10	6:30	5:14	7:10	4:36	7:45	4:27	8:04	4:49	7:49	5:25	7:05	6:02	6:08	6:40	5:14	7:22	4:37	7:50	4:36
25	7:41	5:11	6:59	5:55	6:08	6:32	5:12	7:11	4:35	7:46	4:27	8:04	4:50	7:48	5:26	7:03	6:03	6:06	6:42	5:12	7:24	4:36	7:50	4:37
26	7:40	5:12	6:57	5:56	6:06	6:33	5:11	7:12	4:34	7:47	4:28	8:04	4:51	7:47	5:28	7:02	6:05	6:04	6:43	5:11	7:25	4:36	7:50	4:37
27	7:39	5:14	6:55	5:58	6:04	6:34	5:09	7:13	4:33	7:48	4:28	8:04	4:52	7:46	5:29	7:00	6:06	6:02	6:44	5:09	7:26	4:35	7:51	4:38
28	7:38	5:15	6:53	5:59	6:02	6:35	5:08	7:15	4:32	7:49	4:29	8:04	4:54	7:45	5:30	6:58	6:07	6:00	6:46	5:08	7:27	4:35	6:51	4:39
29	7:37	5:17	6:53	6:00	6:00	6:37	5:06	7:16	4:32	7:50	4:29	8:04	4:55	7:44	5:31	6:56	6:08	5:58	6:47	5:06	7:28	4:34	7:51	4:39
30	7:36	5:18			5:58	6:38	5:05	7:17	4:31	7:51	4:30	8:04	4:56	7:43	5:32	6:55	6:09	5:56	6:48	5:05	7:30	4:34	7:51	4:40
31	7:35	5:19			5:56	6:39			4:30	7:52			4:57	7:41	5:33	6:53			6:50	5:03			7:51	4:41

Add one hour for Daylight Saving Time when in use. Prepared by NAUTICAL ALMANAC OFFICE, UNITED STATES NAVAL OBSERVATORY, WASHINGTON, D.C. 20390

Appendix 3
First and Last Dates of One-inch Snow Cover

	Average date of first one-inch snow cover in fall	Average date of last one-inch snow cover in spring
Albert Lea	Dec. 1	March 26
Alexandria	Nov. 12	April 11
Duluth	Nov. 7	April 13
Farmington	Nov. 28	March 27
Grand Rapids	Nov. 13	April 12
Hutchinson	Nov. 22	April 2
International Falls	Nov. 6	April 17
Little Falls	Nov. 21	April 6
Minneapolis	Nov. 22	April 2
Moose Lake	Nov. 20	April 10
Rochester	Nov. 24	April 5
St. Cloud	Nov. 21	April 4
Warroad	Nov. 13	April 13
Winona	Nov. 22	March 26
Worthington	Nov. 10	April 3

Appendix 4
Average Ice-out Dates for Minnesota Lakes

Lake, county	Earliest	Avg.	Latest
Big Sandy, Aitkin	April 12, 1968	April 21	May 3, 1975
Big Stone, Big Stone	March 27, 1961	April 10	April 26, 1975
Clear, Waseca	March 7, 1931	April 8	April 27, 1951
Crane, St. Louis	—	May 5	—
Detroit, Becker	March 23, 1910	April 24	May 17, 1950
Fall, Lake	April 10, 1945	April 29	May 19, 1950
Gull, Cass-Crow Wing	April 12, 1976	April 23	May 4, 1979
Gunflint, Cook	April 25, 1969	May 9	May 26, 1966
Lake of the Woods	—	May 9	—
Leech, Cass	April 9, 1945	April 29	May 23, 1950
Mille Lacs, Mille Lacs	April 13, 1968	April 25	May 8, 1975
Minnetonka, Hennepin	March 11, 1878	April 15	May 5, 1858
Minnewaska, Pope	March 25, 1942	April 15	May 7, 1950
Mitawan, Lake	April 18, 1958	May 1	May 20, 1950
Osakis, Todd-Douglas	March 13, 1878	April 22	May 14, 1950
Ox (big), Crow Wing	April 9, 1973	April 23	May 5, 1975
Pokegama, Itasca	April 15, 1973	April 28	May 7, 1975
Shetek, Murray	March 20, 1966	April 8	April 22, 1975
Sisseton, Martin	March 17, 1966	April 5	April 26, 1951
Vermillion, St. Louis	April 10, 1945	May 2	May 23, 1950
Waconia, Carver	March 30, 1968	April 14	May 1, 1965
White Bear, Ramsey	March 29, 1981	April 16	May 4, 1950

Appendix 5
Windchill and Humature Charts

		Actual thermometer reading (°F)											
Wind speed		50	40	30	20	10	0	-10	-20	-30	-40	-50	-60
Knots	mph	Equivalent temperature (°F)											
Calm		50	40	30	20	10	0	-10	-20	-30	-40	-50	-60
4	5	48	37	27	16	6	-5	-15	-26	-36	-47	-57	-68
9	10	40	28	16	4	-9	-21	-33	-46	-58	-70	-83	-95
13	15	36	22	9	-5	-18	-36	-45	-58	-72	-85	-99	-112
17	20	32	18	4	-10	-25	-39	-53	-67	-82	-96	-110	-124
22	25	30	16	0	-15	-29	-44	-59	-74	-88	-104	-118	133
26	30	28	13	-2	-18	-33	-48	-63	-79	-94	-109	-125	-140
30	35	27	11	-4	-20	-35	-49	-67	-82	-98	-113	-129	-145
35	40	26	10	-6	-21	-37	-53	-69	-85	-100	-116	-132	-148

Wind speeds greater than 40 mph have little additional effect

LITTLE DANGER (For properly clothed person)   INCREASING DANGER   GREAT DANGER

How cold it is! Use this chart to determine the windchill.

Windchill Factor—An index of the cooling power of the wind. Temperatures are expressed in terms of the equivalent temperature without wind.

TEMPERATURE	0	5	10	15	20	25	30	35	40	45	50	55	60	65	70	75	80	85	90	95	100
140°	125																				
135°	120	128																			
130°	117	122	131																		
125°	111	116	123	131	141																
120°	107	111	116	123	130	139	148														
115°	103	107	111	115	120	127	135	143	151												
110°	99	102	105	108	112	117	123	130	137	143	150										
105°	95	97	100	102	105	109	113	118	123	129	135	142	149								
100°	91	93	95	97	99	101	104	107	110	115	120	126	132	138	144						
95°	87	88	90	91	93	94	96	98	101	104	107	110	114	119	124	130	136				
90°	83	84	85	86	87	88	90	91	93	95	96	98	100	102	106	109	113	117	122		
85°	78	79	80	81	82	83	84	85	86	87	88	89	90	91	93	95	97	99	102	105	108
80°	73	74	75	76	77	77	78	79	79	80	81	81	82	83	85	86	86	87	88	89	91
75°	69	69	70	71	72	72	73	73	74	74	75	75	76	76	77	77	78	78	79	79	80
70°	64	64	65	65	66	66	67	67	68	68	69	69	70	70	70	70	71	71	71	71	72

RELATIVE HUMIDITY %

It's not the heat, it's the humidity! "Humature," or the temperature-humidity index, is the summer equivalent of windchill. Instead of factoring in the wind speed, the humature index looks at relative humidity to compute how you will feel. The greater the humidity and the more moisture there is in the air, the more difficulty your body has evaporating perspiration and staying cool. That old saying is absolutely true!

Appendix 6
Colleges and Universities That Offer Meteorology Programs

UNITED STATES

Alaska, University of, Fairbanks, AK 99775. Geophysical Institute and Physics Department. Master of Science, Doctor of Philosophy.

Arizona, University of, Tucson, AZ 85721. Department of Atmospheric Sciences. Bachelor of Science, Master of Science, Doctor of Philosophy.

California at Davis, University of, Davis, CA 95616. Department of Land, Air & Water Resources. Bachelor of Science, Master of Science, Doctor of Philosophy (in Atmospheric Science).

California at Los Angeles, University of Los Angeles, CA 90024. Department of Atmospheric Sciences. Bachelor of Science, Master of Science, C. Phil, Doctor of Philosophy

California at San Diego, University of, La Jolla, CA 92093. (See Scripps Institute of Oceanography). Master of Science, Doctor of Philosophy.

Central Michigan University, Mt. Pleasant, MI 48895. Department of Geography. Bachelor of Science.

Chicago, University of, Chicago, IL 60637. Department of the Geophysical Sciences. Bachelor of Arts, Master of Science, Doctor of Philosophy.

Colorado State University, Ft. Collins, Ft. Collins, CO 80523. Department of Atmospheric Sciences. Master of Science, Doctor of Philosophy.

Colorado at Boulder, University of, Boulder, CO 80309. Departments of Astrophysical, Planetary and Atmospheric Sciences & Geography. Bachelor of Arts, Master of Arts, Master of Science, Doctor of Philosophy.

Columbia University, New York, NY 10027. Department of Geological Sciences & Lamont-Doherty Geological Observatory. Bachelor of Arts Master of Arts, Master of Philosophy, Doctor of Philosophy.

Cornell University, Ithaca, NY 14853. Meteorology Unit/Department of Agronomy. Bachelor of Science, Master of Science, Doctor of Philosophy.

Creighton University, Omaha, NE 68178. Department of Atmospheric Sciences. Bachelor of Science, Master of Science.

Delaware, University of, Newark, DE 19716. Department of Geography & College of Marine Studies. Bachelor of Arts, Master of Arts, Master of Science, Doctor of Philosophy (in Climatology; in Oceanography).

Denver, University of, Denver, CO 80208. Departments of Chemistry, Geography & Physics, and the Denver Research Institute (Laboratory for Applied Mechanics). Bachelor of Arts, Bachelor of Science, Master of Arts, Master of Science, Doctor of Philosophy.

Drexel University, Philadelphia, PA 19104. Departments of Chemistry & Physics and Atmospheric Sciences. Bachelor of Science, Master of Science, Doctor of Philosophy.

Florida State University, Tallahassee, FL 32306. Departments Meteorology & Oceanography. Bachelor of Science, Master of Science, Doctor of Philosophy.

Georgia Institute of Technology, Atlanta, GA 30332. School of Geophysical Sciences. Master of

Science, Master of Science (in Geophysical Sciences), Doctor of Philosophy.

Harvard School of Public Health, Boston, MA 02115. Department of Environmental Science and Physiology. Master of Science, Doctor of Science.

Harvard University, Cambridge, MA 02138. Center for Earth & Planetary Physics. Bachelor of Arts (available with concentrations in Applied Mathematics or Engineering Sciences), Master of Science, Doctor of Philosophy.

Hawaii, University of, Honolulu, HI 96822. Departments of Geography, Meterology, Oceanography. Bachelor of Arts, Bachelor of Science, Master of Arts, Master of Science, Doctor of Philosophy.

Illinois at Urbana-Champaign, University of, Urbana, IL 61801. Department of Atmospheric Sciences. Master of Science, Doctor of Philosophy.

Iowa State University, Ames, IA 50011. Department of Earth Sciences. Bachelor of Science, Master of Science, Doctor of Philosophy.

Jackson State University, Jackson, MS 39217. Physics & Atmospheric Sciences Department. Bachelor of Science.

Johns Hopkins University, The, Baltimore, MD 21218. Department of Earth & Planetary Sciences. Bachelor of Arts, Master of Arts, Doctor of Philosophy.

Kansas, University of, Lawrence, KS 66045. Department of Physics and Astronomy. Bachelor of Arts, Bachelor of Science, Master of Science (all in Atmospheric Science).

Kean College of New Jersey, Union, NJ 07083. Department of Geology & Meteorology. Bachelor of Arts.

Lowell, University of, Lowell, MA 01854. Department of Earth Sciences. Bachelor of Science.

Lyndon State College, Lyndonville, VT 05851. Department of Meteorology. Bachelor of Science.

Maryland, University of, College Park, MD 20742. Department of Meteorology. Master of Science, Doctor of Philosophy.

Massachusetts Institute of Technology, Cambridge, MA 02139. Department of Meteorology & Physical Oceanography. Master of Science, Doctor of Philosophy, Doctor of Science.

Metropolitan State College, Denver, CO 80204. Earth Sciences Department. Bachelor of Science (in Meteorology).

Miami, University of, Miami, FL 33149. Div. of Meterology & Physical Oceanography. Master of Science, Doctor of Philosophy.

Michigan, University of, Ann Arbor, MI 48109. Department of Atmospheric & Oceanic Sciences. Bachelor of Science, Master of Science, Doctor of Philosophy.

Millersville University of Penn., Millersville, PA 17551. Department of Earth Sciences. Bachelor of Arts, Bachelor of Science.

Missouri, University of, Columbia, MO 65211. Department of Atmospheric Sciences. Bachelor of Science, Master of Science, Doctor of Philosophy.

Missouri-Rolla, University of, Rolla, MO 65401. Graduate Center for Cloud Physics Research. Master of Science, Doctor of Philosophy.

Naval Postgraduate School, Monterey, CA 93940. Departments of Meterology & Oceanography. Master of Science, Doctor of Philosophy.

Nebraska-Lincoln, University of, Lincoln, NE 68583-0728. Center for Agricultural Meteorology and Climatology & Department of Geography. Bachelor of Arts, Bachelor of Science, Master of Science, Doctor of Philosophy.

Nevada, Reno, University of (Desert Research Institute), Reno, NV 89557. Department of Phys-

ics. Master of Science (in Atmospheric Physics), Doctor of Philosophy (in Atmospheric Physics, Optics).

New Mexico Institute of Mining and Technology, Socorro, NM 87801. Department of Physics. Master of Science, Doctor of Philosophy.

New York University, New York, NY 10003. Department of Applied Science & Courant Institute of Math Sciences. Master of Science, Doctor of Philosophy.

New York at Albany, State University of, Albany, NY 12222. Department of Atmospheric Sciences. Bachelor of Science, Master of Science, Doctor of Philosophy.

New York at Brockport, State University of, Brockport, NY 14420. Department of Earth Sciences. Bachelor of Arts, Bachelor of Science.

New York at Oneonta, State University of, Oneonta, NY 13820. Department of Earth Science. Bachelor of Science.

New York at Oswego, State University of, Oswego, NY 13126. Department of Earth Sciences. Bachelor of Arts, Bachelor of Science (in Meteorology).

New York, City College of, New York, NY 10031. Department of Earth & Planetary Sciences. Bachelor of Science, Master of Science, Doctor of Philosophy (through Dept. of Physics).

New York-Maritime College, State University of, Bronx, NY 10465. Science Department. Bachelor of Science.

North Carolina State University, Raleigh, NC 27695-8208. Department of Marine, Earth & Atmospheric Sciences. Bachelor of Science, Master of Science, Doctor of Philosophy.

North Carolina, University of, Asheville, NC 28810. Department of Atmospheric Sciences. Bachelor of Science.

North Dakota, University of, Grand Forks, ND 58202. Department of Atmospheric Sciences. Bachelor of Science.

Northeast Louisiana University, Monroe, LA 71209. Department of Geosciences. Bachelor of Science.

Northern Illinois University, De Kalb, IL 60115. Department of Geography. Bachelor of Science,

Master of Science.

Nova University, Dania, FL 33004. Oceanographic Center. Master of Science, Doctor of Philosophy.

Ohio University, Athens, OH 45701. Department of Geography. Bachelor of Science.

Oklahoma, University of, Norman, OK 73019. School of Meterology. Bachelor of Science, Master of Science, Doctor of Philosophy.

Old Dominion University, Norfolk, VA 23508-8512. Department of Oceanography. Master of Science, Doctor of Philosophy.

Oregon State University, Corvallis, OR 97331. College of Oceanography & Department of Atmospheric Sciences. Bachelor of Science, Master of Arts, Master of Science, Doctor of Philosophy.

Pennsylvania State University, University Park, PA 16802. Department of Meteorology. Bachelor of Science, Master of Science, Doctor of Philosophy.

Plymouth State College, Plymouth, NH 03264. Natural Science Department. Bachelor of Science.

Princeton University, Princeton, NJ 08542. Program in Geophysical Fluid Dynamics. Doctor of Philosophy.

Puerto Rico, University of, Mahaguez, PR 00708. Department of Marine Sciences. Master of Science, Doctor of Philosophy.

Purdue University, West Lafayette, IN 47907. Departments Agronomy & Earth & Atmospheric Sciences. Bachelor of Science, Master of Science, Doctor of Philosophy.

Rhode Island, University of, Narragansett, RI 02882-1197. Graduate School of Oceanography. Master of Science, Doctor of Philosophy.

Rice University, William Marsh, Houston, TX 77251. Departments of Geology & Space Physics and Astronomy. Master of Science, Doctor of Philosophy.

Rutgers University/Cook College, New Brunswick, NJ 08903. Department of Meteorology & Physical Oceanography. Bachelor of Science, Master of Science.

Saint Cloud State University, St. Cloud, MN 56301. Department of Earth Sciences. Bachelor of Science.

Saint Louis University, Saint Louis, MO 63156. Department of Earth & Atmospheric Sciences. Bachelor of Arts, Bachelor of Science, Master of Professional Meteorology, Master of Science, Doctor of Philosophy.

San Jose State University, San Jose, CA 95192. Department of Meteorology. Bachelor of Science, Master of Science.

Scripps Institute of Oceanography, (University of California at San Diego), La Jolla, CA 92093. Physical Oceanography Curriculum. Master of Science, Doctor of Philosophy.

South Dakota School of Mines & Technology, Rapid City, SD 57701. Department of Meteorology. Master of Science, Doctor of Philosophy (in cooperation with Colorado State University)

St. Thomas, University of, Houston, TX 77006. Departments of Meteorology & Oceanography. Bachelor of Arts (in Meteorology; in Weather Communications).

Texas A&M University, College Station, TX 77843. Department of Meteorology. Bachelor of Science, Master of Science, Doctor of Philosophy.

Texas Tech University, Lubbock, TX 79409. Atmospheric Sciences Group. Master of Science, Doctor of Philosophy.

Texas at Austin, University of, Austin, TX 78712. Department of Civil Engineering. Master of Science, Doctor of Philosophy.

U.S. Naval Academy, Annapolis, MD 21402. Department of Oceanography. Bachelor of Science.

Utah State University, Logan, UT 84322. Department of Soil Science & Biometeorology. Master of Science, Doctor of Philosophy.

Utah, University of, Salt Lake City, UT 84112–1183. Department of Meteorology. Bachelor of Science, Master of Science, Doctor of Philosophy.

Virginia, University of, Charlottesville, VA 22903. Department of Environmental Sciences. Bachelor of Arts. Master of Arts, Master of Science, Doctor of Philosophy.

Washington State University, Pullman, WA 99164–2730. Laboratory for Atmospheric Research. Master of Science, Doctor of Philosophy.

Washington, University of, Seattle, WA 98195. Department of Atmospheric Sciences & School of Oceanography. Bachelor of Arts, Bachelor of Science, Master of Science, Doctor of Philosophy.

Wisconsin-Madison, University of, Madison, WI 53706. Departments of Meteorology & Oceanography & Limnology. Bachelor of Science, Master of Science, Doctor of Philosophy.

Wisconsin-Milwaukee, University of, Milwaukee, WI 53201. Department of Geological/Geophysical Sciences. Bachelor of Science, Master of Science, Doctor of Philosophy.

Woods Hole Oceanographic Institution, Woods Hole, MA 02543. Departments of Physical Oceanography, Ocean Engineering, Geology and Geophysics, Chemistry & Biology. Doctor of Philosophy, Doctor of Science (in conjunction with the Massachusetts Institute of Technology).

Wyoming, University of, Laramie, WY 82071. Department of Atmospheric Sciences. Master of Science, Doctor of Philosophy.

Yale University, New Haven, CT 06511. Department of Geology & Geophysics. Bachelor of Science, Master of Science, Doctor of Philosophy.

CANADA

Alberta, University of, Edmonton, Alberta, T6G 2H4 CANADA. Department of Geography, Diploma, Bachelor of Science, Master of Science, Doctor of Philosophy.

British Columbia, University of, Vancouver, British Columbia, V6T 1W5 CANADA. Departments of Oceanography & Geography. Bachelor of Science, Diploma, Master of Science, Doctor of Philosophy.

Dalhousie University, Halifax, Nova Scotia, B3H 4J1 CANADA. Department of Oceanography. Master of Science, Doctor of Philosophy.

Guelph, University of, Guelph, Ontario, N1G 2W1 CANADA. Department of Land Resource Science. Master of Science, Doctor of Philosophy.

McGill University, Montreal, Quebec, H3A 2K6 CANADA. Bachelor of Science, Master of Science, Doctor of Philosophy.

McMaster University, Hamilton, Ontario, L8S 4K1 CANADA. Department of Geography. Master of Science, Doctor of Philosophy.

Saskatchewan, University of, Saskatoon, Saskatchewan, S7N 0W0 CANADA. Institute of Space & Atmospheric Studies. Masters of Science, Doctor of Philosophy.

Toronto, University of, Toronto, Ontario, M5S 1A7 CANADA. Department of Physics. Bachelor of Science, Master of Science, Doctor of Philosophy

Reprinted with permission of the AMERICAN METEOROLOGICAL SOCIETY, 45 Beacon Street, Boston, Massachusetts 02108–3693, USA

Index

Note on the symbols: *(p)* means that a photo of the phenomenon is on the indicated page; *(ch)* means that a chart or illustration of the phenomenon is on the indicated page.

Moonrise in December. *Marc Swanson, Grantsburg, WI.*